PN
3331
D4

 side College Library

Riverside, California

1. All students and faculty in the school are entitled to use the library and draw books.

2. Reference books, such as encyclopedias and
dictionaries, are to be used only in the library.

3. Reserved books may be borrowed for one
period, or at the close of school, and should be returned before nine o'clock the following school day.

4. All other books may be retained for two
weeks.

5. Five cents a day is charged for each book kept
overtime, and five cents an hour for Reserve books.

6. Injury to books beyond reasonable wear and
all losses shall be paid for by the borrower.

7. No books may be taken from the library
without being charged.

THE WORLD OF FICTION

THE
World
of Fiction

BY BERNARD DeVOTO

Riverside College Library
Riverside, California

HOUGHTON MIFFLIN COMPANY · BOSTON

The Riverside Press Cambridge

1950

PN3331 .D4
De Voto, Bernard Augustine,
1897-1955.
The world of fiction.

808.3
D51

COPYRIGHT, 1950, BY BERNARD DEVOTO

ALL RIGHTS RESERVED INCLUDING THE RIGHT TO REPRODUCE THIS BOOK
OR PARTS THEREOF IN ANY FORM

The Riverside Press

CAMBRIDGE · MASSACHUSETTS

PRINTED IN THE U.S.A.

TO BEATA RANK

"Between the fire and the prisoners,
there is a raised way."

Vro 10.10.50   3.50 .3

You have shown me a strange image and they are strange prisoners.

Like ourselves, I replied; and they see only their own shadows or the shadows of one another.

The Republic, Book VII

ACKNOWLEDGMENTS

CHAPTERS I and II expand to about three times the original length articles that were published in my column, the Easy Chair, in *Harper's Magazine*. A few paragraphs in the succeeding four chapters are based on parts of other Easy Chairs. I am indebted to *Harper's* and to Little, Brown & Company for permission to use them here.

The bulk of Chapter V is from my book *Mark Twain at Work* and is reprinted by permission of the Harvard University Press.

In the summer of 1937 I published in *The Saturday Review of Literature* eleven short editorials under the serial title, "The Novelist and the Reader." I have used them as the basis of Chapters VII through XI, but they supply less than a fifth of the bulk of those chapters. My thanks to *The Saturday Review* for permission to use the material.

I believe I am tolerably familiar with the literature of psychology and with treatments of fiction by literary critics, but the basis of my discussion in this book is the shop-talk of psychoanalysts and the shop-talk of novelists and editors. I have known few psychiatrists whom I did not eventually call on to discuss fiction. I have most often discussed the problems dealt with in this book with Dr. Lucie Jessner, Dr. Lawrence S. Kubie, Dr. Beata Rank, Dr. Eveoleen Rexford, and Dr. Gregory Rochlin. However I may have manhandled their teaching, I am grateful for it and, of course, they are completely exempted and exonerated from responsibility for anything I say about fiction, psychology, or psychiatry.

It was in 1932, I think, that a kind of specialization began at Treman Cottage, from 5 P.M. for as long as anyone could take it. My thanks to scores of novelists and editors who in various concentrations of Booth's and Noilly-Prat have laid bare there what at the moment they held to be the secrets of their trades, and especially to the Old Hands, Edith Mirrielees and Helen Everitt, Theodore Morrison and Fletcher Pratt and William Sloane, and a New Hand, Mark Saxton. And to many novelists with whom in many places I have talked through many nights.

The chart of the time-scheme of *B. F.'s Daughter* is by Parian Temple and I am additionally indebted to her for her ability to remain good-natured while working long hours at dull stuff and for her stoicism under the pressure of my prose.

I have inclosed in quotation marks a number of observations made to me by Garrett Mattingly, whose ideas I have been expropriating for twenty-two years. It seemed to me, however, that various other remarks he wrote to me about some of my topics were much too good to be publicly accredited to a historian in such a context as this and I have therefore passed them off as mine.

PREFACE

THIS BOOK has a single, deliberately limited, and clearly
defined purpose. It is not a treatise on the psychology
of fiction nor a handbook on the writing of fiction, though it
involves both psychology and technique. I do not understand it as belonging to esthetics or literary criticism, and I
ask the reader not to label it with those names but to regard
it solely as an analysis of the relationship between the person
who writes a novel and the person who reads it. I especially
ask him to recognize that I am not generalizing beyond the
immediate reference of my text.

More than that, I ask him to open his mind to all novels
while he is reading what I say about fiction. We all know
that some novels are better, more important, more worthy
than others, are the work of more gifted men, have more
significant things to say. I have freely expressed my prefer-
ences here when I could do so without endangering my
analysis. But the analysis is conducted with as few refer-
ences to comparative values as I found possible and none at
all to absolute values. It will be misunderstood if any are
imposed on it. From the point of view maintained here, all
novels are valuable in that they are read. The act of read-

ing brings the novel to completion: it is not a novel until someone, someone who has no vested interest in fiction, has read it. My subject is an illusion which has proved so necessary to mankind that we refuse to do without it. My book is interested in the illusion wherever it is produced.

I am not trying to tell the whole truth about fiction. This is one way of looking at novels; I believe that it is a valid and useful way. There are many other valid and useful ways of looking at them. My discussion is not presented to the end of competing with any of them or excluding any, but merely as true in its own terms, so far as it goes. No one need tell me, in addition, that the things said here are obvious. They are so obvious that I thought it time for someone to say them.

BERNARD DeVOTO

Cambridge, Massachusetts
August 1, 1949

CONTENTS

I

RUTH MARTIN
AND THE SEVEN DREADS

RUTH MARTIN AND THE SEVEN DREADS

I N ANY CITY of fifty thousand you will find the store of T. M. Kirby, Office and Mimeographing Supplies, Stationery, Favors, Souvenirs, Greeting Cards, Lending Library, and — diminuendo — Books. Toward midafternoon Ruth Martin comes into Kirby's, buys a box of correspondence cards and a dozen bridge pads, and pauses before a shelf labeled "Recent Fiction." Ruth is the wife of the cashier of the First National Bank. She is thirty-six and has three children, the youngest of whom is five years old. She is an A.B. of State U; she is head of the local Episcopal charities; she once broke 95 at the country club; and against Bob Martin's express command, she voted for the Fourth Term. After ten minutes of indecision she buys two new novels at three dollars apiece. One is the latest work of John Dos Passos, William Faulkner, Evelyn Waugh, or John Marquand. The other is by a newcomer of whom she knows nothing except he was reviewed in last Sunday's *Times*. By the end of the week she has read both novels and Bob, who is fundamentally serious-minded and had a cold on Saturday, has read one of them, the newcomer's.

Ruth's purchase and the fact that she will repeat it within

a month are the foundation that supports the publishing business and the trade of novel-writing. We are not concerned with the economics of her purchase, though they are remarkable, but with the motives that led her to pay three dollars for forty cents worth of paper, binder's cloth, and labor charge. She herself has no doubt what they add up to: she likes to read novels. Reading them is one of the durable satisfactions of her life. She can count on it with greater assurance than she can on most accustomed satisfactions; with the confidence of an addict she knows before she opens a novel that the odds favor her enjoying it. She reads fiction because she enjoys it; she reads for pleasure. And, sir, professional and semi-professional literary people aside, no one ever read fiction for aught else.

Consider some of the ways in which that same satisfaction is being invoked elsewhere in Ruth's town at the moment when, after leaving little Bobby's door open just a crack so that he will go right to sleep, she sits down to make the economic system produce the exchange value of her purchase. Bob Martin may have stopped off at Kirby's on his way home and picked up the new Raymond Chandler at the lending library. Or he may be rereading a book that he enjoyed some years ago, *Oliver Wiswell,* say, or *Beat to Quarters.* A few doors down the street someone — and he belongs to an organized fellowship that circulates a devotional literary criticism much more esoteric and pedantic than any published in such organs of pure thought as *The Kenyon Review* — has settled down with Mr. van Vogt's *The World of $\bar{A}$.* A teacher of literature at the local college, having finished this issue of *The Partisan Review* and being therefore fresh out of articles which challenge the objections raised in other articles to opinions in recent articles approving attributes of James T. Farrell's novels which they have not got, is rather apprehensively enjoying a novel. Let us say it is *La Peste*, for if it is he will be able to justify his illicit because first-hand pleasure by reflecting that Camus is known as an existentialist. A high-school teacher is reading *Main Street* or *The Ordeal of Richard Feverel* and one of her freshmen girls (if no one has assigned it to her) is caught up in the ecstasy of *Vanity Fair*. Elsewhere in town *Vingt Ans Après* and *Cranford* are holding readers in thrall —— and *O Pioneers, The Wind in the Willows, La Terre, Tarzan of the Apes, Looking Backwards* — Sartre, Balzac, Mary Webb, Graham Greene, Anatole France, Sax Rohmer. It is conceivable too that someone who was reading *The Fountainhead* has not fallen asleep.

And it may be that in Ruth Martin's town tonight someone, on opening a novel, has found himself reading for the first time "Call me Ishmael" or 'You don't know about me without you have read a book by the name of . . ." Or "Alexey Fyodorovitch Karamazov was the third son of Fyodor Pavlovitch Karamazov. . . . " Or "Well, Prince, so Genoa and Lucca are now just family estates of the Buonapartes." Or "For a long time I used to go to bed early."

When evening quickens in the street, that is, it wakes diverse appetites for fiction. Before we are done here we will find that the bridge lamps are shining on some extremely odd facts, but none is stranger than the basic one common to all readers, that they have looked at printed type and found people feeling and acting. But let us begin by asking what is this an appetite for? Why do people like to read novels? What is this pleasure bound in cloth for which they pay three dollars?

*   *   *

Professional and amateur literary people must be excluded from the inquiry: we must deal with the pure, the unforced and uncontaminated, experience. Poets read poetry by living writers, one comes to think, primarily to resent it. Novelists feel a similar jealousy but are less primitive about it: they sublimate it and they are also fortified by an awareness of where better novels can be found on their shelves. Also they have more adult motives: they read one another's novels to keep abreast of fashion, to appraise materials, to enjoy (or learn from or feel agreeably superior to) a display of professional skill, to argue and to refute and to agree. The semi-literary, the dilettanti and hangers-on, read fiction primarily in order to talk about it as if they were novelists or, better still, literary critics. Literary critics have vocational motives — one comes to believe that they have no other. To either the writer or the non-literary reader of novels they seem, so far as he can make out from the formalized abstractions of their prose, to have the strangest of all objectives. We may summarize it by saying that, at least on the higher planes, the interest of criticism in a novel is to find in it the novel that isn't there.

Ruth and Bob Martin have none of these motives, however, and we will be wise not to attribute to them some of the motives that literary people do. Thus novelists, reluctant to think of themselves as mere entertainers who provide amusement for people's leisure time, will tell you that readers come to them in search of beauty and truth and to acquire a philosophy of life and guidance in its application. The idea holds solace for novelists but how true is it? The Martins are not self-conscious about beauty or truth, and if they were they would probably consider fiction at best only an indirect source of either. Their philosophy of life has mostly been imposed on them by forces stronger than fiction, by family and friends, by school and church and other social institutions, by their experience. As for guidance, it seems out of the question. I knew a man who, when he had to take sides in the divorce of two friends, went to the *Nicomachean Ethics* for help in making his choice and seemed to find it there. But there cannot be many like him and I doubt if anyone would turn for such an answer to Jim Farrell.

Yet there is a way in which these contentions of novelists are true, though it is a way of metaphor. They are on still firmer ground when they say that readers ask them to interpret experience, though they are still speaking in metaphor. What they mean here is what Ruth herself means by the last of three reasons which she would give offhand if you asked her why she read novels. She would say straightway that she likes a good story: that is the comprehensive reason, the one that includes all the others, and the effort of this book is solely to find out what it means. With a slight embarrassment, feeling that the admission is a little unworthy, she would add that she wants to keep up with what people are talking about, especially educated people who have been taught that literature is important. She would feel no embarrassment, however, when she went on to say that she reads novels also because she wants "to keep up with the world." Here she acknowledges the truth of the novelist's contention, though both he and she have incorrectly identified something they both feel. What Ruth actually means by her third reason is that she reads fiction in order to keep up with the story of her own life.

Reading a novel is an act of the mind, it is a psychological phenomenon. There are few simple psychological phenomena and few simple motives. Only a little introspection is required to reveal behind acts less complex than reading a novel a composite of motives. Why did you go to Maine for your vacation? Why did you break a date? Why did you sit in a chair facing the window? It is a commonplace that many motives went into the decisions which produced those actions. It is a commonplace that the more closely you examine them, the more they elaborate like root systems and the more parts of your personality they bring in. They go back in time and down in the mind and they form patterns. No doubt if Ruth persisted in her introspection she would uncover a formidable mass and variety, but for the moment it is enough to say that under the surface there are many reasons for reading novels, and that the pleasure people get from fiction is complex.

Begin with the simple kind of fiction and with people more naïve than the Martins. The aspiration of America is still upward, toward a better job, a finer house, a more luxurious automobile. The aspiration is still realizable — and it is especially and universally realizable in phantasy.[1] So there is a constant need to know what life is like on the next stage above. The attendant of a Socony gas station, say, derives from such fiction as might be serialized in mass-circulation magazines a great deal of information he will need on his way up. He is going to be a field supervisor and later on a district manager, and he must not arrive at his new estate uninformed. He needs many kinds of information — for instance about rituals. How do people act at an executive's desk, at the country club, a restaurant where one must wear a dinner jacket? How do they talk, what do they talk about, what are their sophistications, their nonchalances, their taboos? On this floor certain epithets are insults — is it true that, a couple of flights up, they are merely good fellowship? What remarks or behavior which would notify the girl at the lunch counter that you were making a pass at her are considered only a ceremonial gallantry by the young wives along

[1] Throughout this book the word "phantasy" refers to a psychic process and the word "fantasy" to a literary form.

River Road? What is shocking, up there, and what is good form? What assumptions does one carry to a directors' meeting, a church wedding, the Kentucky Derby, the disclosure of an assistant's treachery? The Socony boy will have to know and he acquires such information incidentally while reading a good story with lots of action in it.

If he marries the girl at the lunch counter, as the novel assures him he will, she will have to be equipped with a body of similar information when they buy a house on River Road. A girl must be able to recognize a pass but nothing could be more embarrassing than to mistake for one what in fact was an initiate's tribute to her social position. To do so might ruin her standing or her husband's career. Even the non-amatory behavior of men in liquor must be handled differently at the country club from the accepted usages of Joe's Cocktail Bar. Just as the wives here make caste distinctions between dress shops, so there are caste marks of belief, assumption, intellectual interest, radio programs, sports, games, and slang, and one must be in the know. Even intonations and vocal emphases are hallmarked. A girl who is born at the top learns the correct ones from her family and the daughter of a rich parvenu gets them at Miss Porter's School. But any aspirant can get them from a novelist's adverbs.

Notice, however, what kind of information this is. It is not the kind provided in such reports by commissions of inquiry as *Elmer Gantry* and *Gideon Planish*. It is even more unlike the information in novels which fictionalize data and to some extent dramatize it. The interest of readers in both kinds of novels is easily accounted for and will be discussed later, but it has no clue for us now.

Whereas there is a clue in the need for instruction in office repartee and the signing of drink-chits at the country club. Ruth and Bob Martin, as sophisticated people, do not need to go to fiction for information of that order. But they do need preparation for other kinds of promotion or trans- formation. There is always, for all of us, a next floor above, Another turning of the stair.

Life goes on. Their own private stories unfold. They are confronted from year to year with the manifold experiences of human maturity and decline. With them comes the human necessity to know, not how to act, since action is imposed, but how to feel about them. If drift and circum- stance transform Bob's flirtation with his secretary to a moment of authentic passion, if a star-crossed summer night finds Ruth and the rector of St. Anne's transfixed by the flesh's agony, there is a turbulence whose supreme need is to be understood. Every strong emotion is new and intolerable to the individual until it is fitted into a pattern of the familiar. Fiction, like the confessional and the conversation of old friends, is a ready means of such assimilation.

No one can stand unshaped emotion. It must be given shape, familiarity, a conduit of the known. So Ruth's re- quirement as she approaches the rector's arms — or the fresh- dug grave of her child, a friend's insanity, or a doctor's diag- nosis that she has cancer of the breast — is not What shall I do? For her behavior is conditioned by forces that for many years no novelist has been able to affect. She makes a more peremptory and more pitiful demand: How do I feel?

One primary service of fiction is that it helps to answer that question. It prepares Ruth and Bob to understand the whirlpools of their own feelings. It orients experience by anticipating it and filling in the gaps. Ruth and Bob grow older, the children grow older too and turn against them or disappoint them or prove to be far different than early parenthood had dreamed. What do I feel about this? What is this agony or ecstasy? Their friends die. They come to see themselves plainer and at last plain — the coarsening of aspiration, the degradation of decency, the eclipse of hope, the trumpery details of loss and suffering and defeat and decay, such achievements as the plot of the inner fiction contains. What do I feel about all this? Delivered over to emotions that exalt and crucify him, the individual is helpless to understand. All emotion happens to him for the first time. His paramount need is to know what it is, to give it contact and fixation in the known. Fiction provides a way of closing the circuit and bringing the known in.

It is here, in moments of exasperation one feels that it is almost here alone, that the novelist may be trusted. Within limits, in part, up to a point, he can answer that desolate question, How do I feel? In part, up to a point, he can tell us what emotion is. His work goes beyond it but we follow him with increasing wariness; the farther beyond he goes the more reason there is to be skeptical of him. He can make arresting pictures of the world but ordinarily an inquirer can get a more trustworthy interpretation of society or its component energies from a dowser or an astrologer. The novelist may describe the appearance of things with fine accuracy, though his description is usually dead as fiction in so far as it is not colored by the very compulsions that make him an artist — and as it may be colored, so it is less to be trusted. And when it comes to explaining the world, to explaining anything except the impact of experience on individual people and the emotion and behavior it begets, he has in support of his compulsions only temperamentally distorted theorems learned in Sunday school, in college courses or in conversations which he participated in some years ago but didn't understand very well. At best he can give them little resemblance and less life.

But if fiction has fixed or clarified any emotion, from the trivial to the transcendent, then it has done something inestimable. For the reader has incorporated the clarification in himself. A novel has become part of his destiny and part of his understanding of human destiny. It has even, one believes, had a submicroscopic part in reconciling him to both.

*   *   *

The Martins are not yet done with the novelist. Though we have already arrived at one fundamental of the art of fiction, we have only begun to analyze the relationship between the reader and the novel he reads. We may now take a road fork that at first seems to lead away from rather than toward our destination and talk for a while about fiction's big world and its little world. We may inquire why Ruth Martin obstinately insists on reading some novels that are trivial, unambitious, light-minded, superficial, clearly wrongheaded or untrue, mediocre, or quite bad.

Her obstinacy exasperates some people, all the more so because it strengthens the position of novelists with whom they have no patience. There is a familiar kind of review. A novelist who clearly is not a genius has set out to narrate some interesting events, or to fill a reader's empty hour with some accurate depiction of unimportant but amusing behavior, or to make a mildly humorous exploration of not very deep motives in the hope that readers may enjoy the contradictions. His ambition does not seem reprehensible but there is always a reviewer who cannot accept it, who is impelled to denounce the novelist. You have spent three hundred pages (and an acre of pulp spruce) describing the feuds of clubwomen in Scarsdale — do you not know that the world is still to be saved? You have wasted your time, mine, and the reader's giving us a slight yarn about seduction in

Hollywood — would Proust have done that? Mr. Edmund Wilson, not a man to propose anything lightly, once proposed that novelists be forbidden to write the frivolous and meretricious form called the mystery novel. He raised interesting questions. One wondered whether the prohibition would be best effected by Executive Order, Act of Congress, or Constitutional Amendment. One wondered why a brilliant interpreter of Proust needed protection against Erle Stanley Gardner. But since fiction exists only to be read, one wondered more strongly: What if someone wanted to read a mystery novel? There must be a mystery novel for him to read and a novelist to write it.

What if the novelist did not want to write about a summer romance at a beach resort in the manner of *Madame Bovary?* What if he was unable to? What if the reader did not want him to? Surely there is only one absolute in the criticism of fiction and that is the individual reader's response while he is reading a novel. And surely it is naïve to expect that either novels or novelists will occur in any different frequencies than those which arrange all the excellences and activities of man in the bell-shaped curve. Most novelists — the statistical novelist — will be found along the median line. As we move out toward the right, in the direction of expertness and wisdom, of the deepest demands to be made of fiction, there will be progressively fewer of them.

Does it not show a niggardly spirit to reject novels of the median line on the ground that they lack what those at the extremity of the curve have? It seems best to be grateful for what we can get — a few scenes in which we recognize the emotions as true and to which we can respond with emotion of our own, passages in which true things seem to be happening to actual people, passages that have some wit or grace in them, some beauty of prose, characters who sometimes rise up out of printer's ink and resemble people we know. At any rate, that is what the reader *moyen sensuel* does, what Ruth Martin does. Why?

I have said that we need emotional preparedness for the next turning of the stair. We may get it for turnings we are never called on to take. We may feel in novels, and come to ask to feel, emotions we never feel at first hand in our own lives. If so, then there is disclosed a strange and important attribute of fiction. The light will focus on it best if we recall an experience we have all had — all of us elders, that is. We reread a novel that we remember, from reading it ten or twenty years ago, as a very fine one, perhaps a great one. Sometimes, happily, we find it even better than we remembered: it is richer, more profound, more real than we were able to perceive when we were younger. We have caught up with the novelist. But sometimes we find it tawdry, lifeless, false, or all three. In that event, one or the other of two things has probably happened. We are now able to perceive as we weren't twenty years ago that the novelist did not deal justly with the experiences of his characters. (Nothing is flatter than fiction whose characters we recognize as butts or straw men created to the end that the novelist might ridicule them.) Or else our capacities have grown beyond the novelist's. Love, grief, death, loss, failure — they have come into our own lives by now with such impact and finality that we know more about them than the novelist did, or at least more than he was able to express. By comparison with what we have learned all too sorely, love and loss and grief in the novel are thin, or insufficiently meaningful, or false.

At such a second reading, whether the novel pleased or disappointed us, what we invoke in judgment of it is the realities we have come to know. I now know how one feels when his child dies of pneumonia: clearly the writer knows too or clearly he doesn't. We were not able to invoke those realities twenty years ago but we did know that they existed in human experience and were potential in our lives. Children do die of pneumonia and we would probably be parents; at twenty Ruth Martin was potentially such a mother as the novel shows at the deathbed of her child. So we accepted what the novel said, in the good faith of readers that its emotions must be true — but also because we felt a thirst for experience that had to be slaked. Somewhere between the points of trusting expectation and the actual experience itself, the same thirst and goodwill of readers lead off in the direction of experiences we will never have and emotions we will never feel. A novel is a story: it is an account of imaginary events in the lives of imaginary people. And it leads on. At twenty Ruth Martin could be the mother of a dying child only in phantasy, but the phantasy was of an experience wholly possible to her in the future. Whereas neither at twenty nor at any other age will she be, say, a prisoner at Buchenwald, or a *femme fatale,* or a woman dying of tuberculosis, or the mother of a genius or a thug. But, if only in phantasy, there is always latent in her the potentiality of being any or all of these women, of being many other women. Fiction is both her permission and her means. From nothing human will she turn away — if some way can be found to attach her to the imagined story of such people in the acceptance or engagement of readers.

Once she is attached to the story she will follow it with a reader's good faith. She will follow it because what is happening to one character in that imaginary story, or more than one, is happening to her too. It is a wide thirst or hunger, this desire to follow the lives of people who are not ourselves but who in some degree we become while following their story. It is so strong a desire that it will hold Ruth to innumerable novels which the indignant reviewer repudiates because they are not *Remembrance of Things Past.* It induces her to follow with equal acceptance the imaginary annals of a Negro woman in some Southern slum and the annals, fully as alien to her, of any Lady Ashley fiction has invented. It does not matter to her in the least whether the novel that contains the annals is good or bad by someone else's standards. All she requires is a reader's engagement, a sublimal belief that what happens in the novel is, in a way, happening to her. It is only in a way.

Obviously, then, for our purpose we must think not of the novel as a thing in itself but of the relationship between the novel and its reader. That relationship is composite but also, and this counts more, it is dynamic. In a way, as I have already said, the events of the novel are occurring to the reader, which means that he has partly identified himself with one or more of the characters. In a way, the novel blends with some of his images or phantasies of himself. Some of the emotions in it correspond to his or to emotions latent in him. And in some part of the exterior line or outline of the story itself he finds a symbol, however crude or fragmentary or wrenched out of shape, of his own life.

The terms "wish-fulfillment literature" and "literature of escape" are frequently applied to certain kinds of novels. It is not clear that they have much meaning or relevance in regard to any kind. In the sense that it turns away from real to imaginary experience, every novel is an escape, though in a very important sense which I will mention later on it may also be a return to reality. Anyone who is willing to consider the writing of a novel neurotic may well hold that it is an escape for the novelist, but unless it acquires the force of hallucination for a reader, in which event he is pathological, it can be at most only a brief vacation for him. And certainly every novel is full of wish-fulfillments for the reader; he cannot read it with acceptance unless its organized and developed phantasies attach portions of his own unorganized phantasies. In any sense useful to psychology or (I think) criticism, the silliest Cinderella story and *Anna Karenina* are both on the same side of a fixed line. No man ever escaped so believingly into any novel that he tried to kiss the heroine. It is impossible to imagine him reading it in fulfillment of a wish while his beloved is present in the flesh. If that seems an unjustified extension of the phrase, put it this way: if Ruth Martin's wishful phantasies are to stray from Bob, they will focus on the rector of St. Anne's or some other person who is not type but flesh. It is superficial to say that, toward the fulfillment of desire in phantasy, she identifies herself with Scarlett O'Hara to the end that she may surrender to Rhett Butler or to anyone for whom he stands. It is superficial because the energies at work are more complex than that — and darker. It is superficial because those energies cannot blur the distinction between a real person and an imaginary one. But for the immediate point all we need consider in them is the symbol and the sanction.

All we need consider now, that is, are the reader's partial identification and the phantasy induced in him which the partial identification legitimizes. Or, to use a less pretentious phrase, we are talking now about an induced sympathy. The gently reared parishioner of St. Anne's will never be, for instance, a prostitute but there are in her personality the elements of which prostitutes are made. Her husband the cashier will never abscond with bonds which belong to the First National Bank but he has in him what at times compels every man to make the familiar acknowledgment, There but for the grace of God go I. This is the nexus, the bridge, the contact-switch. A reader will follow with belief a story in which he feels that the characters, the emotions, the events are but for the grace of God. But observe that the emotional preparation acquired here incidentally is not for the expected or foredestined but for the *as if*. That is to say that fiction has offered Ruth an opportunity to be a prostitute in safety and security, giving her the emotions in part while exacting no payment she cannot easily afford. But it is also to say that fiction has widened not only her awareness and not only her understanding and not only her sympathy — but her experience as well.

It should be clear then, why a reader may enjoy some novels whose content seems to someone else trivial or dull, and some novels whose content is at the other pole from his own temperament and experience. But if you hold this fact to the light at another angle it reveals something fully as central in the purpose that fiction serves as the need for emotional preparation we first isolated — and, one thinks, more important and altogether astonishing. Or altogether magical. For in a way, up to a point, the reader has proved willing to accept imaginary experience as real.

*   *   *

I said "no payment she cannot easily afford." She does pay, of course, a small or larger price, spread over a short or longer period — in shame, we may say, or in anxiety, suffering, or sorrow. And the fee will be larger as the novelist is able to make experience poignant or tragedy profound, or as she is able to identify herself more completely with the imaginary characters of his book. But it is easy to see that in the end this is no pain at all. It is, in a cliché, one of the experiences of art. It is one of the pleasures of reading fiction.

Have all the principal satisfactions that Ruth Martin gets from reading fiction now been accounted for? She is cast here as a moderately well-educated, normally intelligent, normally balanced, normally conventional woman, with such interests, curiosities, reticences, and anxieties as may be implied. Is it accurate to say that such a woman enjoys reading *The Idiot* as we may fairly say she enjoys reading, well, *Tess of the d'Urbervilles?* One doubts if it is and the doubt approaches certainty when one moves on to grossly repulsive novels, novels preoccupied with extreme brutality or cruelty, novels about shocking depravity, novels clearly of themselves diseased, and novels whose content is so contemptuous of humanity that such a word as anthropophobia has to be invented to describe them. If there be pleasure in reading such books it must be different from any we have touched on so far, and the needs and motives must be different.

Yet with every outward appearance of enjoying them Ruth Martin, like people both more and less sophisticated than she, does in fact go on reading just such novels, bad ones almost as pleasurably as good ones — plowing through fiction opaque to her understanding, perhaps ineptly or tritely or repetitiously written, and so alien to her own experience that it must be primarily fable or allegory to her. Publishers and novelists can always count on her to spend three dollars for another version of a fable already wearily familiar to her, or a fable whose implications are terrifying, or one so at variance with her own experience that she cannot consciously come to grips with its true content at all.

Precisely there is an explanation. For if Ruth has a deep need to know just what this emotion is that engulfs her at some intense event in her own life, she has an even deeper need. That emotion, though formless till understood, is conscious — but she is under a steady need to slake desires and assuage terrors that never rise to the threshold of awareness. If a novelist is a person who by anatomizing his emotions enables her to identify hers, he is also one who sinks a shaft into his unconscious self for the stability of hers. We have observed an identification that enables her to understand emotions she does not feel directly and sanctions her to follow them till they take her to alien experience, and we have seen her finding in the exterior outline of a fictional story living if fragmentary symbols of her own private story. These are tolerably open facts, they lie near the surface, compared with those that correspond to them in the region we now enter. It is a domain where the relationship between the reader and the novel is fully as immediate and perhaps more intimate but where the communication is almost always by indirection and always by symbols.

In this realm, when the mysterious energies of the personality make an identification on Ruth's behalf it is not with one character or two but with the sum of all the characters and with the relationships in which they are placed. They can make such an identification only on a plane of the personality that is buried far below the shadow-play of conscious phantasy. Down there among the mind's pre-Cambrian quicksands it may be inaccurate to speak of personality at all, and certainly there are no characters either of fiction or of the real world. There are only wills, blind and frustrate wills, and a child crying in fear. It is the child who was left behind when Ruth grew up and is now only a wraith — a wraith not seen as Ruth goes about her daily life but heard as a voice whispering and felt as an impulse exerted on all she does. There in that Lyonesse of the soul, where no light ever penetrates the waves that cover it but the cathedral chimes sound so that they can just be heard when the wind is right, fiction does a great charity to the human spirit. It is a means by which the child to whom all time is one may find achievement, joy, expiation, and reconciliation. It is one of art's handmaidens to the child who must not live and cannot die.

Thus Ruth Martin reading a novel about a daughter's rebellion against her parents is not only a mother in 1950 who greatly needs to know what this is she feels about her own children's rebellion. She is also a child in 1924 rent by will and terror to destroy a parent who died in 1931 — who has been dead these nineteen years, but not to the child's knowledge. On upper planes of the mind the novelist has fascinated the mother in 1950 by dramatizing his own maternal woes and therefore hers; just as surely, on the deeper planes he has gratified her childish need, which is outside time, by forming his own into images. Ruth will raptly follow, say, William Faulkner through a hell's brew of frenzy, mutilation, murder, and disembowelment that should disgust the parishioner of St. Anne's — because from severed roots far below the communicant's awareness grow out just those monstrous blossoms in a child's terror and necessity. She will follow John Dos Passos through a chronicle of events she does not understand occurring to characters who never touch her adult heart — because many times in that chronicle events and characters symbolically evoke relationships, currents of desire thwarted or gratified, guilt felt or anticipated, fear assuaged and ecstasy achieved when the child who is now a wraith confronted the unknown, and because that child still quivers with them in the unlighted void. She will follow the brutalities of *Studs Lonigan* and the horror that underlies the delicate poetry of *Winter*

Orchard with the same intentness, because over and beyond the fictitious events occurring to imaginary characters in them, both books permit the spellbound child to raise a curtain, in safety and some comfort, on a stage where a child's dreads played out their drama years ago.

This in all novels. The mole burrows deeper than we can ever follow it but in every novel there are Snow White and the poisoned comb, there is a thumbling loosed with his sword in the giant's house, there is an impetus and handhold for the child Ruth used to be. If it chances to be a fine novel it will fuse these pitiful symbols with the real objects of an adult's world. But it need not be even a good novel to provide channels for the insatiable cravings and surcease for the seven dreads. It need only attach the marionettes to their strings and turn out the lights, leaving the rest to childhood. For it is fiction's charter that children accept fairy tales as true. And it is a reader's reprieve and absolution that novelists, whatever else they may be besides, are also children talking to children . . . in the dark.

2

FROM DREAM
TO FICTION

Riverside College Library
Riverside, California

———————— 2 ————————

FROM   DREAM   TO   FICTION

W HAT KIND OF PERSON is a novelist? Why does he write novels? What happens when he writes one and what does it mean?

A moderately extensive acquaintance with novelists will teach anyone that there is no uniform exterior resemblance among them which it is safe to fix on, and that statements about interior resemblances must be made with extreme care and qualification. There are novels as extroverted as *Gil Blas* and others as introverted as *Ulysses*. There are novelists as extroverted as anyone you have ever known and others so introverted that they seem incapable of any perception that lacks direct personal reference. Many kinds of people write novels. Many kinds of people write good novels.

But it is safe to say that some of the characteristics popularly attributed to novelists are uncommon. Thus, though you may know a novelist who is a close and accurate observer of the exterior world, who perceives the appearance of things more comprehensively and exactly than the average layman, you do not know many such. A popular fallacy induces the aspiring young to carry notebooks about jotting down "significant details" of the physical scene in the hope that they will later be striking in some fictional scene, recording tragedies which they think they see in the faces of people in subway cars, and pausing in the midst of symphonies and sunsets to make notes for scenes as yet unimagined in novels to be written sometime. Typically, a novelist listening to a symphony will be so engrossed in elaborating a reverie with some association which the music has initiated that nothing significant in its structure or emotion will get through to him. It will be like the "background music" of a movie, making the drama on the screen more vivid by raising the threshold of attention in regard to exterior stimuli and inducing in him a state of consciousness remarkably like the one called hypnagogic. Typically a sunset will not impel him to search for words that can poetically express the gradations of color. He will have serviceable words ready at hand when he needs a sunset in his novel and why should he bother about the actual sunset when any manufactured one will do? It is more likely to evoke in him such a thought as "I should have grabbed her and kissed her right then"; she may have been yesterday or twenty years ago but he will repair his ignominious failure at once. The face in the subway is less likely to set him reconstructing the tragic life of the scrubwoman whose face it is, with her varicose veins and her drunken husband and her crippled son who wants a college education he can never have — than it is to bring surging into his mind, well, let us say, "Her glazing eyes, staring out of death, to shake and bend my soul. On me alone. The ghostcandle light on the tortured face. Her hoarse loud breath rattling in horror, while all prayed on their knees."

By extension this postulated talent for observation is supposed to make novelists so sensitive to human relationships that they cannot come into a group of people without at once perceiving the stresses and strains, hopes and frustrations, and unfinished dramas in that group. It seldom works out that way — and is the friend you turn to for sympathy or understanding in a period of distress likely to be a novelist?

I think not. In the exterior circumstances of life and in personal relationships as well, a novelist is a person wearing a placard which reads "Dramatist at work." His wife can tell tulle from chiffon at sight and always remembers the evening dress Louise had on the other night. That is why he automatically appeals to her when he reaches a passage where a character named Miriam will have to wear an evening dress. The exasperated complaint of all wives, "For God's sake, don't you ever notice *anything?*" applies specifically to a novelist's aesthesia and anesthesia — and so does the reciprocal remark, "You simply couldn't get your eyes off that skirt of Louise's, could you?" Dress or skirt has got to have a personal reference (the skirt is easy) before he will even see it; it has got to have implications for the dramatist at work. The service to fiction thus performed by wives, that of providing inert detail that will be accurate, is provided outside their specialty by a varied corps of assistants. A novelist is a sedentary man — he has to be — and frequently one force that helped to make him a novelist was timidity. He may make a trip to a factory after his drama of the oppressed worker is in first draft, to check his descriptions, but more often he will go to the library, where there is less chance of accident and infection, or to the telephone. Certainly he has never seen a fight between finks and strikers. The violent strike scenes that move you so much when you read them derive their objective exactness from newspaper files, where reporters who have been trained to observe accurately put them at his disposal. And you have admired a good many scenes of passion whose physical details, because the novelist's experience was defective, rest on the appendices of Havelock Ellis.

As for the recognition of emotional nuances, one is sometimes tempted to believe that a reliable reading of a novelist's talent could be taken from the degree of his initial insensitiveness to them. You cannot conceal a quarrel with your wife from your secretary, a society reporter, or the neighbor next door, but it is safe from an average novelist's awareness though he may enter in the midst of it. He will get there in the end but not by unusual sensitiveness to the signs and implications of emotion. I have never attended a Rotary Club luncheon with Mr. Sinclair Lewis but I doubt if he could correctly report the color of the chairman's hair or suit, acceptably summarize the speaker's argument against farm subsidies, or say what the menu was. He would be too busy developing a fictitious luncheon more vivid than the actual one. The actual luncheon would serve as the bridge to the creation of a far better one, which would not much resemble it. Similarly if William Faulkner happened to enter a shabby Mississippi drawing room during the early stages of such an intrigue as the one that produces doom in his last chapter, he would probably be unaware of the incest or mass murder that a good observer could deduce from the evidence. An inferior novelist might see the Rotary luncheon with eyes less blinded by the finer one or might deduce the gathering horror from the behavior of the crazed Southern châtelaine. But novelists as good as Mr. Lewis and Mr. Faulkner do not. They are withheld from doing so by the fact that they are actors in and spectators at similar but much more absorbing dramas.

Unless, that is, some way can be found of attaching them to the real emotions immediately at hand. In good novels

there are subtlety, tenderness, concern, understanding of relationships and their emotions surpassing those we usually
get from our friends. That is why fiction is able to illuminate and clarify emotions for us. The understanding of
them we get from a novel, frequently greater than our own,
is the novelist's. The key that unlocks meanings for us is
his. Whatever the novel says about experience is said by
him. He is a guide to griefs and satisfactions whom our
reading of his book proves we are willing to accept as having
authority. If we cannot get directly from him in our lives
the wisdom put at our disposal in his books, he nevertheless
has that wisdom and it would be available to us directly if
a way of closing the circuit could be found.

If you ask a novelist where he got the motives and behavior of his characters — in the book as a whole or in a
single scene — you are likely to get one of two answers. One
novelist will tell you that they rest on his study of human
nature, which is here concentrated, purified, and focused on
the characters of the novel. Another novelist will indig-
nantly repudiate such a suggestion, denying that he has
summarized a hundred case histories in this scene, and will
tell you instead that he "made them up." The second one
is defining the act of artistic creation, and it will be safer to
follow him.

Psychologists and in particular those who have developed
dynamic psychology are parvenus. They are latecomers on
the scene. Artists have been using the material they deal with
so long as there has been art, which means so long as the
human imagination has found any expression at all, and the
kind of artist we deal with, the novelist, has been practising
the psychologist's trade with marked success ever since language evolved from grunts. In his arrogant moods a psychologist seems to him little more than an amateur novelist with

a repulsive vocabulary and a reckless willingness to make guesses. For a thousand years before there were psychologists, for two thousand before there were dynamic psychologists, you necessarily had to go to artists, and in particular to poets and novelists, if you wanted to find out what men and women are and how they feel and what makes them act the way they do.

That last sentence paraphrases an anonymous novelist whom I am unable to identify but who published in *Harper's* some years ago an excellent discussion of this basic fact. He added that in the mass people still go to novelists to find out about those things, rather than to psychologists, and remarked, "nor can I find it in my heart to say that is an unwise preference." He then went on to say:

> *Sure it implies that novelists know better than you do what the human being is and how he gets that way. Sure it implies that in so far as I am a novelist, just so far I am wiser than you [he should have said "than most of you"] about the human soul. Don't think that any novelist will manage his own life or understand his friends any better than you do. [This supports what I have just said, but I think a novelist is likely to manage his own life less well than you.] But, in common with most other literate people, you have got from novels a part of what you know and a greater part of what you believe about the human race. From novels. From books written by men and women who, in frustration or impotence or despair it may be, but somehow, were more sensitized than most others to how people feel and why, and who have made that sensitivity a means of giving you more understanding and more pity than you had before.*

He is right and in some moods psychologists are prompt to acknowledge that he is right. In an exurberant moment Dr. Theodor Reik speaks of Dostoyevsky as "a psychologist whose knowledge of human nature surpassed that of all the members of the International Psychoanalytic Association." If an ordinary reader is willing to accept the imaginary experience in novels as real, in a way, up to a point, for a more or less brief period, psychologists are frequently willing to accept it as completely valid, as experience to which they can apply without alteration or adjustment the same tests they apply professionally to real experience. Freud took from a character in the poetic drama, which is to say from fiction, the name he gave to the constellation of energies that constitutes the basis of his psychological theory. His works and those of his associates and successors contain a good many passages which discuss the imaginary emotions and behavior of characters in novels exactly as if they were those of actual people undergoing analysis. The technical literature of psychoanalysis and other psychologies frequently turns from emotion and behavior observed in the consulting room to those which never had any existence but are described in novels, with no regard for the fact that the substance is completely different.

In less arrogant moods the novelist is astonished by this amiability of psychologists but it is nevertheless justified. A novelist is a psychologist. He is, in the word I have just quoted, "sensitized" to human feeling and behavior. The better novelist he is, the truer results this sensitivity will lead to — the more dependable will be his report on the emotion and behavior he creates for imaginary characters. There is no difference in truth, accuracy, or profundity between what a great novelist at his best perceives in human nature and what a great psychologist at his best uncovers there.

Under a perfectly useful system of classification the novels of, say, Tolstoy or Proust could stand on the same shelf with treatises of, say, Freud. Ever since there were great novelists they have been divining the sources of action, the motives, and the secret behavior of men. So long as there have been novelists of any kind, many of them have worked with equal validity if less deeply.

But in bringing our inquiry of what a novelist is to this point we have run into a dilemma. He is liable, I have said, to be tone-deaf and unperceptive in the presence of actual emotion or to have only a superficial understanding of behavior that he sees occurring, and yet he is capable of creating characters so truly that their emotion and behavior will illustrate and explain the very ones he missed or misunderstood. It is only a slight dilemma. The reader, we found, needed some means of achieving engagement with the imaginary emotions of the novel. The novelist needs a means of engaging himself with those imaginary emotions and also with actual ones. The bridge or contact-switch turns out to be the same for both novelist and reader.

*   *   *

A novelist works at home and the machinery of the household involves innumerable things which in the eyes of his wife and children are considerably more important than his work. This may be sound literary criticism but it is before the fact. In any event domestic common sense seldom scruples to interfere with an apparently unoccupied man's occupation. A daughter's wheeling her doll carriage up and down the hall once led Mark Twain to wonder whether it was not a mistake for an artist to have children. A novelist remarked to me of his wife, who had probably asked an idle man to carry the laundry upstairs, "I can't make her understand that if I'm staring out the window I'm working."

He is working — harder, probably, than when he is at his desk. He is working most of the time. During his most intensely busy moments he is likely to seem to an outsider a loafer wasting time as pointlessly as the crowd that watches a steamshovel excavating a basement.

You and I are the wittiest people, half an hour too late. We have never lost an argument, in the end. Intellectual power takes us straight to the heart of every question that proved too involved for a dinner-table conversation to untangle, along about one A.M. We make sure that our excellences get adequate display on the way home or after going to bed, when we brilliantly supply the insight or repartee that was not at hand when we needed it. We redress grievances so forcibly that friends, strangers, and superiors tread on us at their peril, and there lurk in all of us courage, skill, sagacity, and cunning that are the admiration of mankind or would be if we could find some way of getting them into the open. Of our unvarying success with women it would not be seemly to speak here.

These are phantasies and they ring us round. They lurk along the edges of consciousness and we constantly turn to them from the reality of the moment. A thousand stimuli in the day's routine plunge us momentarily into more vivid, more consoling, more exciting, or more terrifying products of an invention that is seldom quiet. Something in what a friend says may call up in our mind an imagined scene so engrossing that we no longer hear him talking. The music of a hurdy-gurdy on the street corner, the swirl of a woman's skirt, or light glinting from the windshield of a car may raise the curtain on a similar drama. Nor do we need exterior stimuli. A stream of reverie flows beside the main channel of consciousness and at times floods over into it.

When psychologists speak of the stream of consciousness, in fact, they mean the river in which the streams have joined. The Mississippi of the mind is always below the mouth of the Missouri.

Moreover everyone "makes up" stories from his phantasy. We have all died lingeringly and seen someone stricken by remorse; we have all cast ourselves under the wheels of loco-motives as the result of pitiful events. There is no man alive who has not cleared the bases with a homer in the ninth inning, carried a child from a burning house, avenged with courageous cruelty the slights put on him by wife or sweet-heart — and suffered with a sensitiveness or nobility not gen-erally accredited to him by the coarse world. There is no woman who has not surrendered after a long flight which she conducted with more art and power of sexual attraction than the world sees in her or she in fact has. These may be very extended stories, a serial of the ego. Yet experience has taught everyone (except neurotics) to pursue such phan-tasies as an off-hours diversion only. Everyone recognizes them for what they are. They are understood to be a transi-tory means of gratifying impulses which it is inexpedient to express in action — or impulses that would produce more discomfort than, on the whole, one cares to undergo. Or a means of correcting the providence that has given us less than we deserve. Most of all they are seen to be fragmentary, their logic is seen to be fallacious, and they drift where they want to go of their own will. They are not dreams but they are like dreams in that they are not subject to the control of the one who makes them, the subject of them who is also their object.

In this way, then, everyone is his own novelist but an unsatisfactory one. An actual novelist is a person who not only has a gift of phantasy more highly developed than other people but also has an ability to organize his phantasies in coherent sequences and to bring them closer to the realities. It is fair to say too that with him there are times when phantasy is not "less real" than what happens but "more real." This is not to say that he is an obsessive or any other kind of neurotic, and we must not suggest that a novel is a delusional system. But the phantasies out of which it is made are sometimes what connect the novelist with the objective world. At such times they are more immediate than the world of friendship, nutrition, and fatigue in which his body exists and they are frequently superior to it. At such times they form the conduits by which realities reach him. At such a time Mr. Lewis would only vaguely see what was happening at the Rotary Club; that luncheon would be less real than the Rotary inside him.

Such phantasies are the basis of every novel. They are generated by the impact of the novelist's experience on his ego. They flow from what has happened to him in relation to his needs, urges, impulses, disappointments, desires, fears, hopes, anxieties, and ambitions — in relation to the sum of these from infancy on. Necessarily therefore a novel steams and ferments with its author's personal history.

Novels, then, are autobiographies? Of course they are. Where would the novelist get the emotion that moves you in his characters' experience except from inside himself? What is the psychology that a novelist practises professionally except a conscious, semi-conscious, and unconscious examination of himself? Or a need to release in print the greatest character he has ever created, himself? In a way the title of a novel is always *Confessions of Jean-Jacques Dos Passos.* But we must be careful how we understand that statement and what we mean by autobiography. We have thus said that every novel is a *roman à clef* but who can find the key? Except in trivial aspects of the novel — minor characters or relationships that have only an accessory function, small episodes tiresome to write but necessary in the preparation of more highly charged ones, stage business which it is mere economy of energy to set down from the literal — the key is likely to be beyond the reach of a critic or an inquisitive friend.

Actual *romans à clef,* novels in which the writer intends the reader to identify the fictitious characters as actual living or historical persons, in fact, supply a flagrant clue. They are exceedingly hard to write, so hard that few good ones are written. In the others the reader is able to make out very easily either a mediocre novelist or a compulsive motive. Most of them belong to the species of light satire which the reader enjoys precisely because he sees that the novelist has distorted the characters and falsified their motives. No minute scrutiny is required to reveal that the novelist is symbolically paying off grudges or avenging hurts, and no deep introspection is required to reveal that the reader's pleasure comes from their correspondence to his own grudges and hurts of about the same importance. That is one reason why light satire is short-lived, why it is dead and usually irritating or absurd when we come back to it later: fiction's grudge-fights and revenges must be on a deeper plane if they are to endure.

Whereas a better novelist or one working more deeply finds it increasingly hard from page one on to keep imaginary characters congruent with actual models. He may set them in a situation that reproduces the essentials of an actual one or so clearly symbolize them that a reader can identify it, but he will find the situation changing as he writes and it is likely to go on changing till the resemblance becomes merely formal or disappears. He may do his utmost to dramatize just the characteristics of an actual Jane Smith that her friends regard as her truest self and the very conduct that he wants to deride, punish, or avenge. But by page

50 it has become hard for Jane's friends to believe that she could act in the way alleged and by another hundred pages she is beyond recognition. The Miriam of the novel who represents her has Jane's red hair and some of her verbal mannerisms but she has become a different woman.

On page one Jane Smith was swept into the turbulence of the novelist's phantasy as we have described it. So Miriam becomes a composite of many women he has known in fact and phantasy and she is doubtless a displaced part of himself too — and, as well, she has acquired an identity of her own. The same is true of the other characters, once actors in a drama of real life. The grudge that had to be paid off or the wound that had to be healed, it turns out, was deeper down. The novelist has made a deeper engagement with his materials than he intended to and the needs served by this novel have proved to be necessities. There is more of him here than there was meant to be, and in a different light, and the fable he set out to write had a sharper point — it was, if you like, more desperate. Finally there has come into action one of the attributes of fiction that entitle it to be called, in the strict denotation of the word, magic. For the novelist found that he must hold Jane Smith against the complex necessities of a complex whole, whose dynamics set requirements of its own for the role that Jane had to play. That is an additional and astonishing reason why Jane was transformed into an individual Miriam.

On behalf of all novelists we need one more item from this process and from the novelist who undertook to create characters identifiable as actual people, living or dead. How would he set out to make Adolf Hitler, or the headmaster of his prep school (who appears to have scared more novelists than ever Hitler did), or that girl he almost married — how would he set out to make any actual person a character in a novel? How would he set out to make you one? Or, to say

it in full, what is the bridge that would enable him to understand the painful episodes or emotions in your life to which
we said some pages back he is so often tone-deaf?

Clearly he must begin in phantasy and we have seen the
conduit, the wire which the current travels. He must make
an identification with you and, seemingly, he must do so by
one or the other of two acts of imagination. They are radically different although they are not necessarily separated.
Surely it is by phantasy, by in part identifying myself with
you, that I may share your delight or sorrow — that they become alive and real for me — that I may answer your human
need for sympathy. Surely also there is a difference between
my responding to what happens to you by imagining what I
myself would feel in your case, and my responding by
dramatizing your feelings as imaginatively mine. Both responses are identification. Both mean that, in a way, in part,
up to a point, I have succeeded in becoming you emotionally. Well, a novelist gives his characters life by the same
identification, and here also there are the same two kinds.
It is likely that they are seldom pure, that both processes are
involved in any given act of a novelist's imagination. Nevertheless in any novelist's imagination one will predominate
over the other. For our immediate purpose that fact makes
little difference — we are now merely stating how the wire
becomes a live wire — but it sharply defines a basic difference. Fiction's autobiography is always amplified. There
are novelists who amplify it primarily by incorporating in
themselves the experience of others. There are novelists
who amplify it primarily by projecting their own experience
on others.

*   *   *

Let's get on with autobiography. But first a stop-sign must
be set up, one that will recur at intervals from now on. We

are concentrating on the psychological sources of fiction in the hope of describing the relationship between novelists and their readers. But, as I have said, we must not think of a novel as made by automatic machine tools or of its author as an automatic switchboard. Neither is a closed system ready for Dr. Norbert Wiener's study. It may be that by the minute probing of psychoanalysis every item in a novel could be found to have at least a slight color of reference personal to the novelist and that a complete if invisible conditioning of the novel could be established. It may be, and once or twice psychoanalysts have advanced that idea to me as a theoretical possibility — but I doubt it. I will give my reasons when we come to free will. Here it is enough to say that people have conscious minds too and novelists use theirs, whatever embittered friends may suggest to the contrary. That fact is to be remembered as we go on burrowing.

Chemists recognize a phenomenon that will be useful as an analogy. A chemical element has properties wholly its own: that is what makes it an element. But compounds, which are made up of elements, also have properties entirely their own. The properties specific to a compound are different and distinct from those of the elements that compose it. Furthermore, as more complex compounds are built up, the chemical system — the relationships and equilibrium among the components — has properties which determine the activity of its constituents. Its characters, so to speak, have experiences or emotions that derive from the chemical system itself, not from the compounds in the system or from elements in the compounds.

Well, that is a novel. A novelist has thought and felt characters into existence. He has grown them into relationships and situations that produce forces of their own. He lives with them in the dynamic relationships they themselves live in; he overhears, he watches, he feels. A force begins to operate which is distinct from the one interior to him that set things in motion. His sophistication consists of an ability to incorporate with his own emotions material which takes life from them by induction — or chemical combination. He fuses public and private elements into something new, something different from both. Unless he is a primitive type (disregarded for the moment but taken up farther along) his autobiography will not be history but symbols.

Except when such primitives (Folsom Man of the Asheville Site) are in question it would be naïve to suppose that the antipathy between characters named Joe and Herbert embodies or represents the novelist's quarrel with his best friend. The cruelties inflicted on the character named Miriam are not a confession that a woman capable of being identified once treated him badly. The career of another character named Patricia does not confirm the rumor that he had an affair with a movie actress. And Bill, the hero, is not the novelist as he wishes or imagines himself to be.

Or rather, Bill is indeed the novelist — but he is also an almost infinite number of echoes and reflections of other people who have affected the novelist's life. More than that, he is further compounded from needs and desires and compensations and penalties and dreads, some of them private to the author but others picked up elsewhere and worked in here because they are of the same tone, are on the same wave-length. In the same way the cravenness of the character named Herbert is an act of revenge on various people who have injured the novelist, a defiance of some who have frightened him, a public confession of guilt that is both expiatory and safe — and, as well, fragments of all these from lives exterior to the novelist, fragments that appear here because the identical emotion has made them fluorescent. Similarly with Miriam and Patricia. In both are vestiges of many actual women; and each is also a complex image of longing unfulfilled, desire unsatisfied, and revenge taken, or the converse of all these; and each is a compulsive projection of part of the novelist himself. Similarly with all the others, the little boy on page 60, the old family servitor, the straw boss, the threatening crowd offstage. When they walk and talk it is the novelist walking and talking — but in costumes that will disguise him from research. They are, in addition, compounds in which elements entirely outside him have united by attraction. Finally, they are images projected from the swarm within him, deposits left on him by contact with many lives — and also something straight from the core of desire and fear that throbs below his consciousness.

The psychological substance is infinitely divisible. We are wise to search for the smallest particles, which will set the tone of a relationship or an episode in a novel, not write a scene. They may be displaced from the novelist so far that they will be merely a transformed feeling which gives life to a symbol. But they are there: autobiography is a magnet beneath the page and filings form round it . . . let us not forget, in lines of beauty as well as force.

But by now the phantasies have been organized into an exceedingly complex system. Here are characters, wholly imaginary people, who live, feel, and act according to the needs and logic of themselves and of the relationships that bind them together. This is a long way from the shapeless bits that drift from a stream of reverie into more central areas of consciousness. There is no word for it except the battered one, art. But, at even this early stage of our inquiry, it should now be possible to say something else. To turn from the job one is doing, say cooking an omelet or adding up a column of figures, and float for a moment with that shapeless bit of phantasy is indeed to turn away from reality. But if an organized system of phantasies moving under its own momentum and according to the laws of its own metabolism is not insanity — and assuredly a novel is not — then it may be a strange and momentous thing, it may be an effort to achieve reality.

*   *   *

We must look at something else that happens when someone writes a novel. It leads to a segment of experience which we have previously reached through the person who reads a novel. Since we reach the same destination by such different roads we are sanctioned to believe that it is fundamental in the art of fiction.

Every reader of fiction divides novels (however else he may also classify them for other purposes) into two groups, a small group of good ones and a large group of the mediocre or worse. In mediocre novels a phenomenon occurs with sufficient frequency that one tends to think it is revealing. In many run of the mill novels the scenes that deal with childhood are better done, more convincing, more real and alive, than the other parts. Novelists often write more authoritatively about childhood than about maturity. It is as if their own adult lives had proved less important than the enchanted (or bewitched) years, or as if a compulsion lingering on from childhood were stronger than their adult wills. Or again, the characters of a mediocre novel are sometimes preposterously simple in motive or behavior, as simple as a child thinks adults are. Or they seem to feel a child's emotions when a grownup's are called for. Or they seem to be not warm, fallible, and contradictory human beings but just creatures in a fable, a child's fantasy of virtue, evil, heroism, villainy, danger, muscular power, or destruction. What happens to them is as uncomplicated, or has as little relation to what happens in this world, as a child's image of what would happen if its secret thoughts were to find expression.

In short, a peril of one who has an unusual gift of phantasy is that he may be emotionally fixed in some part of his childhood. A bad novel may be a regression toward infancy. A really good novelist — as a mature, non-literary reader will use the adjective "good" — must have many talents and their proportion varies. But the common essential is this: that he must so far transcend his childhood as to impart to the phantasies from which his books are made the emotions proper to adults. There is no such thing as a complete delivery from childhood, and it is true of all arts that the generative force of the artist's phantasy derives from the years in which there is little distinction between the world of experience and that of the imagination. So that, though a mature novelist's personal history cannot be recovered from his books, as we have just said, their pattern nevertheless expresses a pattern that was fixed during his childhood. No novelist ever has more than one story.

As he goes on writing novels that story may be modulated, transposed, reversed, displaced, wrought into symbols till the books that embody it are dissimilar to the outward view. But its outline is fixed and most simple. Look at the collected works and you will find in all of them the assertion of some magnificent simplicity: doom precipitated or doom averted, desire fulfilled or unfulfilled, cruelty or tenderness triumphant, the world conquering or the world conquered, life stable or life flowing away. It is a fable as elementary as one spelled out with the alphabet of a child's blocks. For thus the world was in dread or dream when the novelist was young and thus it therefore has to be now that he is writing books. But the mature artist is one who can modify the dream — who can turn it toward reality. An inferior novelist writes fables in compliance with a child's urges: a mature novelist has made those urges obey the teaching of experience.

In every novel the shapes of childhood will be walking, and as we have already seen, part of such power as it may have for any reader will be the response of a child meeting another child. But in a fine novel there is a stronger force, that released by meeting adults, children who have grown up to be men, who are no longer controlled by a child's fears and wishes, in whom dream has been shaped to conform to what really is. A fine novel is a victory for the reality-principle, for the faculty of control, for the human will.

It remains a vicarious triumph, since it is won in printer's ink. But art is the world of vicarious experience, and if only in that world are some of the achievements of maturity possible for the artist, that condition of his life is a benevolence to the rest of us since it makes those achievements possible for us too. None of us has ever completely silenced the little monster from whom he grew, but sometimes in a mature novel we can break all the chains that bind us to him. If a novel is sometimes the only place in which its writer can be altogether grown up, it may also be a place where a reader can put away childish things altogether and be what he will never be in his own person, a whole man.

3

ALICE'S ADVENTURES IN UTOPIA

ALICE'S ADVENTURES IN UTOPIA

THIS INQUIRY has a narrow base. The facts we have been dealing with are background facts and they must not be allowed to get out of proportion to the whole. This is a good place to remember that people read novels for pleasure — for fun — and that novelists write them professionally. Some of the experiences of art — a phrase that must not be printed with capital initials — enter the life of everyone, but most of them never enter the lives of most people at all. At the utmost, even among people who value it most highly, fiction can play only an exceedingly small part in anyone's life. For most people who read it, it is a slight unimportant thing. Anything that anyone says about it can be true only to a degree and the degree varies.

Because its illusion is private, because one reads a novel to oneself, fiction cannot be a mass art, though we may say figuratively that it approaches mass art as it reaches large numbers of people. Several hundred novels are published in the United States every year. Shall we say that an average sale is eight thousand copies and extends over three or six months? At the end of a year twenty-five thousand people may have read this statistical novel. Thereafter it will be only another book on the shelves of private or public libraries, read only by chance or at the suggestion of someone who remembers having liked it, eventually disposed of to make room for another one which is already fading from remembrance. It vanishes: it becomes merely a physical entity, smeared paper for which there is no use.

The chances are that such a novel represented the best work of a writer who was trying to deal honestly with experience as he understood it. He simply did not feel deeply enough, or understand well enough, to command more than a transient attention. He was entangled in the pain and necessity of human experience, he felt joy and grief intensely, but his report on them proved to be superficial and commonplace, and probably also he was not a sufficiently good workman to achieve his intent. Among the twenty-five thousand people who read his book there may have been every degree of engagement with it but for only a comparative few was the degree more than slight. Certainly for every novel there are some perfect readers, people who by the permutations of chance have been prepared to find themselves in tune with it and to respond in a conviction that some of the meaning they have derived from their lives is here confirmed and clarified. The simplest, the most trivial or casual, the most superficial symbol may evoke our deepest feelings and beliefs, as we demonstrate when we are stopped short in the street and half-paralyzed by regret, overhearing a phrase from some cheap song that was associated with an intense experience long ago. But in the main the statistical novel meant little to those who read it. It sufficed to amuse the statistical reader for a few hours, to protect him from boredom, to divert his attention from the aches of influenza, to sharpen the outline of his interior drama while he was reading it, to facilitate the processes of digestion, to accelerate the effect of a Nembutal capsule taken at bedtime. His engagement with it was shallow; it left no deposit on his mind. He has only a hazy remembrance of it and could not tell you Miriam's last name or why she felt so sorrowful. This may be a small return for the effort of a novelist's total personality but it is one of the conditions under which he works.

This, however, is only to voice a platitude, that fine artists are rare and that the full experience of fiction is possible to only a few people. We are back in fiction's little world. Of the several hundred novels published in any given year not more than twenty-five undertook to get out of the little world into the big one, to deal meaningfully with the depths of human experience, and it is a good year if three make the grade. Yet the twenty-two that were turned back at the frontier were efforts in the direction of truth — and I must emphasize that most of the annual production were efforts in the direction of less important truths. In the little world the aims of novelists are humbler and more limited and their capacities are fully visible. The novels are insubstantial, they deal weakly with important aspects of life or they deal only with less important and ephemeral aspects, their characters are less deeply conceived, their actions are less significant, the illusion is less real and less lasting. But it is important of fiction's little world that if less is given here, less is also asked.

Nevertheless, these novels were read. However limited their purpose or the effect they achieved, readers made the engagement with them we have described, and in that engagement all the forces we have isolated were operating. They are the background facts where the foreground is a person reading a novel, no matter what other and conscious reasons he may have, no matter what the novel may be about. They were all there while he was reading, if only faintly, and the illusion held, if only just. The proof is absolute: the reader did not shut the book.

Statistically, he never will. For though at one end of the curve the demands mankind makes of fiction may be slight, trumpery, ridiculous, or meretricious, they are nevertheless, together with the demands made at the other extremity of the curve, eternal. We may conceive the first novelist as still too timorous to stay out of the trees for any length of time. But he is telling a story of imaginary events occurring to imaginary apes. And in the eyes of those gathered round him in a circle to listen you will see fear, excitement, and delight — born of the simple magic that in so far as it happens to any ape, it happens also to me. The audience will go about its business in a few minutes but the succession will never be broken. So long as the ape's inheritors can see themselves mirrored in the cast of characters, however dimly or momentarily, they will always be under the necessity of finding out what happened in the mirror's next chapter — and to themselves.

A novel is a story of imaginary events occurring to imaginary people — *plus* a reader who follows it with recognition and surprise. It leads on. All novels are adventure stories: they deal with strange occurrences in a strange world, occurrences that raise your pulse-beat and make your breath catch with suspense. They are all detective stories: they work toward the solution of a mystery. They are all fairy stories too, and they are all parables.

I repeat: although the reader's engagement with the novel may be slight and shallow, it invariably includes all the energies we have so far described, though some or indeed all of them may be operating only on the far margin. As fiction widens toward the mass audience, it is probably the simple outline-symbols and the direct phantasies they stand for that count most, and probably also the engagement is most temporary. I am not clear that anyone is therefore licensed to pass by on the other side.

The enormous circulation of some novels that has been such a striking phenomenon in recent years must in part be explained on other grounds than the nature of fiction. Many people read *Gone With the Wind* and *Forever Amber* for the same reason that they bought Lucky Strikes or Pepsodent: extensive advertising told them to and so they did. Many others read them for the same reason that they wore a particular kind of hat or played certain dance records on their phonographs: a lot of other people were doing the same thing at the same time. But neither advertising nor fashion can be much of an explanation. There are always fashions in the writing as well as the reading of novels. As this is written a late fashion has produced a number of novels which explore the psychic adventures of alcoholics and a number of others which explore those of the inmates of insane asylums. None of them has been first-rate or even, in any critical sense, serious. The best of them have achieved the authenticity of documents in social anthropology, a species of fiction I have already classed as humble; the others are, critically speaking, frivolous. But surely neither advertising nor fashion can explain the widespread interest in them. On a plane simple enough to be easily intelligible they are the kind of fiction I have called but for the grace of God. In a time of trouble and anxiety, it has been possible for large numbers of troubled, anxious people to make the necessary engagement, to find in these novels an embodiment of some of their own phantasies, and to get from them one of the fundamental experiences of fiction, if only temporarily. They would have to be better novels than any has yet been for the experience to go very deep or the effect to be more than transient, but a lot of people got as much as they could from as much as was there.

Documentary and anthropological fiction always works under that limitation. For instance the tensions and dangers of interracial friction can make good novels only as they may become experience of individual people who live as characters in their own right. Novels are about people, not themes or problems: themes, problems, social ideals, a sense of moral urgency are not of themselves fiction. Yet the outline-symbols of comparatively undeveloped novels may induce the engagement of many readers who have been favorably sensitized by the currents of thought and feeling round them. Take Miss Laura Hobson's *Gentleman's Agreement*. Expert in surface technique, this book got the dividends that good contrivance will always earn but it was a frivolous novel. That is to say, its characters were shallowly conceived, of no great reality, presented as two-dimensional exponents of a theme. They were forced into an adventitious situation so that the psychological experience they were asked to work through was unreal. The author dealt with that experience after the manner of the slicks, she answered the question it posed by avoiding the issue. Miss Gwethalyn Graham's *Earth and High Heaven,* which also dealt with social anti-Semitism, was a more serious novel, was almost a serious novel. Its theme was embodied in the experience of its characters, their experience was true as individual experience and it was therefore moving, and Miss Graham dealt justly and rigorously with it through four fifths of the novel — when she too refused or proved unable to meet the issue she had herself set up. A first-rate novel on the subject common to these two would have come to grips with life as they did not, would have to hide the theme behind the living characters so completely that it would not be visible to the eye. But both set up a symbolical fable to which many people could respond, if not often deeply or more than transiently.

With such a novel as *Gone with the Wind* the process is simpler and clearer. All its characters, instrumentalities, and effects were familiar, old and even ancient in fiction, and no one will say that any went deep or, on reflecting after the fact, that any had much reality. But Miss Mitchell gave us a sharp reminder that a novel is a story of imaginary events occurring to imaginary people — that so long as events *do* occur to characters that resemble people, there will always be a handhold for the ape's successor to fasten on in his eagerness to follow the story. In a novel of improbable length there were few emotions that were real and none that were deep or strong, but she took us through it because her storytelling was expert and because the stories she told had enough elementary symbolism to help the narrative persuade her reader that they were happening to him. For a moment.

Nothing so elevated can be said of *Forever Amber*. It is hard to imagine a novel which would have fewer of the qualities that any common criterion of fiction calls good. Miss Winsor has little skill at storytelling: her narratives have only a mechanical movement and even that movement is undependable, it repeatedly stalls. If Miss Mitchell's characters are assembled from the conventions of fiction that have proved reliable through the centuries, at least they derive some life from the conventions, whereas Miss Winsor's have hardly a surface appearance of life. Throughout that mass of pages it is hard to find a moment of emotion: the novelist keeps proclaiming it but her Honest Whore and the rest of the cast neglect to feel it. If readers think they

find its appearance there, one is tempted to believe, they do
so like the buyers of consumers' goods, because the adver-
tiser, here the novelist, keeps on telling them to. A reader
always writes the greater part of any novel — the skill of the
novelist is to make him write the novel intended — but he
can seldom have been required to write so much of it as he
is forced to here. It embarrasses the literary view that so
many hundreds of thousands of readers have at an obviously
inept novelist's bidding looked at wooden figures labeled
Aristocrat's Honor or Irresistible Muliebrity and bestowed
on them enough belief to turn the page. But what does
turning these particular pages mean? Clearly that the need
which the inheritors of the ape feel for fiction they can hang
their phantasies on is so desperate that if they get even such
a peg as this they will put up with novel-writing about as
unskillful and unreal as it is is possible to be. . . . We need
not be dismayed: it is only for a moment.

   Forever Amber has brought us to the far perimeter of fiction, to the frontier province where the inhabitants are
called the Rover Boys or Lanny Budd. On the way there
we passed without pausing a species of novel even more
annoying to the literary view. Let us not misrepresent the
Reverend Lloyd Cassel Douglas, especially to ourselves. He
can write narrative, no inconsiderable talent and one which
a good many better novelists possess in smaller measure. He
can take such stockroom dolls as Miss Winsor vends and
make them behave with great liveliness, as she cannot.
Twenty years [1] during which booksellers have seldom
ordered his works in lots of less than twelve dozen gross have
proved that readers will stampede to accept his fictions, and
with rejoicing. That, in the literary view, is precisely why
the case is so dreadful. For if Miss Winsor merely makes

---

[1] *Magnificent Obsession*, 1929.

conventionally sentimental assertions about experience, Mr.
Douglas's figurines falsify experience.

Not, of course, by Mr. Douglas's intent. Some kinds of
fiction can be written with little or no conviction of the
novelist that what he says is true, but Mr. Douglas's kind
cannot. Years ago Don Marquis put it for all time when he
wrote in regard to the novels of Harold Bell Wright, from
whose roots Mr. Douglas has so gorgeously flowered, "It's
Moral Worth that wins the Mazuma. And it can't be faked."
The essence of this kind of fiction is the fervor of the novelist's own belief in its axioms. Without that there could be
no throngs to follow the kind of big fisherman he is. When
Mr. Douglas's *Green Light* appeared I undertook to explain
the phenomenon to subscribers of *The Saturday Review*.
The explanation holds good and I quote part of it here:

> *He tells us: one increasing purpose runs. He tells
> us: let not your heart be troubled. He tells us no more
> — but do not be disdainful. . . . Millions want to be told
> just that. . . . He gives them what they need and des-
> perately desire: assurance. In a time of economic chaos
> [this was 1935] it is comforting to be told that the Long
> Parade is Moving Onward in God's plan. In a time of
> disaster, it is comforting to be told that one is being
> Dragged Up. It is always comforting to frightened,
> weary, and discouraged men, to be told that they are
> the masters of their fate, that they have a spiritual
> power which will bring them through, that they have
> the Kingdom of Heaven within them, that the God-
> spirit of which they are a part has given them unused
> and even unguessed capacities for heroism and eventual
> success. It is comforting and, when told in terms of
> metrical and crepuscular vagueness, it is convincing.*

Thoughts so noble, so impalpable, so incapable of precise statement must be true.

Comfort is what his readers ask of Mr. Douglas and comfort is what they get. His books could not sell by the carload . . . unless his public found what they were looking for. . . . He works with the humbler symbols of art but they are eternal symbols. Their success on the lower levels of literature, in the sub-basements where yearning and exhortation and incantation dictate their form, requires no explanation. Does Molly-Make-Believe *need to be explained. Or* St. Elmo? *Or* Tempest and Sunshine? *Or* If Winter Comes?

But let not your heart be troubled, either, for again it is only for a moment.

In an area where fiction approaches a mass art, then, we have found three if not indeed four varieties of novels in which the imaginary experience drew progressively farther away from the realities of experience and made itself progressively more congruent with elementary, and perhaps compulsive, phantasies of the reader. With at least the last variety the reader is, even if at his own behest, misled. As we say, life is not like that. But is not this reprehensible of fiction? Is not fiction behaving viciously or even criminally? Can any good come from bearing false witness against experience, from falsifying truth? Is it not weakness in a reader to desire such falsification and evil of a novelist to gratify the desire?

There are always those who believe it is evil.

*   *   *

I was once a guest at a small dinner where another guest was Miss Frances Perkins, then Secretary of Labor. Three novelists were present, one of them a novelist good enough to be named Rebecca West. It was Miss Perkins's mood to spend an hour explaining that writing novels was an occupation proper only to children and reading them an occupation proper only to the old. Surely, she said, it was the duty of adults to act, to get something done in the world (and to improve it if they could), and writing novels was the very antithesis of action. And not only that: it was anti-social behavior besides, for the deplorable thing was that people insisted on reading fiction and so the novelist kept them from the very action of which life is intended to consist. Novels gave young people false ideas about life and so tended to unfit them for life. It was even more culpable of adults to surrender to the seduction of unreality. Theirs to be up and doing, facts were better than dreams, man was created in order to will his own activity — and fiction was a narcotic drug. For the old, yes: they could no longer act and it might be that in the loneliness of age the dreams which fiction makes up could have some consolation, some value as a substitute for action. Yet Miss Perkins could see no way of licensing novelists to practice their childish trade for old people only, there would always be the danger that young people and adults capable of action would get hold of the drug and fall victim to it. I felt that if she had been running the New Deal there would have been no Writers Project.

There has always been formidable support for the Secretary's ideas. Of the two literary critics who have been most influential throughout the history of literature, one held the same views. Novels, he said, were falsehoods; they dealt with the appearance of appearances, not with realities; they were at least three removes from truth; and they might deceive children. It was beyond the power of novelists "to educate and improve mankind." Indeed the case was worse still, for novelists necessarily perceived things falsely and

therefore must communicate false impressions to their readers. Their art, in fact, consisted solely of misinterpretation,
misrepresentation, and the corruption of the reader that
must ensue. Their art was magic — black magic. It worked
on "that weakness of the human mind on which the art of
conjuring and of deceiving by light and shadow and other
ingenious devices imposes, having an effect on us like magic."
Even worse, it worked on one of the inferior principles of
the soul — and it increased the conflicts there. "The soul
has been acknowledged by all of us to be full of these and
ten thousand similar oppositions occurring at the same
time."

This begetter of more than two thousand years of literary
criticism went on to say that, worse still, the novelist actually
prefers "the passionate and fitful temper" of the soul. So he
will unman us, giving us dreams instead of realities. We
must be up and doing, we must not be children past our
time. Take, for instance, the manliness with which we
ought to meet misfortune. The shadows that are fiction, its
appearances of appearances, will undermine our wills and we
will give way to the softness with which lingering in its
dream-world has infected us. Whereas properly we should
"when the dice have been thrown order our affairs in the
way which reason deems best, not like children who have
had a fall keeping hold of the part struck and wasting time
setting up a howl, but always accustoming the soul forth-
with to apply a remedy, raising up that which is sickly and
fallen, banishing the cry of sorrow by the healing art." (The
healing art is here understood to be the power of the soul to
penetrate through illusions to the realities and its preference for realities over fictions.) And this brings the critic to
his severest accusation. Fiction has a power "of harming
even the good" and this "is surely an awful thing." Fiction

is evil; novelists are evil. As in a city when the evil are permitted to have authority and the good are put out of the
way, so in the soul of man the novelist "implants an evil
constitution, for he indulges the irrational nature which has
no discernment of greater and less, but thinks the same
things at one time great and at another small — *he is a man-
ufacturer of images and is very far removed from the truth.*"

Wherefore, in the judgment of a character named Socrates
in a *roman à clef* by Plato, wherefore and quite literally the
novelist be damned. Socrates is engaged in composing one
of the most moving fantasies in literature, he is imagining
the Perfect State. To that State he will not admit novelists:
they are for illusion and against reality, they impair reason
by awakening and nourishing and strengthening the feelings. And yet Socrates remembers that there are ends to be
served and so he attaches a rider to his bill of exile. Novelists may hold citizenship, he decides, provided they will
write novels which are solely "hymns to the Gods and praises
of famous men." In the Perfect State of fantasy, as in the
only perfect state the world has yet seen, novelists will be
tolerated so long as they follow the party line.

And how does Plato bring to climax the *Republic*, one
of the noblest of all books? [2] Immediately after this passage
on the arts, he has Socrates say, "I will tell you a tale." And
Socrates then goes on to tell a story about a hero, Er the son
of Armenius, and the symbolic journey of the soul willing
its own destiny — and how the soul grapples with fate and
necessity, how in scorching heat it crosses a barren waste
called Forgetfulness and pauses by the river of Unmindful-
ness (which, like the shifting images of any dream is somehow the plain as well as a river), and how at last it passes

[2] Noble, that is, as exalted thinking and noble in the moments of the
ideal. But it is first systematic treatise on totalitarian government.

over that river to maintain itself undefiled. . . . It is not clear whether Socrates and Plato should be admitted to the Perfect State. For they both turned novelist when the chips were down. As novelists they had to find symbols, appearances of the appearances of appearances, when they came to communicate what they felt to be the meaning of human experience. Against the health of the State they set up images to which an inappeasable urgency in the phantasies of readers has responded ever since, carrying them entirely out of the real world to one which existed only in Plato's imagination.

If only, so far as their readers go, if only for a moment now and then.

For Miss Perkins, then, all fiction is bad because it is a dream that gives some readers false ideas about life and withholds all readers from action. For Plato, here writing with the absolutism that schematic critics have adopted ever since — shall we say establishing the idea Critic? — there are right novels and wrong ones. Mr. Douglas's novels are acceptable since their images conduce to religious piety, and so are such historical novels as may express a patriotism that will improve civic virtue. But most novels are evil, so great an evil that the State must suppress them, because they cannot but report falsely. They cannot help corrupting the mind by misrepresenting reality. They give people false ideas about life. (There is an ambivalence here. Homer is acceptable when he praises the gods but it is the nature of Homer that he cannot know experience at first hand, that he cannot report truly on what a cabinetmaker or a physician feels, and so he cannot educate and improve mankind. Admitted to citizenship on one count, Mr. Douglas is banished under bill of attainder on another one.) The schematic critics who have come down from the Platonic archetype and today play the highbrow-quarterly circuit have invariably held that there are right and wrong kinds of novels and right and wrong ways of writing novels. They have usually, however, permitted fiction more than two functions. True, they always ask novels to praise virtue, though the virtue that must be praised changes with a probably calculable periodicity.[3] But they are usually willing to certify several kinds of novels as right, proper, and good — though with fair uniformity they usually reject others on precisely the grounds that made most kinds offensive to Plato. As their objection to comic books is platonic, that "they may deceive children," so they would find Mr. Douglas, Miss Winsor, and Miss Mitchell dangerous (if not Miss Hobson as well) because they represent life as it clearly and demonstrably is not. In common with an enormous amount of fiction recently described by one critic as "cultural sewage that is manufactured for the tastes of the lowbrow and lower-middlebrow . . . the oafish classes," the novels of these writers falsify reality and give readers incorrect ideas about life, softening and no doubt corrupting them.

A number of psychiatrists who have wanted to suppress comic books because they may deceive children have gone on to warn us against fiction that misrepresents reality. According to them it confirms the unreal and compensatory phantasies of readers, readers who when they come to it may already be but poorly equipped to distinguish phantasy from reality. Novels that do this confuse people. They report falsely on human experience, they make the unreal

---

[3] The novelist whom I quoted in the second chapter was probably speaking flippantly when he said that the cycle of critical absolutes had a recurrence of three and a half years. I once made a serious effort to work out the periodicity in American criticism since 1900. I got a figure of eight years and that is certainly the upper limit. Perhaps the novelist's figure represents an epicycle.

appear real, they give incorrect answers to the questions readers ask them. So they may seriously and even disastrously betray a reader's trust. They may make him interpret himself and the world incorrectly. They may increase the power of the unconscious forces in his mind that impel him away from reality. They may deceive and victimize him — so seriously, perhaps, that he will suffer impairment. They may so blunt the weapons with which he must fight the always desperate battle against unreality that he will lose it. Novels may tell lies to readers, although as Plato said it is the duty of the soul to search out the truth.

I am afraid we must go along with these thinkers, part of the way. We cannot deny that much of what fiction reports about life is false or that much fiction is read because it is expected to give false reports. A wide acquaintance among novelists has suggested to me the possibility that a few of them may not be infallible in perception or understanding. Some write novels out of an inner disorientation that probably makes it impossible for them to apprehend or represent reality. Some write novels with the deliberate intention of telling lies about life. In any event, most novelists occur along the median line, where they share the median ignorance, superstitions, and errors of mankind. And those to the left of it may, though with the purest aspiration, be even more deceived and therefore more likely to deceive children and adults. Along the median we must expect to find novels in which artificiality and honest but inevitable error mingles with trustworthy reporting on what is real. I see no way out, however, except the suppression of fiction on behalf of the good life proposed by Plato — but I see no reason why we should take that one. There is no reason why we should grant philosophers, critics, or psychiatrists plenary power over novelists. The reader of novels, I judge, has got to take his chances, to run the risk. Apart from fiction, he is used to it. He lives in and is forced to accommodate himself to a world where the realities are incorrectly reported to him by every kind of authority and specialist he appeals to. He must make his way as best he can among the errors of, say, dentists and economists. Not all that philosophers and literary critics have said about life has turned out in the end to be true, and we may guess that an occasional psychiatrist has been wrong in his understanding of experience.

But for the moment let us give philosophy, criticism, and psychiatry the whole case with a plea of *nolo contendere*. All right, novels sometimes misrepresent experience, either unintentionally or deliberately. Sometimes they give readers false ideas about life. Sometimes they support and strengthen the unreal phantasies of readers. Sometimes, even very often, they represent life as it certainly is not but as many readers deeply, if with deplorable weakness, wish it were. How evil is this? Is it evil at all?

It would be possible to waive these questions and the whole problem they involve as perhaps saddening but nevertheless irrelevant. We might say that the hunger of mankind for fiction indicates a necessity for precisely the drug-action that is declared to be deplorable or dangerous, and we might add that since it is a necessity nothing can be done about it on behalf of either reality or the good life. There are those who hold that alcohol is a grave danger too, we might say, and yet mankind has insisted on drinking it, despite all that philosophers and physicians and schematic critics could do for prohibition, ever since the processes of fermentation and distillation were discovered. The race has always drunk alcohol and smoked tobacco, we might say, though both are drugs and both have been called evil. We might add that Freud ranks the art of fiction higher in the scale than drugs and the alcohols, in a pasasge where he discusses the absolute necessity of human beings, in order to stay alive, to find such pleasure as they can in a world which makes happiness almost impossible for them.[4] Finally, we might point to that circle of apes listening to a story, and to the generations that have succeeded them. Pointing to them, we might say: there is no answer to that.

But there is no need to give the case away and the meaning to be found in the circle of listeners is altogether different. Part of it is implicit in what we have said before this. We will cheerfully turn over to the psychiatrists the people who cannot distinguish between phantasy and reality: they are the insane. It is precisely because as sane people we know very painfully the infrangible distinction between them that we invoke fiction. Precisely because we know that no princess will let down her hair for us from a tower, we are lead to read a story which we should not read if we could persuade ourselves one ever would. This fact is illuminated by the novels that are classified as fantasies. Certainly a novelist is not misleading any reader to his hurt when he notifies him at the beginning: the rules are suspended for three hundred pages and I am writing this story *as if*. As if the Food of the Gods could produce such monstrous growth; as if the Man Who Was Thursday could watch a man named Sunday produce such transformations of himself and exert such powers in a world otherwise subject to natural law. The illusion of fantasy can be as binding as that of the most realistic fiction and a reader can follow it with as much engagement and belief. He will feel an

4 This passage, however, leads to a much more important conclusion about the arts, a conclusion which negates the assumption Freud here makes as a way of focusing the problem. I shall be quoting it later on.

emotion just as strong when a rat the size of a St. Bernard runs across the floor as he feels when horror impends in a novel by Emile Zola.

The reader of fantasy has accepted an open falsehood. For this date and train only, for eight or ten hours, men are going to be horses, a woman is going to be a fox, earth-men are going to inhabit an asteroid, snow is going to fall steadily for weeks, all men but one are going to be sterile, or a girl is going to grow tall or tiny at will by nibbling the edge of a mushroom. We cannot convict Lewis Carroll of "harming even the good," sapping the human will, or victimizing honest burghers by giving them false ideas about life. He published legal notice that he was about to practise a deception in the public square and a reader who supposes that the blonde is actually being sawed in two is on his own. But if the novelist is thus cleared, can we on the other hand suppose that the reader who has rushed to embrace illusion has suffered injury? Confronted by a person who thought that the saw was actually cutting through the blonde's midriff, we would straightway call an ambulance and have him confined. An enthralled reader is not accepting as true the false idea that Alice can grow tall by sipping something from a bottle that is labeled "Drink me." There is a lie here but it is a permissive lie. The reader assented to it when he picked up the book.

There is an act of assent when he picks up any novel and it makes whatever deception the book may contain, whatever phantasies may expand or strengthen his own, permissive. He will go along with Mr. Douglas too — provided Mr. Douglas can give the phantasies force. He will do so gladly. Here for a time, as we say, dreams do come true, virtue really is rewarded, and man is master of his fate. It is only for a time — every reader knows that a term is set. He may gratify his own unreal phantasies with these unreal ones but only for a time; it cannot indefinitely escape his attention that he has shut the book. "As a rule," a friend writes me on this point, "the daydreams of fiction are less misleading than those we invent for ourselves. For the normal organism they are an inoculation against the more injurious private phantasies, and the more obviously they follow the superman and cinderella patterns the less likely most of us are to mistake them for reality." That is certainly true, and I would lay even more stress on the idea of inoculation than on the extremely important idea that the phantasies of fiction may be a substitute for phantasies, not for realities. The principle of inoculation or immunization joins hands with a principle I have several times pointed out, that the reader of fiction may gratify phantasies in safety.

Neither psychiatrists nor literary critics (I remember no philosophers who have dealt with the subject) have hesitated to inform us that the reader of a detective story may be gratifying symbolically, but therefore safely, a lamentable wish that none of us escapes feeling at times, the wish to murder his wife, mother, or sister. We cannot suppose that the false idea of life sedulously propagated by the mystery writer succeeds in persuading him that he has killed his wife, or even that there is a better chance he can kill her. Can we intelligently suppose that because inside the covers of a novel he has by a permissive phantasy slept with the heroine he therefore believes he has slept with Jane Smith in the flesh or will have a better chance to if he tries? I think not. And I doubt if anyone who has just finished reading a set of artfully constructed false ideas about life which for some hours permitted him to marry the boss's daughter, take over the firm, and buy a house on River Road, feels any impulse to phone an imaginary wife whom he has not got that he will meet her at a country club to which he does not belong. I doubt, too, if he will conduct himself in any increased belief that presently he will be able to. The false ideas of cheap fiction are much less dynamic than those plentifully supplied to everyone by religion and sociology. They have much less force, for they are understood to be dream, a dream which we recognize as such all the more certainly because when we picked up the book we volunteered to dream it.

Moreover, if these false ideas about life are an inoculation, as my friend says, they provide an additional defense against "more injurious private phantasies" in that they have had order imposed on them. Private phantasies are blobs that' drift where they will, but these have been given what in better fiction is called artistic form. They have inner organization and logic. That is why they are safe: they permit the injurious private phantasy to discharge, as it is not able to do by itself because of its confusion and contradictions. They are a healthier form of mental life in that they are organized, and they are still healthier in that they procure the discharge of phantasy. The false idea about life is not only self-limited, a terminus ad quem — it also inoculates against the possibility of action on false premises since it has produced symbolic action.

It therefore seems reasonable to amend the constitution of the Perfect State so as to confer citizenship on the most sentimental and the most dishonest novelists. But there is something more to be said, for in dealing thus with rudimentary fiction we have uncovered another fundamental of fiction, one which is a final justification of the best.

It is an ingredient I have so far left out and the last but one that I must deal with in this analysis. It is simply this. What we agree to call false ideas in trivial fiction, I have

said, are given organization, logic, and form. Because they
are, the reader can accept the phantasies they embody. But
of course the same thing happens on the higher planes of
fiction. In a novel irrelevant experience is cleared away;
what happens is all relevant to the lives of the characters
and to the web of life in which they are enmeshed. It could
not be otherwise, for many years in many lives may have to
be represented and in any event ten hours of reading time
is a shorter period than the novel's time-lapse in terms of
real life. Even if he wanted to, a novelist could not help
dealing solely with what is relevant to his book: he has no
space for anything else. But the extinction of irrelevance
clears the way for the ultimate magic. A reader's own life
and all the lives he knows about in the flesh are packed
with irrelevant experience, so much of it that he may come
to doubt whether experience can have meaning. By the
magic of fiction he may find meaning in life.

4

AM I NOT CHRISTOPHER SLY?

AM I NOT CHRISTOPHER SLY?

T HE MIND has its own logic but does not often let others in on it. Writing a novel is a long psychological process. It may, I repeat *may*, produce interior behavior that amazes the novelist and exterior behavior that exasperates, bewilders, or disgusts his friends, or gives them doubts of his sanity. We are working toward the activities of a novelist that are conscious and controlled, toward the part of the relationship between him and his reader that is subject to his will. Before we get there we will have to make another speculative excursion through mental activity that is more or less unconscious. Now, however, we must examine experiences of a person who is writing a novel that oscillate between rationality and irrationality and are doubtless conscious and unconscious at the same time.

Of the long process of writing a novel, the actual reduction of it to words on paper is only a fraction — a third, a twentieth, a hundredth, what you please. The preparation for writing any given novel may take years. Parts of the eventual novel will turn out to be composed of material that antedates the preparation — made up at random long ago for no specific purpose or designed to belong to earlier novels and found unusable. As we have seen, some elements will go back to childhood, and the writer's entire life up to now must be counted as, in a way, preparing the preparation.

But there comes a moment when random feelings of anticipated pleasure (or anticipated grandeur), unfocused intentions to do something about a generalized idea or subject or situation or character, scenes or fragments of scenes that have composed themselves with a splendor never to be attained on the drab page, impulses, intimations, urge, will — there comes a moment when these coalesce and he has begun to "think about" a novel. We may say that what has begun is the period of preparation and that from now on it is a series of complex psychic acts. They are frequently intense. Small wonder if sometimes, they produce moods objectionable to his family or friends, if they lead to expressions of egotism or vanity or jealousy or temper, if his behavior seems childish or irrational or idiotic. All men who work hard must sometimes work under strain but writing fiction has especially intimate and powerful strains, since it is a direct expression of personality whereas designing a bridge, say, or performing an appendectomy is at most an indirect expression. They will be the greater as the writer is more serious, as he may determine to do in full exactly the job he has undertaken or to express in fiction the truth about life as he sees it.

It is dangerous to write a novel. Parts of the personality resist expression, sometimes with powerful weapons of defense. Thus it is not unusual, it is even routine, for a novelist to, as he says, "get stuck" while writing a novel. He comes to a place where for a short or a long time he cannot solve his immediate problem and get on with the job. Usually the reason is near the surface. He has not sufficiently

thought out his technical procedures. Or he has mistaken
the function of the passage. Or he has not lived long enough
with his characters and must now suffer suspense and frustration while he feels his way into an emotion or a situation
that he would be inside if he had let the book ripen further
before trying to harvest it. But there may be darker reasons. F. Scott Fitzgerald once said that it requires the novelist's greatest sagacity to determine when to throw a story
away and when to force himself to keep at it in spite of
whatever difficulties may have developed. This, however,
can be true only of the less serious stories, when the writer is
only lightly engaged with his material; with others the
dilemma may not be so simple.

"Getting stuck" may mean a psychic block. The novelist
may be on the way to saying something that a part of him
does not want said. He may be dealing with a theme that
frightens a part of him. He may be trying to confess something that a part of him insists on keeping private. The
resistance may be so strong that he will have to abandon
the novel, though usually he will find some way of flanking
the defense. If he does abandon it, he may come back to it
years later and find that the difficulties have disappeared —
in which event the unconscious conflict has been resolved
without his knowledge or the unconscious alarm has been
found unwarranted. But, more likely, years later he will
find that a novel he is writing is the one which stopped him
but is that one in symbols that make it wholly different on
the surface. (Our next chapter describes one such instance.)
The mind is thrifty and willing to be deluded: it does not
like to waste material and it will feel no fear if danger wears
a reassuring mask. Nevertheless the block can be absolute:
some novels cannot be written. In defense of something that
it holds to be more important the mind has said, The rest is

silence. We may respect the profundity of such an utter-
ance — it may confer on the novelist a dignity that he had
not had — but it has cost literature a book. And more than
that. There are many reasons why a novelist may give up
his trade, among them weak creative impulse, lack of confidence, belated discovery that he has no vocation, and relax-
ation of the pressures that first turned him to fiction. But
we have probably lost some good novelists because their
desire centered on themes too painful or too terrifying to be
borne.

Such energies are never far away when a novelist is at
work. He works under innumerable threats and must deal
with them as he can. An irrational ritual may be a defense
against a threat, a kind of bulletproof vest. One novelist I
know writes elaborate biographical sketches not only of his
characters but of many imaginary people besides who never
enter the novel even by implication — the heroine's great-
grandfather who marched with Sherman, the millionaire
who gave the town a park where the lovers will meet, the
first owner of the house where the hero grew up. There can
hardly be even a pretense that either the novel or the novelist
needs them but they are all typed and arranged alphabetically
in a loose-leaf notebook. The notebook is obviously a fetish,
a protection against unnamed beings of malice and ill-will,
but we may more decorously think of it as an insurance
policy. He knows that he will have no use for it, but how
reassuring to have it on his desk, just in case.

One reason why Eugene Gant had to count all the people
in Boston and begin a worldwide census may have been
that he was thinking about writing the novel in which he
appears. Why does Mr. Kenneth Roberts have to have, besides a library of supporting source documents, the journal
of a soldier who was in the regiment he is using as a model,

before he can write the scenes in *Rabble in Arms* which take his characters from Arundel to Ticonderoga? He says that when he found such a diary, after a prolonged and despairing search, "the moment I read it, those hitherto static figures came to life, laughing, grumbling, sleeping in the bushes, rain-soaked, mud-splashed, hungry, ragged, needy." [1] Clearly this is irrational and ritualistic. The novelist has imagined all this behavior already and has wrought it into scenes; he has even (apparently) written the scenes, but they remain lifeless and unacceptable. Then a ritualistic act, of a kind habitual with Mr. Roberts, propitiates the off-stage Something that has inihibted him from writing well and the scenes begin to live. The diary shows, too, that Mr. Roberts always writes in an *angst,* a condition of strong

[1] *I wanted to Write,* p. 227. A few pages later (he is quoting from his diary) he states what he regards as the original impetus that started him to work on this novel, and the purpose it has in his mind: that he wanted "to give in fiction that can be read by any schoolboy, a complete picture of a military campaign that is imperfectly grasped or understood by many advanced students of military tactics." I am sure that Mr. Roberts is entirely honest in this statement but I doubt if it is true. No analyst, I think, would hesitate to say that this is a screen, and not a thick one, over the real reason, and most analysts, I dare say, would guess that the dominant motive (in a cluster of subsidiary ones) that set him to writing not only this book but all its predecessors and successors through *Oliver Wiswell,* is repeatedly revealed earlier in *I Wanted To Write,* his strong identification with his Maine ancestors. Whether or not that is true, Mr. Roberts's insistence on documenting his novels far more extensively than any other historical novelist I know about seems to me irrational and ritualistic. Only when he has made this minute documentation, apparently, is he able to write. But, of course, the minute historical accuracies which he insists on, which he must obtain as permission to write a novel, are entirely devoid of importance for a reader. The reader does not care by what exact route Robert Rogers reached the Connecticut after burning St. Francis, though that indifference may classify him among the halfwits and morons of whom the human race is mostly composed in the more anxious entries of Mr. Roberts's diary. He is interested in people; he wants to know the sufferings, dangers, and heroisms of Rogers and his companions, on their return from St. Francis. Mr. Roberts, a gifted and skillful novelist, could have completely satisfied that desire if he had sent them on a different map-route or an entirely imaginary one.

anxiety. It is, I have pointed out, dangerous to write a novel.

From simple irrationality we may go on to something more revealing. In a novel by a friend of mine that deeply moved me I was puzzled by the similarity in the early chapters of two characters who thereafter were radically dissimilar. In the first part of the book they spoke in much the same rhythms, they acted much alike, their personalities were twinlike, and, what was more striking, they seemed to be serving the same function, though presently they diverged and by the end of the book had become foils and counterbalances. There are ways of inducing novelists to talk about their work — one way being to refrain from speaking for thirty seconds — and eventually I learned the explanation. It was the question of function. As he went ahead with the first draft my friend had found the novel increasingly unsatisfactory. He had the heady feeling of being on top of the job that is the exhilaration of the trade. The thing flowed easily, his daily output was copious, the right scenes and devices came to his pen at the proper times, he could objectively admire a brilliance that was unusual even for him. Nevertheless he was aware that the thing was not jelling. It was not coming together and he had the premonition of an old hand that presently it would diffuse into formlessness. By the end of the first third he became aware (it usually is a process of gradual enlightenment, not sudden illumination) that a principal character was being called on to do too much. In the superb novel already written in my friend's mind, the perfect thing of which the written novel is always a wretched parody, that character had been given two functions. In support of them he had been endowed with attributes so contradictory that they were making him a split personality. As soon as he realized this, the novelist was able to separate the twin personalities and assign to each its proper function. Then, richer by one character, he went back to the beginning and started over. Thereafter he wrote straightforwardly and in comparative comfort to his intended end. But in his haste to get on with the job he borrowed too freely from his first draft, did not sufficiently differentiate the two characters in the opening chapters, and thriftily assigned to the new one scenes and experiences that had been written for someone else before he existed.

This is an example of sloppy workmanship — of the failure to "put the thing through the typewriter again" that allows much fiction to issue to the world before the chips and shavings have been cleared away. But the point is that a character had split mitotically while the author was writing. Evidently the process that made the novel change while it was being written was both conscious and unconscious. As he wrote, the novelist was matching the daily chore against the intended effect with the self-criticism of a good workman and with the feel for the whole that is any skilled person's scrutiny of the job he is doing, which is conscious too but so complex and swift that it seems like a reflex. But also something was going on below consciousness that enabled him to recognize the problem and find the answer.

I once served American letters by telling the author of a subsequently celebrated novel what he was writing about. He brought me a first draft in the suicidal depression of any writer who feels that he has done a job badly and therefore knows that he has lost his grip and the world will end before midnight. Most writers — all young writers — who ask friends to read their stuff do not want objective criticism and violently resent it if it is provided. Candid criticism has broken more literary friendships than jealousy, Pulitzer awards, or adultery. What the writer who rings your doorbell with a manuscript in his pocket wants is to be told that a new, faint doubt that he may not be as good as Proust is absurd.[2] This one, however, was in earnest. The problem that had baffled a first-rate novelist and reduced his mind to chaos proved simple. Any good editor or any experienced writer who looked at it impersonally could have solved it. I said, in effect and at not much greater length, "This is Miriam's book, not Bill's." After a period of conflict and self-searching, it proved to be Miriam's book. In the process of thinking the novel into order, the novelest had oriented a story of complexly interwoven lives by the wrong character.

Experienced novelists do not often have such an experience but it frequently happens to less seasoned ones. A skill of editors is to point out to such bewildered souls what they are writing about. (The best teacher of writing I have ever known, Miss Edith Mirrielees, always begins by asking, "What is this story *about?*" Though a writer can seldom answer it in full he will be in for trouble unless he can answer it approximately.) The process of thinking and feeling a novel into existence is in part blind and it is always

2 Another rough classification of novelists would divide them into those who secrete their manuscripts from everyone till they are finished and are reluctant or even unable to talk about them (a rare and essentially superstitious but blessed breed), and those who force them on all their friends, especially of the other sex. The latter simply have to be, in the idiom, built up — repeatedly, over and over. They are not unduly exhibitionistic, they are revealing a temporary but severe anxiety neurosis. One of the most widely praised of living novelists requires the support of a whole corps — his editors, a couple of professional literary coaches (who are all gyps), and as many friends as do not see him coming, especially women friends — with whom there is no suspicion whatever of sexual involvement. (Though a psychiatrist would raise an eyebrow at the symbolism.) By the time the last fair copy of his manuscript goes to the printer (after the last copy readers have told the author for the last time that it is his masterpiece and the capstone of American literature), it has passed through the hands of at least twenty-five people who have found no flaw in it. Meanwhile hypertension has reduced his life-expectancy. Actually he knows what he is about better than his editors. None of these people can do anything for him except tell him that he has made Tolstoy an also-ran. There are a good many like him.

stumbling. Frequently a good editor can shine a light in places where the novelist is unable to see. A novelist must always listen to his editor with the greatest respect, though if a disagreement proves incapable of adjustment he must always in the end follow his own ideas — for, though editors sometimes forget the fact, the novel is his.

To some degree all novels are still blind when the actual writing begins, and we need not confine that statement to novels. A friend of mine, a geneticist, told me he was writing a book and when I flippantly asked why said a true thing: "In order to find out what I know about genetics." The reason why a novelist cannot answer Miss Mirrielees' question in full is that only by writing the novel can he find out, in full, what it is about — what he knows about these people, what their emotions and experiences are, what life the lens is refracting. It is a sad truth that when the book is published no two readers will read the same novel, but it is a more important one that no published novel is ever quite the one that the novelist set out to write. Sometimes it is a radically different one. The novelists for whom I (personally — I do not want to commit anyone else) have the greatest respect are those who, above and beyond the feeling for life that makes them novelists, have in the greatest measure the ability that makes them artists, the ability to subject their material to control. But there was never yet a novel that in the end had followed the blueprints exactly, however disciplined and fastidious the artist who drew them. The novel changed at the moment when he picked up the pen and it kept on changing. The change may make but a small sum but it always occurs. In part it occurs because of the interplay between consciousness and the unconscious. And in part it occurs because as the novel goes on it develops requirements of its own, independent of the novelist and so not foreseeable.

A common experience manifests this fact. In a novel by another friend of mine which I liked, I especially admired the development of one character. He began as a minor character, an occasional spectator on the edge of a scene used for comment on that scene or as an instrument for getting ahead with the action, and his personality as we saw it was unpleasant, even obnoxious. But as the novel developed he became more central in the action, coming to exert a decisive influence on it, and we slowly perceived that behind the unripe cynicism of his early manner there was a subtlety and a capacity for deep emotion that made him strikingly sympathetic. Now this sort of thing is first-rate novel-writing, it deserves the highest praise, and if the book had been written by the first novelist I mentioned, the one whose character split in two, I should have assumed as a matter of course that it was deliberate, the exercise of highly skilled techniques. But I had my doubts about the novelist who wrote it; as I knew him, he had no such virtuosity. So the first time I ran into him I said, "You rather fell in love with Bill, didn't you?" He said, "Another hundred pages and there would have been nobody else left in the book." A minor character, a mere device, had come to be a central character. Disregarded by the novelist in the period of preparation, apparently destined to serve only a mechanical function, he came to express a large part of the book's meaning.

Many novelists have comparable experiences. Believing when they begin to write that Bill is the principal character, the one who is to be most fully developed or with whom they are most in sympathy, they find out that it is really Joe — and, what is more surprising, that it has been Joe all along. Or the web of personal relationships they took to be central turns out to be subsidiary to another one, yet the new one seems to have been what they were driving at all the time. Or the true theme they are exploring proves to lie deep beneath the one which they undertook to explore, to which they devoted so much thought in the period of preparation. Or, thinking ahead as they write, they become aware that at about page 200 a crippling inconsistency in character or situation is going to be revealed by the developing action, or that a technical problem which can no longer be disregarded is going to prove insoluble. But, approaching that sad event with the fatalism of a good professional who will play out the game he is losing, they find on the morning of the dreadful day that there has been no inconsistency, there is no problem, everything is quite all right. They were writing more truly than they were aware. They knew more than they believed.

All this indicates the simultaneousness of conscious and unconscious thinking. But it does more than that: it indicates that writing a novel is *in itself* experience. Both halves of it. Both are experiences of the novelist's total personality. Both are dynamic.

Exactly how any given novel grows in a writer's mind will always be, I think, beyond research. But certainly the process is in large part one of accretion, of feeling for the true thing in emotion and action, of testing and modifying and amplifying it, of fumbling through the false or the merely plausible to the true or, if you like, the apparently true. Characters grow in the mind, not unlike embryos growing in the womb. Scenes form for the expression of emotion, meaning, or significant event. The scenes grow and develop and proliferate. Additional meanings besides the originally intended ones are revealed in them. They form sequences and these come to be seen as necessary. There is rejection, substitution, adaptation, adjustment. Content is being shaped into form; form is developing out of content.

Now unquestionably all the private energies of the novelist we have noted are at work, but unquestionably there is
also at work a process that originates in the material, a
process that is initiated by the material, that is its own
determinant. Right here is the greatest mystery of creation
and again there is no word to identify it but art. The
merely felt is clothed with flesh, if imaginary flesh. The unshaped takes shape. A firmament begins to divide the waters
from the waters. Certainly the roots are deep in the unconscious but certainly too there is a conscious and critical invention, a making-up to fit.

So with the second half of the experience, the writing. It
too is a dynamic, evolving, proliferating process. We have
seen that the conscious act of putting into words what one
has prepared to be put into them may uncover material
which was prepared unconsciously. But there are also sur-
prises, new developments, unforeseen emphases or changes
of an entirely different kind. They represent not the unconscious of the novelist nor his critical faculty but the interior requirements of the novel. Not only the act of preparing a novel and the act of composition are dynamic: the
novel itself is a dynamic system.

The fact that writing a novel is in itself experience creates
the cleavage between the way novelists think of fiction and
the way literary critics usually think of it. The formal inquiries of schematic criticism, its postulates, its abstractions,
its aims, its methods and judgments are on a plane wholly
alien to a novelist. He does not question the legitimacy of
the critic's effort but he has no way of telling how valid the
results may be. At best he can make out that the critic is
trying to do at second hand what he does at first hand, and
he wonders why life, which is his subject, is not a better
subject than his novels for the critic. But that is at best, and
commonly the novelist is bewildered by the critic's efforts to

relate his work to formal systems of thought, to general ideas highly abstracted, to theories of knowledge or of metaphysical reality, to economics, or sociology, the one and the many, the Holy Ghost. When he himself wants instruction in such matters he turns to treatises that deal directly with them, not to the novels of his fellow craftsmen. He is incapable of reproaching one of them for having misconstrued the moral of the atom.

Critic and novelist, that is, do not speak the same language nor are they talking about the same thing. A novelist thinks about his novel from within, as a dynamic process, at the moment of occurrence — which is continuous, since the title of every novel he writes will remain Work in Progress till he dies. The critic thinks about the same novel after the fact and from outside. I was speaking in the novelist's name when I said that the interest of schematic criticism is to find the novel that isn't there. The novelist would add that the critic usually finds it. The significances, private or public, that the critic uncovers in a novel are seldom those which the novelist believes it has. Those which the critic reproaches it for not having were never within the novelist's intention and are frequently outside his understanding. As for what criticism has to say about the novelist's intentions, failures, successes, and procedures, and what it has to say about the realities and unrealities of the novel and about its place in any scheme of ideas — they are, the moment they become more generalized or systematized than the immediate response of any intelligent reader, meaningless to the novelist. They may have meaning for others but not for him.

Mr. William Faulkner put this fact succinctly when an interviewer showed him a passage from an intrepidly abstract inquiry into his art. He shook his head: what the critics said had no relevance to the books Mr. Faulkner had written, at least none that he himself could make out. He was not a literary man, he told the interviewer, he was a writer. To a writer a novel is experience and it is not experience to the critic. Bearing a child is experience to the mother but her obstetrician is a literary man.

*   *   *

All general psychologies, I believe, hold that everything in the psychic process is determined. Psychology abhors accident: it will not permit any action of the conscious or the unconscious mind to be without a cause. The proposition seems necessary; without it, psychological inquiry would be meaningless. But our inquiry need not touch that proposition. Instead it asks how much of a novelist's work is subject to his free choice, and especially how much of it can be thought of as not determined by his own personal needs. A quantitative answer would make no sense. But we require some rough qualitative idea of what choice implies.

I remarked earlier that occasionally psychoanalysts have advanced to me as a theoretical possibility the idea that by the minute probing of which psychoanalysis consists every item in any novel could be found to have at least a slight reference personal to the novelist. Take a passage that seems altogether of the novel and follow it patiently enough, that is, and eventually association or dream or symbol will show that the passage not only is colored by the unconscious derivations of the novelist but actually acquires its energy from them. It is conditioned from within his private experience.

This theoretical idea is sometimes implied as a working principle in the psychoanalytical literature. I have heard it advanced as an absolute at psychoanalytical seminars I have had the privilege of attending, though always by young analysts in training, who are more adept than their elders at unearthing absolutes. When, on being admitted to the general discussion, I have sometimes suggested that the data were being over-interpreted — that, say, there may have been moments when Herman Melville's castration-anxiety and the oral phantasies which stemmed from it looked away long enough for a few sentences of the novel to slip through by themselves — I have been told that we need only peel off another layer of the onion. If we go a little deeper we will find the little Melville biting the nipple and so Ahab must lose his leg and the anxiety will leave its spoor through the collected works — the name of Plotinus Plinlimon was foredestined long ago and the adult Melville will strike out an awkward phrase in his second draft at the dictation of those unhappy years. The psyche may hesitate for a moment but the deletion of a comma was determined.

It seems to me that there is a tendency to mistake the nature of the conditioning. But at the moment it is enough to say that there must be different degrees. Certainly there are novelists who seem unable to exercise much control over what they write and in whose work one suspects that the direct personal reference is seldom far below the surface, Thomas Wolfe for instance.[3] His writing was a torrential outburst, in his own words it poured from him "like burning lava from a volcano." He says that he found it almost

---

[3] Here I must make a personal statement. In the *Saturday Review* for April 25, 1936, I published a 2500-word article called "Genius Is Not Enough." It was a review of Wolfe's *The Story of a Novel*. Before that I had devoted a paragraph to him in a review of James Boyd's *Roll River*, which uses certain symbols that are also used in *Of Time And The River*. I have not alluded to him more than cursorily in any other context. I have refrained from writing more because it is firmly established in literary folklore, on the basis of a single review, that I spent most of my time for years attacking Wolfe. The notion is now embedded in college textbooks, which speak of my "relentless pursuit" of him. Thirteen years is a gratifying life for a book review but the folklore has estopped me from discussing Wolfe's books when they were germane to comments I was making on literary subjects. They are germane to some of the subjects I discuss here and this seems a proper time to call the attention of students to the facts.

impossible to control what he was writing. The efforts of his first editor, Maxwell Perkins, to get him to revise and condense a passage of freight-train length frequently resulted in his producing not a condensation but a substitute passage four times as long. (Mr. Edward Aswell, his second editor, appears to have had somewhat better luck.) Though Wolfe insists, almost correctly, that "it is impossible for a man who has the stuff of creation in him to make a literal transcript of his own experience," he also repeatedly declares that his novel (there was only one) is an autobiography — and no one who reads it can doubt that it is only slightly fictionalized. His peculiar force comes from the fact that he dramatizes with the giantism of an essentially infantile mind, but he is able only slightly to transform his autobiography or to direct its expression. He was, in my opinion, a bad novelist, if tragically a bad one, but let us set him up as one limit. A great novelist, Dostoievsky, appears to have been of the same kind. Here the uncontrolled outpouring was an inner, not an outer, autobiography, and it was forged into symbols that speak for the depths of the mind and so are able to free the power that abides there. That in itself is a definition of one kind of greatness in fiction, but Dostoievsky's evident inability to objectify his own literary processes was the reason why Turgenev dismissed him as an amateur.

At the other pole we might set up a writer of formula stories. He can find well-established sets of characters, emotions, and sequences of action in the conventions. He need hardly engage himself with them beyond choosing among conventions and rearranging the interchangeable parts, and this would not appear to involve specific conditioning from within himself. But that will hardly do and let us take instead such a novelist as Mr. Somerset Maugham, whose cool professionalism is obviously subject to his complete control. His work shows an eager interest in so many lives and so many experiences certainly not his own that it would be precarious to find in it the confessions of Mr. Maugham. There may be a confession in his choosing one rather than another set of lives or experiences to write about, but even here one must go warily for an experienced writer's sagacity may tell him where fruitful material is to be found. Fruitfulness may refer to his skill, the past responses of readers, or a purely intellectual challenge that is like a chess problem, as often as to the echo of the writer's past or the urgency of his needs. With such novelists it would appear unsafe to look for the autobiography anywhere but in the basic fables, what we have called the outline-phantasies. It is unsafe because everything else has been subjected to the selection, transformation, and invention of professional skill — of criticism and craftsmanship. If the simple fables are brought together and examined for uniformities it may be possible to say something about the determinism exerted on the novelist. Perhaps something more may be obliquely revealed by the very tirelessness of such a writer's need for to admire and for to see, for to behold this world so wide. But when a need is so tireless that we think it significant, it is also so capacious that we should be wary of identifying and labeling any individual item it picks up.

Similarly with so different a novelist as Henry James. (Or, in direct opposition to Dostoievsky, his contemner Turgenev.) The publication of James's notebooks enables us to speak with some confidence. In them we can see the impact on him of people he meets, stories he hears about them, situations they have been a part of. Thereafter we can frequently follow "the drama" when an item proves to be alive — when his imagination gets to work on it. We can watch it becoming "the little idea that I have for these few

years past carried in my brooding brain." His imagination
is indefatigable. No one ever probed more exhaustively the
emotions whose presence or effects he had noticed. No hack
was ever more sedulous to apply to them the entire bag of
mechanical tricks, surefire devices, conventions of the cheap
theater and the slick magazines, dodges, formulas, clichés.
(Nor was the usefulness of the stockroom for fine fiction
ever more clearly demonstrated.)   The flagella of his mind
are never still. They are constantly reaching out to seize
from the flux something that may elaborate and enrich the
drama — the drama which James is always pushing ahead.
He is constantly building scenes and sequences. While doing so he is constantly matching items against one another,
testing them against the immediate context and the whole
so far and the ultimate structure and effect intended —
matching, altering to fit, selecting, rejecting, reshaping. In
this process the wholly extraneous and the clearly false or
mechanical will serve him as well as anything else. For if
sometimes it is rejected as worthless at other times it acquires authenticity from the complex to which it has been
added — the graft takes life. In some we can follow the development of "the little idea" all the way to the completed
story.

What is it just to say? This, I think. Certain emotions,
situations, and elementary phantasies were tremendously
important to James, so important that they must have con-
stituted the general conditioning of his fiction. But in the
end-product, in the novel he writes, beyond the outline
phantasy, they are usually present as color and tone only.
Usually everything else has undergone a process so meta-
morphic, so controlled by the wisdom and skill of the novelist, so responsive to the world outside that identification of
James himself would always be arbitrary and nearly always

wrong. The novelist in person is not to be recovered from the novel because the novel has been written by the artist. Though we may repeatedly encounter evidence which suggests that a few simple psychic drives determined the novels Henry James wrote there is little trustworthy evidence that any fictional experience in them must be referred to his own, symbolically or otherwise.

This is enough to establish rough limits within which the question we have been asking about the act of writing a novel makes sense for our purposes. Let us say that a novelist is about to write a scene which is to take place in Central Park, and that what happens in the scene itself is the point. The novelist would appear to be free to have a character enter the Park at Eighty-Ninth Street or at Ninetieth Street as he may choose. We will repeat that writing a novel is an act of the total personality and that everything in the psychic process is determined. Still, if the scene itself is the point, it would be precarious to decide that the number 90 has a psychic necessity for its author that is not present in the number 89. The choice appears to be open, and we may extend the area of freedom. Fifty-Ninth Street, 110th Street, Fifth Avenue, Central Park West — the character may reach the Park at any of its boundaries without, necessarily, obeying the unconscious dictates of his creator. He may get there on foot, by bus, by bicycle, taxi, or private automobile without, necessarily, serving the novelist's inner needs or employing a symbolism that the author finds soothing. If he has to get the character there by any means other than simply saying he is there, the novelist would appear to be free, ordinarily, to consult the novel he is writing and not himself. To get the character to Central Park with reference solely to the requirements of the novel up to the scene he is about to write, of the scene itself, or of the novel from there on. As a minimum at one extreme, the mechanical details, the stage lumber, of the work in progress are ordinarily outside the novelist's private determinism.

As a maximum at the other extreme, to exactly the extent that it is a product of the novelist's unconscious feeling and thinking, clearly it is determined. To a degree it is also determined in other ways as well. The basic fable, the outline-phantasy to which I have frequently referred, is unconscious and beyond choice. When we think of theme or subject, the *kind* of thing written about, we reach a different matter. A novelist may write about a subject lightly or profoundly, frivolously or seriously, believingly or skeptically, ironically or hortatorally. There is choice here but how much? Whatever his engagement with his subject, he must choose in part because he is the person he is. Mr. Maugham chooses one set of an interested bystander's observations in preference to other sets, but to say that he is more interested in one set is to say that the choice is not wholly free. Even the pulpwriter's choice among formulas cannot be altogether free. From there on as a novelist deals the more deeply with his subjects, as he becomes more engaged with them, presumably his choice is progressively less free. The canyon narrows and as the walls approach each other we may guess that they increasingly restrict freedom. Where they meet — I decline to locate that point on the map — we may say that a novelist does not choose his themes or subjects. They are chosen for him.

But there is a more striking phenomenon. If a tolerably good novelist has been an intimate friend of yours for a long time, you may come to realize that in subtle ways his novels may sometimes be autobiography not only by confession of the past but also by prediction of the future. Why not, since character is destiny? Since his gift is to derive the truths of emotion, no one should be surprised if sometimes he works out imaginatively a series of events which embody emotions he has perceived in friends of his, events that literally or with an unmistakable symbolism parallel events which occur later on to those friends. It should be much less surprising if emotions more important to him, his own, are sometimes so truly rendered in imaginary experience that some small arc of his own future is foretold.

We have seen how complexly characters in novels are made, from what diverse perceptions of many people they may be assembled, what an intricate web of associations they may represent. Let us say that one such composite character in a novel has lacked an emotional experience of a particular kind and has a deep need of it, and that both lack and need are derived from the novelist himself. Part of the novel charts an imaginary relationship with an imaginary woman who is able to answer that need and to give the male character exactly the emotional fulfillment he has not had before. A sequence of entirely imaginary events embody the emotions of this relationship, its ecstasy and its tragedy. Then some years later the novelist himself has precisely the experience his novel has imagined with precisely the kind of woman imagined in it — has that experience almost literally or in a form that the novel unmistakably symbolizes. Or in another novel the stress of imagined circumstance reveals weaknesses in an imaginary character that develop through personal decay to personal degeneration — and later on just those weaknesses produce just that decay and degeneration in the novelist himself.

I am thinking, of course, of two novelists who were friends of mine and are now dead. I could describe comparable instances among living novelists, one of whom recently remarked to me, "I'm never going to write another novel —

it's unlucky." No prevision, foreknowledge, clairvoyance, or extrasensory perception is implied. It is merely that the novelist's hold on emotion was so sure that he made a true if wholly imaginary extrapolation. The growth sleeps within the seed. Character *is* destiny and the truth of fiction may sometimes be seen, in retrospect, to have been a prophecy of fact.

We need not carry the exploration of unconscious determinism into other areas. These, with what was said in Chapter II, are enough to suggest what the nature of the private determinism is. Such energies are at work in the writing of a novel. I need not inquire how far they may inclose or affect the working energies that are subject to the writer's conscious control. No doubt they are in relationships of mutual dependence but I doubt if anyone will ever be able to make out wherein and how. A quantitative inquiry has no application.

Come back to the character who was headed toward Central Park. I said that if the scene which is to occur there after he arrives is the point, then ordinarily the novelist is free to get him there by any convenient means. That was a minimum statement of free choice, since practically all technical procedures (again excepting the torrential primitives) and many other parts of the long processes of thinking a novel into existence and then writing it are obviously at the writer's will. Even so, something is required to effectuate his will — and here we reach another kind of determinism, if a radically different kind. If the novelist does not simply open the scene with the character present in the Park, I said, he may consult the convenience or requirements of the novel in order to get him there by one means or another, at one entrance or another. That implies convenience or requirements. And if the scene is the point, then what happens in it — how the character behaves and how he feels — is required. "Everything in the psychic process is determined" — but now, though the novelist is still making up phantasies, and though the aim of all phantasies is fulfillment, he is making them up not to satisfy his own needs but to satisfy the requirements of his characters and of the novel. The fact is central in the act of creation. But it is often disregarded by psychologists who analyze fiction and by critics who interpret it. It limits the applicability of anything said about the novelist in person.

I must repeat emphatically: a novel is a dynamic system. As such it has an interior logic, a metabolism, necessities of its own that must be satisfied. Take a novel of direct and mostly physical action, the species, say, of *Treasure Island* or *The Three Musketeers*. Mere plausibility, to go no deeper than that, requires that at any moment what is happening must be the necessary outcome of what has happened before. An antagonism aroused in the third chapter will produce a fight in the fifth chapter, which lead to a flight in the seventh and a pursuit in the eighth, which will bring on miscalculations in the ninth, from which the struggle in the eleventh will develop. It is not otherwise with *Remembrance of Things Past*.

The soul insists that what happens to us is not by chance: "not without reason is our journey to the deep." The truth of fiction is the necessity of what happens, and therefore in the writing of a novel the largest part of the creative process is the determination of necessity. The period of thinking the novel into being is an effort to discover the true emotions, the true motives, and the behavior and action and change that result from them — of search, tentative experiment, error, criticism, rejection, renewed search, to the end that imaginary people may feel and act truly. That their feelings and actions may be faithful to their nature as the novelist understands it, faithful to the relationships he has put them in, faithful to reality in the experience of mankind . . . as he understands it. In this process of laying bare and of building up he will exert the utmost conscious, critical intelligence he is capable of, whatever unconscious elements of his mind may be simultaneously at work. And writing the imagined thing, putting it into words and form, is also an effort to discover necessity, to find the best way of laying bare and building up for the reader's sake. Except for the primitives (or the possessed) it will be consciously critical to a greater degree than the earlier stage. But in neither stage is it just to separate acts of the mind that are reciprocal. In both stages the novelist is trying to find the true and therefore necessary thing, and so to avoid the adventitious and therefore false thing.

When (to his capacity or satisfaction) he has found the necessity in what he is writing about, it is from then on outside himself. Whatever was conditioned in him may partly or totally inclose the novel. But there is a dangerous verbal fallacy in stating it in those terms — and in any event it no longer interests us here. For if an occasional novel may be seen to have been a prediction of its writer's destiny, all novels must be seen as a prediction of their characters' destiny, and on the way to the fulfillment of it every page is history. The growth sleeps within the seed. The novel, in fact, is the visible germination and growth.

I cannot too emphatically point out that it is d'Artagnan, Babbitt, Swann, Stephen Dedalus whose destiny the reader sees unfold, it is not their creators'. In so far as they are true, they are subject to the laws of their being, not the novelist's. Or let us modify that statement in the direction of caution: his may be the conditioning but the process is theirs. They may enact a symbol that is his as well as theirs but they enact it as themselves. At any moment the reference and significance of what happens are within them. Put a novel into motion — write "Call me Ishmael" at the top of page one — and from then on the inertia that keeps it moving is its own. It travels its own route. Its energy is from within itself.

No other psychological phenomenon is quite like this one: outside the arts no other resembles it much. The psychic substance has been so changed and fructified that it has become something new. From now on what must be dealt with at first hand is not the novelist but the novel. Character, emotion, behavior, action are imaginary — invented, created — but the first reference is always to themselves. The unfolding, the necessity, the destiny are theirs.

The fact sets a limit beyond which psychological inferences about the novelist are not reliable, for the characters are themselves, not him. It sets a limit beyond which the inferences of criticism are not safe, for the activity of the novelist is to uncover and display the truth about these people, not about society or about general ideas. And at the line that marks this limit the reader re-enters. He is indifferent to the novelist and if something is to be inferred about ideas or the world, he will make the inference after the fact, not of it. He is participating in a magical operation. He has entered a world governed by its own laws under the strictest construction. He has joined hands with its inhabitants and is walking deathward with them as if with friends.

5

THE PRECIPITATE

5

THE PRECIPITATE

THERE ARE more secrets in my trade than in most,"
Henry Thoreau said, "and yet not voluntarily kept."
He would require of every writer, "a simple and sincere
account of his own life, and not merely what he has heard
of other men's lives; some such account as he would send to
his kindred from a distant land, for if he has lived sincerely,
it must have been in a distant land to me." So presently he
begins to write a simple and sincere account of his own life:
"I long ago lost a hound, a bay horse, and a turtledove, and
am still on their trail. Many are the travelers I have spoken
concerning them, describing their tracks and what calls they
answered to. I have met one or two who had heard the
hound and the tramp of the horse, and even seen the dove
disappear behind a cloud, and they seemed as anxious to
recover them as if they had lost them themselves." Others
must abide his question, Thoreau is free.

We have seen some of the processes at work in the act of
creation. Perhaps we have chalked out a few short sections
of the boundaries that inclose it. We have seen enough to
feel sure that most of it is beyond scrutiny. Now our inquiry
has reached a stage where the inscrutability of the process
is a barrier in our way. For our next step should be to examine the energies we have isolated working jointly to trans-

form a novelist's experience into fictional experience. Unhappily the transformation takes place where it cannot be seen: the dove disappears behind a cloud.

All known approaches to the problem are static and after the fact, whereas only a dynamic one could inspire confidence. The technique of psychoanalysis is dynamic but when it is applied to a novel it is uncontrolled. You cannot psychoanalyze a book; the novelist is not present and the book makes no answering response. I do not question that the application of analytical ideas to novels yields much brilliant interpretation, but it can be reliable only within fixed and fairly clear limits, and I am skeptical of the results when it tries to get at the novelist by way of his work. Too much stands in the way. There is the fact that the novel has its own necessities and these must deflect inquiries about the novelist. The diffusion of the autobiography I have pointed out makes identifications precarious. More important still, when an analyst deals with a living patient he is forced to pursue the autobiographical realities through the lies, inventions, disguises, projections, displacements, and fragmentations that constitute resistance and may need several years to hunt them down — but a novel is a resistance that cannot be broken down. We are forced to regard as unverifiable conclusions about the working of a novelist's mind that are made solely on the basis of the novel. The analyst, whether professional or literary, may be making gross errors and there is no way of checking his results.

Nevertheless, when proper instruments are lacking, we must use such others as may be at hand. I see no way out except to make a speculative and uncontrolled inquiry. It happens that I once made such an inquiry into the transformation of a writer's personal experience as it worked out in various manuscripts and eventually a novel. This requires some explanation.

For eight years, as editor for the Estate of Samuel L. Clemens, I was the custodian of practically all the unpublished papers of Mark Twain, besides the manuscripts of many of his published books. My first job was to put a good many of them into order, assembling them from the chaos in which my predecessor had left them — it was as if he dumped them in a barrel and stirred them with a paddle. This mechanical effort was what led me to suspect that the manuscripts dealt with here were significant. When I got the papers into order, I spent two years studying this group of manuscripts, following the hints and clues in them through the rest of Mark's writing and through his biography, and applying to them such scholarly and psychological instruments as I could.

In the end I saw that a chapter of Mark Twain's biography had been imperfectly recounted and that a part of his writing had been closed to criticism. Mr. Albert Bigelow Paine had not only failed to appreciate the importance of this group of manuscripts, he had not even understood what they were. He mentions several of them and devotes a few sentences to describing two or three, with the indulgence of one who is willing to concede that a great writer may sometimes have silly ideas and write rather badly. But it never entered his mind that they constitute the most sustained literary effort Mark Twain ever made.

After I had studied the manuscripts exhaustively, I wrote the essay that I reprint here. I published it under the title "The Symbols of Despair" in a book called *Mark Twain at Work,* which also included essays on the writing of *Tom Sawyer* and *Huckleberry Finn.* I did not write it with this present book in mind but its relevance will be evident. Because it focuses on Mark Twain rather than our problem here, it develops some topics further than they need be developed for our purpose, but except for the first page and

a half, which I have covered in these remarks, i let it stand
in full.

I have notified my reader that what follows is unverifiable.
But my speculation is supported by a much fuller documentation, I am sure, than exists for the writing of any
other book by a novelist of the first rank. The documents
include not only the manuscripts described here but a great
many others in the Mark Twain papers, many unpublished
notebook entries (Paine blandly said in his preface to *Mark
Twain's Notebook* that he was printing the notebooks in
full but actually he printed only about fifteen per cent of
what they contain), unpublished letters by Mark Twain and
others, and much else which there is no need to detail, including several manuscripts not by Mark Twain which I do
not feel at liberty to describe. I add that years of studying,
editing, and writing about Mark Twain gave me additional
qualifications for the search. Finally, Mr. Dixon Wecter,
who succeeded me in the editorship, has gone over all the
material independently and his chapter on Mark Twain in
the recently published *Literary History of the United States*
comes to exactly the same conclusions.

I also point out that Mark Twain may not be the best
kind of novelist for our purpose. Perhaps we could focus
the problem we are now dealing with more sharply if he
had been more like Henry James, if he had had some ability
to criticize and correct his own work. He hated revision
and raged about it even more profanely than Mr. Kenneth
Roberts. He abandoned as much of it as he could to William
Dean Howells or anyone else who would work out on his
text. None of his principal books received anything that
can fairly be called a second draft. Such revision as they got
was confined to a few days, interrupted by boiling-point
letters to Howells, of crossing out sentences and paragraphs
and sweating hard over single phrases. Up to the time when

he wrote the manuscripts I discuss here (but, as will presently be clear, not with them), any attempt to rewrite something meant that the job he was doing did not much engage him. Like all novelists he wrote best, and unlike some most freely, when what he was writing was most concerned with his deepest self. But unlike most novelists of his stature he could not write well (in fiction) about anything else. It is even more maddening that he could not perceive any difference in quality between his greatest work and his worst, that in fact he frequently thought the worst better than the best. Finally, the book whose growth and composition I am about to document is a fantasy, whereas our purpose would be better served by a realistic novel, where the autobiography would be transformed into a representation of real experience.

My reader must bear these facts in mind. And yet they are not wholly a disadvantage. That Mark was so little able to modify the writing which expressed his instinctual self may give some of my guesses about the transformation of experience a little more validity than they would have if I were guessing about something that had undergone more critical control. And that what came out of the experience examined here was a fantasy provides new and powerful support for one of the fundamental points I have made earlier.[1]

* * *

A Connecticut Yankee in King Arthur's Court was published in December, 1889. It is the last of Mark Twain's books that we can call certainly of the first rank, and its publication furnishes a convenient date. He was then the most widely known and admired writer in America, and very

[1] The next section of this chapter is my essay "The Symbols of Despair," less the first page and a half. It is reprinted from *Mark Twain at Work* (1942) by permission of the Harvard University Press.

likely in the world. He was at the summit of his personal happiness. His books had won him not only world-wide fame but a fortune as well. He was the husband of a beloved wife, the father of three delightful children, the master of a house famous for its hospitality, the center of a small cosmos of friends, an intimate of the famous men and women of his time, courted, praised, sought after, universally loved. His life had a splendor that marked him as the darling of the gods, and that and the splendor of his imagination made more than one person think of him as a mysterious sojourner from somewhere outside the orbit of this earth. The backwoods boy, the tramp printer, the Mississippi pilot, the silver miner, the San Francisco bohemian had become one of the great men of the earth, the hero of a story more romantic than any of Tom Sawyer's dreams.

Our first concern is the series of catastrophes that came in the eighteen-nineties. Some years before, he had established his own publishing firm, to publish his books. He had expanded it in order to publish the memoirs of General Grant, and the over-extended business required better management than Mark could give it, better management than anyone could give it whom he hired. The firm faltered, the going got worse, and finally, as a result of the freezing of credit in the panic of 1893, it had to go into receivership. It could have been saved — except that a greater loss had drained Mark's fortune and his wife's as well. Always a speculator, a Colonel Sellers who dreamed of millions but was a predestinate sucker for all salesmen of gold bricks, he had poured nearly a quarter of a million dollars into the development of an invention that was going to make him many times a millionaire. This was the Paige typesetting machine, and his grandiose dream was not absurd, considering the millions which the Mergenthaler Linotype has made. But the Mergenthaler machine succeeded, whereas the Paige machine failed altogether and carried Mark Twain down with it, just at the time when his publishing firm went bankrupt. Furthermore, these same years saw a mysterious alteration in the personality of his youngest daughter, Jean, and finally the terrible mystery was cleared up by the discovery of the still more terrible truth, that she was an epileptic. During these years also his capricious but usually exuberant health failed. He was racked by the bronchitis which he was never again to lose, by the rheumatism which was the inheritance of his frontier youth, and by other ailments which were the result of the enormous strain he was under.

So, in 1895, a bankrupt, little better than an invalid, four months short of sixty years old, Mark Twain started on a lecturing tour which was to take him round the world and pay off his creditors dollar for dollar. His wife and one of his daughters went with him, but they left behind them in America their youngest daughter and their oldest one, Susy, the one who Mark felt was nearest him in mind and spirit. Just a year later, the exhausting trip ended in London, and the children were to join them there. They did not. Across the Atlantic from her parents, Susy died of meningitis. And in the months following, Mark's wife began to decline into the invalidism that was to last through the remaining eight years of her life.

The gods had turned against their darling. Such a sequence of calamities might well drive a man mad; there would be little to wonder at if Mark Twain had broken under them. And the truth is that for a time he lived perilously close to the indefinable line between sanity and madness. Passages of his private anguish in the unpublished papers show to what a tautness the membrane of the mind was stretched, and come near breaking the reader's heart. But we are concerned, not with the man's grief but rather with the use the artist made of it.

For, of course, it is obvious that such events as these cannot occur to the man without happening to the artist as well. The rich man had been bankrupted, and the threatened poverty had imperiled his wife and children. The man of great fame had, or so to the tortured ego it must seem, been somehow toppled from his high place, and always thereafter Mark Twain would carry in his heart some remnant feeling of disgrace. Necessarily, his image of himself had been impaired. These blows which had fallen on him, which had been struck at him, had made him something other than he had been — or at least something other than he had seemed to himself to be. A man's position in the world, his various successes, his public reputation are interstitial with his ego; an injury to any one injures all and so injures his secret image of himself. But also interstitial with that image is a writer's talent. In the deepest psychological sense, even in a biological sense, a man's work is his life. That is to say, the sources of his talent are inseparably a part of his feeling of wholeness, of his identity, and even, quite nakedly, of his power. An injury to the man must necessarily be an injury on this deep level of personal power — a blow at his virility. And reciprocally, an injury to the inner picture of the man must be an injury working outward to impair his work as well. In the dark areas where the roots of life go down, the threatened soul cannot easily distinguish among the parts and organs of personality. And if one of them is endangered then the dim mind knows that all have come in peril.

All this is the merest commonplace of experience. Remembering it, we should expect the series of disasters to have a powerful effect on Mark Twain's writing. And also,

remembering that it is the nature of writers to forge their
art out of the materials of their lives, we should expect to
find in his writing some effort to grapple with the disasters.
Art is the terms of an armistice signed with fate. Or, if you
like the words better, art is experience appraised, completed,
neutralized, or overcome.

It was July, 1896, when the lecture tour ended in London.
The lectures had made almost enough money to clear Mark's
debts but not quite, and there remained to write the book
about his trip, *Following the Equator,* which was to complete his task. It was in August, 1896, that Susy died. He
began the book in October. And he wrote to his friend
Twichell:

> *I am working, but it is for the sake of the work —
> the "surcease of sorrow" that is found there. I work all
> the days, trouble vanishes away when I use that magic.
> This book will not long stand between it and me, now;
> but that is no matter, I have many unwritten books to
> fly to for my preservation; the interval between the
> finishing of this one and the beginning of the next will
> not be more than an hour.*

Observe that he was relying on work, on writing, to hold his
grief at arm's length, the grief of Susy's death. But, besides
that pitiful purpose, are we not already entitled to see something else? There seems to me already a hint of what was
soon to be plainer, that part of the necessity to write was to
vindicate himself as a writer, to restore the image that had
been impaired. He had to write: he was under compulsion
to.

Following the Equator is the dullest of his books, and
writing it was a laborious and sometimes agonizing task. He
rebelled at having to write it for money. He rebelled at the
meaninglessness of the pursuit, which was part of the mean-

inglessness of life. For, with Susy dead, life seemed to have no meaning except loss and cruelty. But he kept at work and on April 13, 1897, a notebook entry says, "I finished my book today." But it needed rearranging and on May 18, the notebook says, "Finished the book again." Several pages of notes follow, some of them for a story I shall be describing in a moment. Then on May 23, five days after the end of the book, the notebook says, "Wrote first chapter of above story today." The interval had been a little longer than the hour he predicted to Twichell, but not much.

With that first chapter, Mark had begun the series of experiments and failures that are our central interest. And also he began other experiments and other failures not closely related to them. What the next months show is a man writing in the grip of an obsession, driven to write, flogged and scourged to write by the fierce drive within him — a man under compulsion to write for "surcease of sorrow," but still more to reintegrate a blasted talent, and most of all to restore his private image of himself. But also this compulsive need to write is constantly blocked and distorted. It is so frenzied that it seems aimless — and also it is perpetually frustrated. "I couldn't get along without work now," he wrote to Howells. "I bury myself in it up to the ears. Long hours — 8 and 9 at a stretch, sometimes." That shows the compulsiveness, and we get a glimpse of the frustration when he writes to Howells in August, 1898, fifteen months after that confident notebook entry, "Last summer I started 16 things wrong — 3 books and 13 mag. articles — and could only make 2 little wee things, 1500 words altogether, succeed — only that out of piles and stacks of diligently-wrought MS., the labor of 6 weeks' unremitting effort." But the truth was more serious than this glimpse shows, for the inability to make more than on an average two little wee things come out of sixteen starts was to last longer than he thought. It was to last through 1898 and on to 1899, to 1900, to 1904 — and in fact the jobs that he completed from 1897 on through the rest of his life represent only a small fraction of the jobs he began. From 1897 on there are scores of manuscripts in the Mark Twain papers which begin bravely enough and then peter out, some of them after only a few pages, some of them only after many hundred pages of stubborn and obviously heart-wrenching work. Now it is certain that, as Mark grew older, he did not intend to finish some of them — that he began them merely to amuse himself or to jot down a passing observation or perception, or to find release from some mood in the only remedy he was able to depend on. But other manuscripts, especially those we are to deal with, he meant and desperately wanted to complete. He was impelled to come back to them time after time, take them up again, try some other beginning or some other set of characters, impose some other form on them or some new outcome or some other meaning or some other moral — but get on with them, sweat them through, mould them to an end. So time after time he came back to them. And time after time he failed. He could not finish them.

Now, such a frustration is striking and must be meaningful. There must be a significant reason for the repeated failure of a practiced literary artist, a man who had been writing all his life with marked success. True, Mark Twain had always been subject to enthusiasms and his enthusiasms were short-lived, so that normally he began a good many manuscripts which he never bothered to finish after the going got hard. But this is something else, a repeated and habitual failure, and he did try to finish them — he tried repeatedly, under the compulsion that had enslaved him.

He kept coming back to them — and always he failed. This is no casual or meaningless failure; it is obviously closely interwrought with the fundamental energies of his personality.

The end of our search will come in 1905 but we are most concerned with the two and a half years following that notebook entry of May 18, 1897. During that period he wrote so much that, turning the manuscripts over in my hands and trying to make out their relationships, I have frequently told myself that all of them could not possibly belong to these years, that no man could write so much. But there they are, manuscript after manuscript, a staggering number of them, a still more staggering grand total of words. He actually wrote them during these years. During the same years of course, he also wrote other essays, sketches, reminiscences, newspaper articles, which he succeeded in completing and which were published. But here is a many times greater number of manuscripts which he could not finish.

The force that was impelling him to write was, clearly, both desperate and remorseless. Only a man who was hell-ridden could write so much. Think of the inner desperation this indicates — and think how that desperation must have grown and spread when time after time he was forced to realize that he could not finish what he had begun. His invention ran out, he could not solve the ordinary problems of structure and technique, he could not overcome the ordinary difficulties of his own intentions, he could not push the thing through to an end. Apart from the manuscripts themselves there is only a fragmentary record of his distress, but surely it was a long agony. Secretly, in the hours of black brooding which had become habitual since Susy died, he must have been forever grappling with the most terrible fear that any artist can feel: the fear that his talent has been drained away, that his spark has been quenched, that his achievement is over forever. It is a poison which acts two ways, spreading back to reinforce the poison that begot it. For the failure of the artist must strike close to the identity and potency of the man — and that identity and potency had already been challenged and grievously impaired by the catastrophes we have glanced at. Of course, it must have proceeded out of those catastrophes, or at least been set in motion by them, and few would doubt that his new impotence was related to the impairment he had suffered or that these literary failures issued from the complex sense of failure that had been created in him.

Much of this heap of manuscript is at random. I disregard that part and consider now only what seems significant in the end. And the first support of what I have just said about impairment comes from Mark's attempts to make use once more of the boys who had conferred immortality on his two finest books — and whom he had called upon again, during the anxieties of the early nineties, for two lesser stories, *Tom Sawyer Abroad* and *Tom Sawyer Detective*. So now he put them to work again, involving them in a long conspiracy of Tom's invention more preposterous and much drearier than the one that turns the last part of *Huckleberry Finn* into extravaganza. It is a maze of romance and rank improvisation that is trivial to begin with and speedily becomes disheartening. It is wholly without structure and moves without plan by dint of a feverish extemporization which gets more mechanical and improbable as it goes on. It is dull, humorless, without the enchantment of the great originals. Mark's touch is altogether gone from it and, what points most vividly to the truth, even the prose is dead.

It is pitiful to see a great writer turning back in such a desperate mood to the works of his greatness. And this effort

to repeat what he had done at the height of his power, sum-
moning ghosts from his earlier books, shows the strength of
his fear that power had departed from him. It is more pitiful that the effort to save himself does not save him: the
book is a merciless parody of the great books it turns back
to. He must have realized the true nature of the effort he
was making, and certainly its failure could not be hidden
from him. Nor is this manuscript the only one in which he
tried to use the two boys, as we shall see, nor are *Huckleberry Finn* and *Tom Sawyer* the only earlier books he called
on in his need. Through much of the unfinished work of
this period runs a diluted strain of other books, *Pudd'nhead
Wilson* in particular, and of ideas, devices, stock themes and
treatments which he had found effective in his great days
but which were not effective now when he needed them
most.

It was at this time, also, that Mark began to think seriously about his autobiography. He had written fragments
of it before, notably the account of his publication of Grant's
memoirs contained in the first volume of the published portions. But now he wrote a number of more or less systematic
sketches and planned to buckle down and write the book.
He made many pages of notes for it — lists of people,
character sketches, memoranda of exciting or important or
amusing events. These jottings run through all the notebooks he kept during this period, a long sequence of them
in one book shows a comprehensive plan, and there is a
forty-page catalogue of Hannibal people which is well along
toward actual biography.

Of all this autobiographical material, by far the largest
part concerns two periods of his life. Scattering memoranda
cover many years, but most of them deal either with the
dead child Susy or with the Hannibal of his boyhood. One

long section of a notebook describes the agonizing details of Susy's illness and death, and yearns over the trivial, pitiful incidents of her childhood, the promise of her life, the loss and cruelty of her death. These notes he actually worked up into a biographical sketch of Susy, but he could not finish it. He was to come back to it some years later, and to work much of it into the *Autobiography*. But there is even more about Hannibal, and the friends and neighbors of the Clemenses, than there is about Susy.

What is the importance of these facts for our inquiry? Well, it is significant that, in this time of impotence and failure, his mind was constantly turning over not only his memories of his dead daughter but also his memories of his boyhood. For we know from his books that boyhood was his golden time and that Hannibal was his lost, immortal idyll, not of boyhood only but of home as well. It meant whatever home means of peace, happiness, fulfillment, and especially security. In the time of desolation whose symbol he was not yet able to forge, he turned back to the years and the place that meant safety. Presently we shall understand why.

Finally, it was at this time that he began to write what he called his Gospel. Twenty years ago or more he had read a paper on philosophical determinism to a club in Hartford, and from time to time thereafter he had shown that the idea was working in him. Now suddenly it began to demand expression — and it was to go on demanding it until he died. A large part of the Mark Twain papers consists of argumentative or analytical chapters, dialogues, letters, some of them finished, more abandoned, which develop and embroider the twinned themes: man's helplessness in the grip of the inexorable forces of the universe, and man's essential cowardice, pettiness, and evil. He went on writing them

until within a few months of his death, but actually he began to write them, and wrote the most consecutive of them,
in the period we are dealing with. Probably the greater part
of those which he privately printed in 1906 as *What Is Man?*
were written during these years.

The importance of *What Is Man?* to our inquiry is that
it provides the first dependable indication of what was going on in the ferments that were at work. We have asked
what was the result on the artist of the calamities that had
all but broken the man, and with this book we may make
a start toward an answer. For *What Is Man?* is not only a
treatise on man's instability, weakness, cowardice, cruelty,
and degradation. It is not only an assault on the illusions
of free will, integrity, decency, and virtue with which mankind makes tolerable its estate. It is not only an assertion
of the familiar logic of determinism, the fixed universe, the
infrangible sequence of cause and effect from the beginning
of time, holding man helpless, and unalterable by will or wish
or effort. If that were all there were to it, surely there would
be significance in its getting itself written at this particular
period. But it is much more than that. For clearly *What Is
Man?* is also a plea for pardon. In describing man's helplessness, it pleads that man cannot be blamed. In asserting
man's cowardice, it asserts also that man is not responsible.
In painting man as enslaved and dominated by circumstance,
it argues that the omnipotence of circumstance must answer
for what Mark is inwardly afraid he is being held to answer
for. If man is weak, cowardly, and sentenced to defeat, then
one who feels himself weak, cowardly, and defeated cannot
be to blame. If man is not responsible, then no man can
be held responsible. No one, I think, can read this weari-
somely repeated argument without feeling the terrible force
of an inner cry: Do not blame me, for it was not my fault.

That theme, which is to be repeated in many forms, is sounded clearly in *What Is Man?* So we may now move on to the three groups of manuscripts from whose chaos was to be resolved the answer to that troubled cry. I cannot be sure that my arrangement is chronological — I cannot date all of them in relation to one another. But that does not matter much, for they are variations on themes common to them all, the themes come together in the end, and I can date most of the significant steps in the evolution that is really a debate.

We will follow them rather by idea than by manuscript. A number of ideas are repeated over and over in the various manuscripts, modulated, changed, adapted, blended, and in the end, harmonized.

One of these ideas, and probably the earliest, is that of the great stretch of time which may seem to elapse in a dream whose actual duration, in waking time, is only a few minutes or perhaps a few seconds. And mingled with this idea is another one, which holds the germ of the eventual conclusion, the idea of confusing dream with reality. The notebook entry I have quoted, which says that Mark began the "above story" on a certain day, proposes a story in which a man is to nod for a moment over a cigarette, dream a sequence of events which he thinks has lasted for seventeen years, and on waking from his momentary sleep, so to have confused the dream with the reality that he cannot recognize his wife. Accompanying this entry is a list of characters for the story which identifies many of them as actual persons from Mark Twain's past. The significance of this is made clearer by the fact that, as I have said, Mark was making plans for his autobiography at exactly the same time.

But the story which he actually began to write, though it preserves the framework of the dream, mostly disregards it

in favor of another idea, a different theme, whose significance is apparent at sight and which was to arouse, following this story, his most persistent effort. It is the story of a
world-famous personage who is cast down from his high
estate. The time is shortly after the Mexican War of 1846,
and the hero is the youngest major general in the American
army. His heroism and gallantry have made him a world
figure and destined him for the presidency as soon as he
shall be old enough to hold that office. He is not only
world-famous but very rich as well, fortunate and happy,
married to a beautiful woman whom he worships, the father
of two small girls whom he adores, one of whom is talented
and promising. He falls asleep over his cigarette and in his
dream the family's magnificent house is burned down and,
following that, a greater catastrophe swiftly engulfs them. A
relative of the general's wife, who has been trusted with the
management of their fortune, proves not only to have dis-
sipated the fortune but to have become involved in widespread chicanery and fraud as well. The general's reputation is blackened, he and his beloved family are plunged
not only into abject poverty but into overwhelming disgrace
as well, and in all ways he and they are ruined. He sinks
into unconsciousness, wakes from that a year and a half later,
finds himself and his family living in a squalid log cabin in
California, learns the bitter struggle his wife has made to
support them . . . and here the manuscript breaks off. It had
broken off before this and been resumed, but this time the
break was final. Mark Twain could go no farther.

Already my point must be clear; it hardly needs my statement that the story is crowded with undisguised autobiographical material — lifelong friends of Mark Twain, members of his family, enemies, incidents that had happened to
him, scenes and speeches straight from his life. Notice the

nakedness of the theme: a great and fine personage of unimpeachable integrity is struck down by catastrophe and disgraced in the eyes of all the world. Notice also how it is made clear that the personage was innocently betrayed, that the catastrophe was not his fault.

Following this story, Mark separated out the dream idea and confined it to a sequence that I will describe in a moment, while proceeding to carry the theme of the virtuous man cast down from his high estate into a series of manuscripts which together represent the strongest and most persistent effort in our whole cycle. He kept coming back to this story not only during 1898 and 1899 but as late as 1904. How many different essays he made I cannot say, I can only say that he made them repeatedly. The thing obsessed him and he must get it out. But time after time he found himself blocked and had to quit.

It is too long a story and, as his efforts crisscrossed and failed, too complex a story for me to tell here. It concerns the leading citizen of a town which hardly differs from the St. Petersburg of *Tom Sawyer* and the Hannibal of *Autobiography*. And it concerns not only the squire but another citizen, formerly wealthy, who had suffered the loss of his fortune and is now reduced to poverty but everywhere respected for his virtue and integrity. Through an intricate series of circumstances the virtuous man is led by his own weakness to commit murder, and other intricately wrought circumstances throw suspicion on the squire. The theme is frequently lost sight of in the melodramatic incidents that Mark frantically invented to get it told somehow, or anyhow, and in a flood of other themes from all the other ventures of this period. But the theme is the moral cowardice and hypocrisy of mankind, the liability of everyone, even the most virtuous, to yield to his secret weakness, provided only he is tempted, or there is some seeming necessity, or mere chance comes his way. Back and forth across this theme play related themes from *What Is Man?*

Now see what has happened. The theme of catastrophe has been modulated. The protagonist has been split in two.[2] The victim of catastrophe is no longer innocent, as in the major general's story. He is guilty and knows he is guilty, and a large part of the story is his effort to appease and justify himself. But, though he is guilty, the plea is made for him that he cannot be blamed. In different attempts different reasons are given but they all come to the same thing in the end — that circumstance is omnipotent and what happens must happen, alike to all men. If all men would sin in the given circumstance, then none can be blamed for sinning — the responsibility must be turned back to impersonal fate or to the malevolent God who designed it. But notice that there is here a psychic admission, or an accusation, which the earlier story did not contain. The major general was betrayed by one he had trusted, but the virtuous man of this cycle, though the plea is made that he was not responsible, is cast down by his own act.

This cycle too is crowded with unmistakable portraits and actual events from Mark's own experience. A greater effort is made to transform and adapt them, but they are there. And it should be clear that they are there by the same compulsion that put the admission or accusation there.

Bear in mind that none of the expedients, new starts, or changed devices had worked: Mark had proved unable to bring any version of his story to fruition. Not even when he went back and borrowed from its predecessor. He tried, that is, telling the same story of the virtuous man made murderer and coward and hypocrite by calamity, as some-

2 Like the character mentioned in the preceding chapter.

thing that happened in a dream — in a dream, furthermore, that was to last for a few minutes only, though it seemed to consume many years. So what began as an independent story became essentially the same story, though with the modulation I have pointed out. And that modulation, I think, discloses the secret self-accusation as it is met by a counter-assertion, a confession in avoidance, that all men are guilty as circumstances compel them to be.

We have now got far along in our period and must go back, to where the idea of the dream began a different evolution. A number of apparently aimless sketches which have no surface relationship to our inquiry had dealt with sailors or other people marooned in the vast Antarctic waste of ice and darkness. In one of these there had been introduced a legend of an enchanted sea wilderness in the midst of this eternal winter where ships were caught in a central place of calm, circumscribed by the ice and snow, and held drifting forever there with the dead bodies of their crews and passengers preserved by the unearthly cold. Various components of this idea run back farther in Mark's thinking than I can trace them here, but now they have come together in a striking and terrible symbol of desolation.[3]

Mark had not been able to complete any of these casual sketches, but, whether consciously or not, they led to a re-entry and flashed across his mind the bright hope that he had found a variation of the story that tormented him, a variation which, this time, he would be able to complete. Again we have the happily married man who is the father of two delightful daughters and again he falls asleep and is to waken after a few minutes, believing that years have passed. But this time, before he falls asleep he looks through

[3] Mr. Wecter's biography will probably show that Mark took the symbolism of the Antarctic from the reading he was doing at the time.

a microscope at a drop of water — and that item changes and immensely deepens the story. For in his dream, he and his family are on a mysterious ship sailing they know not where in a perpetual darkness filled with storms of snow and ice. This proves to be an Antarctic waste in the drop of water which he had looked at in the microscope, and in that tortured dream the voyage progresses in mystery and terror — and also in what I feel to be significance. No one knows where they are, no one knows where they are going or for what purpose or under whose command. But they are in the Great Dark at the edge of the microscope's field, a place of unimaginable desolation. And somewhere far off is the horror of the Great White Glare, which is really the beam cast through the microscope's field by the reflector.

Moreover, on this ship there is some recollection of waking life — the world of reality outside both the microscope and the dream. But this fades, and one comes to doubt it, one comes in the end to believe that the reality one remembers was a dream after all, and that the dream one lives in is the reality. Furthermore, there is a supernatural being on board the ship, the Superintendent of Dreams, who has power over both the ship and the minds of its passengers, who steadily, vindictively, cultivates in their minds the doubt of reality which becomes the belief in dream.[4] And in the terrible darkness, monsters roam the freezing ocean, threatening to snatch victims from the ship and devour them. And finally, there are mutiny and betrayal on this ship, trusted officers who will be untrue and produce catastrophe.

This story also Mark could not finish. He came back to it several times, trying to find an effective outcome for it, try-

---

[4] I need not point out that the Superintendent of Dreams exactly corresponds to God in *What Is Man?* Later he becomes Satan.

ing to give it this slant or that, trying to crystallize round these symbols a coherent expression of the dread they had for him. The frustration still held and he could not do it, but what he did write is markedly superior to anything I have previously mentioned. It is a strange, powerful, and moving story, this uncompleted fragment; it holds you fascinated despite some crudities of construction. There is significance for us in the fact that he was able to make it better literature. And there is more significance in the notes that show how he wanted to finish it.

For as the voyage went on, still greater afflictions were to visit the ship. It was to meet other ships caught in the same terrible enchantment. One of them was to contain a fabulous treasure in gold, and this was to madden some of the already mutinous crew. The baby who had been born to our married couple was to be carried off on another ship, the search for the child was to mingle with the crew's mad lust for the treasure, the wife's heart was to break, her hair was to turn white, and she was finally to go mad with grief, during the ten fruitless years while they tried to find the child. They were to catch up with the other ship at last — but in the Great White Glare, where the child and all the crew and passengers of the second ship were to be killed by the heat. And the Glare was to further madden the gold-maddened mutineers and to dry up the sea, the monsters were to gather, and in a final, apocalyptic phantasy of destruction, the two beloved daughters were to be killed, the grief-crazed wife was to die, all remaining survivors of the first ship were to die also, leaving only the helpless narrator and the loyal Negro who was his servant.

Once more, a great part of the detail of this story was from Mark's experience. Most of the characters are identifiable from his life, or correspond to characters elsewhere in our

material who are identifiable. The children's parties, the
servants, the arguments can be annotated. The girl who is
so loved and who is killed with such cruelty dies in exactly
the delirium that the faithful notebooks record of Susy
Clemens's fatal illness. And so on.

The pattern has now been repeated many times. We have
seen Mark's compulsion to write it and the inhibition that
withheld him from working it out to an end. So now, I
think, we may make some judgments. We have seen in fiction the shape of the imprint left on Mark Twain's mind
and heart by the series of catastrophes I began by describing.
For essentially they are the catastrophes that obsess him in
these uncompleted stories. Nor can there be any doubt
which great personage is cast down from his high place,
which beloved wife is maddened by despair, which beloved
daughter dies in agony. But if we recognize all that, then
we must also recognize the terrible accusation that had risen
in his heart. I said, far back, that he walked the narrow
edge between sanity and madness. How close he came to
madness may be understood in this cry, "It must have been
my fault."

We need neither the anthropology of primitive religions
nor the psychology of the unconscious mind to understand,
for in all of us a similar fear and accusation hover about the
margin of the mind, to come forward a little and lose some
of their vagueness in moments when discouragement is on
us or the menace of living has suddenly sharpened. That
primal guilt is of one tissue with our primal despair, but
happily those are brief moments when we are in health. Yet
we all know, of our own experience or experience near to
us, that the shocks of life may sometimes prolong those
moments, bring the accusation into the center of the mind,
delay the healthy reaction from it — and then we have at best
despair and at worst insanity. This close had Mark Twain

come: that there had been set up in him a contention, an accusation he could not bear, a denial he could not make. In the yeasty darkness at the mind's base, he had, of his own fault, brought on himself this disgrace and degradation and humiliation. In the phantasy that underlay both his grief and his rebellion, he was the author of his own fall, and the author also of his wife's and daughters' illness, of his daughter's death, of the unabated agony that had come upon his family.

So now he had found the symbols of despair. Through stormy darkness and hemmed in by ice, directed by some unknown and malevolent will, a ship sails a terrible sea for which there is no chart and where monsters lurk that may strike and destroy at any moment. The ship sails there forever, there is no plan or sense to its voyage and no hope that the agony will end, and the helpless passengers are menaced not only by the Great Dark without but by mutiny and greed and maniac revenge within. And quite surely there will come to them bereavement, the death of their loved ones, the triumph of an idle and unmitigated malevolence whose terrible decoys are love and hope and human warmth, to lure humanity to destruction.

The artist is driven to make what he can of experience: art is the armistice he signs with fate. Yet the compulsiveness Mark Twain shows and above all his frustration make clear that here we are dealing with more than the comparatively simple way of art. The impact of calamity had been too great, he had taken one step too near the edge, and there is evident a struggle not only to make terms with his experience but also to vindicate himself. And not only to vindicate himself but, quite literally, by that vindication to integrate a mind that had been blasted and restore a talent that had been blown asunder.

We have seen his first attempt to still that accusation:

the "It was not my fault" of the story where the major general is betrayed by a trusted relative. That would not suffice: the excuse was too transparent. There followed the assertion in *What Is Man?* that no one can be blamed since the chain of circumstance holds him fast in a plan determined by a vindictive God. That would not move the judge's heart, nor could the voice be stilled by the argument of the cycle to which he returned so often (in the stories of the virtuous man turned murderer) that all men are weak and all men fall when tempted.

But the dream story had brought important modulations. And let me add that at one time, as his notes show, he contemplated going back to the disgraced major general and setting him out also on the dreambound ship in the eternal ice, together with a company of fellow victims living out their diverse fates in the same predestined anguish and despair. He did not write it. If he had begun it, he would not have finished it. For though this addition to the idea had hope in it, he had not yet found the reconciliation.

But he had come close to it. There was a grotesque hope, or at least an alleviation, in the position he had now reached. For this dream idea has two parts, one that dreams are brief though their agony may seem to last forever, and the deeper idea that the reality may fade into the dream, that one may not be sure, that as one wakes from a dream so perhaps one may wake from a lesser to a greater dream. Here the perturbed spirit finds comfort, though not quite enough, in the simple thought, so direct and inevitable, so characteristic of the helplessness of our deepest selves: "It may not be true after all. It may be a dream. Maybe I have dreamed the whole agony. Maybe loss and suffering and despair are false, are only a dream."

Remember that this compulsive writing had produced

other manuscripts, apparently at random and without relation to this bitter debate. Among them was a story about
Tom Sawyer and Huck Finn, which I briefly described. But
that story could not have been altogether aimless and at random. It was, in a way, a premonition. For in his winnow-
ing of his own books and his lost years, he recalled a mysterious stranger in the town of Hannibal. I do not know
much about this man, for he takes various shapes in the
stories and autobiographical notes, but the important thing
is his secret, the fact that there is noble or perhaps royal
blood in his veins. This made him kin to Mark Twain, in
whose veins ran the blood of English earls as well as
that of a regicide. And was not Mark, besides, that most
mysterious of strangers on this earth, a genius, a man born
unlike other men, to a strange destiny? Somehow the image
of this unrecognized nobleman blends with another image
that had fascinated Mark all his life long, the figure of
Satan. And this was a fruitful time to remember Satan, for
Satan is an angel and angels are exempt from loss and pain
and all mortal suffering, they are exempt from guilt and con-
science and self-condemnation, and temptation has no meaning for them and they have no moral sense, and neither
humiliation nor death nor the suffering of anyone affects
them in the least. Moreover, of the angels who were all that
Mark needed most to be, he felt nearest to Satan, the one
who had revolted against the inexorable laws of the universe stated in *What Is Man?* and the one whose insatiable
curiosity about the ways of man kept him going up and
down on the earth and to and fro therein.

So it is not surprising when presently young Satan, a
nephew of the fallen angel, comes to Hannibal and falls in
with Tom Sawyer and Huck Finn. This first manuscript is
not remarkable, being little more than a succession of mar-

velous works done by the young angel for the admiration and stupefaction of the village. But in it and in the notes made for carrying it on Mark found the vital clues, the seeds that were to bear fruit at last. At first young Satan was no more than a vehicle for Mark's derision of the God whose vengefulness creates human pain and for his scorn of the antlike race pain is inflicted on, and an identification, infantile at base, with a supernatural being who can perform wonders that make him distinguished and envied, a being also of irresistible strength. But he became more than that, and the way out of the basic frustration was his miracles. So another manuscript begins with Tom and Huck and young Satan in Hannibal, but this soon breaks off and a longer, better, and more deeply wrought one begins. The same story has been transferred to Eseldorf, in Austria, centuries ago — but if we still needed a key by now, note that this story includes a print shop such as young Sam Clemens worked in when he was the age of these boys. I will say nothing of this manuscript except that it led directly to the one which came through to triumph at last, the book which, after it had been painfully written over and changed and adjusted and transformed, was to achieve the completion denied its many predecessors, the book which we know as *The Mysterious Stranger*.

In those tortured revisions and adjustments, which are part of the same desperate effort to make the story go somehow that I have traced in other sequences, we see the thing finding expression at last. Or, if I may so phrase it, we see the psychic block removed, the dilemma solved, the inhibition broken, the accusation stilled, and Mark Twain's mind given peace at last and his talent restored. The miracles, which at first are just an idle game for the amusement of the boys and the astonishment of the villagers, become finally a spectacle of human life in miniature, with the suffering diminished to the vanishing point since these are just puppets, unreal creatures moving in a shadow-play, and they are seen with the detachment of an immortal spirit, passionless and untouched. And so from a spectacle they become a dream — the symbolic dream of human experience that Mark had been trying to write in such travail for so many years.

So an unrecognized purpose had dominated the chaos of those efforts, after all, and out of it had come *The Mysterious Stranger,* a minor masterpiece, with its clear, subdued colors, its autumnal pity and compassion, its fine, silvery echo of mortality and of hope destroyed and of man's pettiness somehow given the nobility of suffering, the thread of pain binding all living things together. But what is it? Eseldorf — Assville — is just Hannibal, seen far away, softened by the mist of centuries. The boys who are eager and cowardly, aspiring and cruel, are just Tom and Huck once more, which is to say they are what Mark had found best in himself and his long phantasies. The villagers, the human race in little, are just his friends and neighbors, his detractors and enemies and those who had undone him. The deaths died, the injuries suffered and agonies endured — we do not need to inquire what they are, after the innumerable times he had tried to give them meaning in art. Nor can there be any doubt who the immortal Antagonist is, the enemy of God, which is to say the rebel against law — and so against responsibility. Here the dreadful things alleged against mankind, and so made as a confession, in *What Is Man?* are said again, but now they are tolerable, conformable, acceptable, for they have been removed far away, over them broods the peace of distant dream. And now we know that the dream had closed the arc and permitted him to say

what he must say and enabled him at last to live at peace
with himself.

> *You perceive,* now [*Satan says, just before he vanishes
> and the book ends*] *that these things are all impossible
> except in a dream. You perceive that they are pure and
> puerile insanities, the silly creations of an imagination
> that is not conscious of its freaks — in a word, that they
> are a dream, and you the maker of it. . . .*
>
> *It is true, that which I have revealed to you; there is
> no God, no universe, no human race, no earthly life,
> no heaven, no hell. It is all a dream — a grotesque and
> foolish dream. Nothing exists but you. And you are
> but a thought, — a vagrant thought, a useless thought,
> a homeless thought, wandering forlorn among the
> empty eternities!*

The dream, that is, was the answer and the proof. He
had tried to say: It was not my fault, I was betrayed. But the
accusation could not be stayed so easily. He had tried to
say: It was not my fault, for the fixed universe of inescapable
law intended from the beginning that this should happen.
But that was too easily exposed as subterfuge. He had tried
to say: It was not my fault, for anyone would have done
the same, but the remorseless feet that follow, follow after
had driven him from that refuge. He had tried to say: It is
just a delusion, a dream I will wake from — and that had
almost served, but not quite. Susy's delirium was not his
delusion and there could be no waking in forgetfulness of
it — and if that was so, then the terrible accusation still held.

But there was still an answer. If nothing existed but a
homeless thought wandering forlorn among the empty eter-
nities, then his smaller agony and his personal guilt were
also a dream. If everything was dream, then clearly the

accused prisoner might be discharged. The accusation be-
gotten by his experience could be stilled by destroying all
experience. It was possible to uproot terror and guilt and
responsibility from his little world, by detonating the universe. He could end his contention with the vengeful God
and put away remorse forever by reducing all contention,
vengeance, pain, degradation, guilt, sin, and panic to a
lonely dream.

That was the price to be paid for peace. It seems a high
price. But the terms one makes with fate, even in art, are
the terms one can make. At this cost the fallen angel of our
literature, the mysterious stranger who seemed only a sojourner in the cramped spaces of our mortal world, saved
himself in the end, and came back from the edge of insanity,
and found as much peace as any man may find in his last
years, and brought his talent into fruition and made it
whole again.

*   *   *

I do not know what a typical novelist would be or how we
could determine what constitutes a typical example of the
transformation into fiction of personal experience that this
chapter set out to deal with. I judge that in some ways *The
Mysterious Stranger* must be an extreme case. Mark Twain
had become obsessional and had come close to the edge of
sanity as most novelists who forge deep personal experience
into fiction do not. But whatever the typical may be, the
extreme certainly illuminates it.

All the energies we have previously isolated are visibly at
work in this case history. Of the conscious phantasies that
went into it I think it proper to stress three elements: the
persistence of a distinguished and good person; his gradual
modification into a different kind of person, with a corre-

sponding modulation and enrichment of theme, and his eventual division into two persons; and at last the multiple split by which he becomes a whole cast of characters. Note too the repeated and wide-ranging excursions through Mark's personal and literary past, in the effort to find material that will come alive in the projected story. (There are many more of these in the manuscripts than I have had space to mention. For instance, one attempt to tell the basic story incorporated an allegory about free silver and the gold standard, played out on an Antarctic island by the shipwrecked crew. This was clearly the financial panic of 1893 that had had a part in Mark's own downfall.) Finally, the simple outline-phantasy, which we have identified as the novelist's unconscious phantasy, is the same throughout. The circumstances of doom change from manuscript to manuscript but doom itself and the pathway to it are constant.

But the important thing is that Mark Twain's autobiography was forged into symbols. That fact is what makes *The Mysterious Stranger* a novel instead of what I have called a pre-novel.

The transformation has been carried through to completion. The autobiography is completely hidden behind Satan, the boys, and the rest of the dramatis personae, as the psychic autobiography of Dostoievsky is entirely wrought into symbolic character and event. Turgenev called Dostoievsky an amateur and Arnold Bennett used the same word to characterize Mark Twain. But the word "amateur" here has neither its dictionary meaning nor the one empirically given it in art: it merely classifies them as being a particular kind of workman. So far as that sense of the word may limit them they are, perhaps, incomplete craftsmen but they are nevertheless, as artists, complete novelists. The case history shows that Mark Twain is, as an artist, whole. He

succeeds where the novelist I have set up at one pole,
Thomas Wolfe, fails. Satan derives from the same autobiographical necessity that creates Eugene Gant, Starwick, and
Professor Hatcher, for instance, in *Of Time and the River*.
But no one can find any justification for giving Satan a
worldly name, whereas Gant is "I" in the manuscript,
Hatcher's name is George Pierce Baker, and scores of us
could supply the name for which Starwick is an alias and
could point to events which, though somewhat fictionalized,
are untransformed. The scene in which Satan makes
homunculi of clay and sets them to work building a castle
is on a plane so much more mature, so much more complete
as creation, than the scenes in which Gant, Hatcher, and
Starwick claw at one another for fifty pages at a stretch that
we must say there is an absolute difference. One is wrought
into art, the other is not. I conclude that the process of
transformation completed by Mark Twain is typical, though
the experience behind it is extreme. This, I suppose, is how
the imagination of a novelist customarily creates fiction out
of personal experience.

Satan, the boys, Father Adolf, Father Peter, the other persons in the drama of *The Mysterious Stranger* are not complex characters. They do not have to be for they are characters in a fantasy. But they are too complex and too thoroughly themselves alone to be identified. They have been
created by the processes we have been examining; identifications and incorporations have been so diffused that they have
disappeared. A student of Mark Twain does not hesitate to
say what they signify and symbolize, but except as symbols
they are of themselves and of the novel, they are not of history. Moreover, the developing content of the novel is in its
own terms. As symbol and conception it is entirely conditioned by the autobiography, but as fiction it is entirely

at the novelist's choice and of its own necessity. I doubt if a novel more certainly the expression of the inner biography can be found; it is at the extremity. It is autobiography so unmixed that the absolute need to write it was repeatedly frustrated by an equally powerful refusal to confess in public. The mind that had to write it found the confession too shameful and too terrible to be borne and so inhibited it. It could not be written until Mark Twain found symbols that were safe. But even at this extremity and even with a novelist so little self-critical as he, there is never any question that the action, the drama, the specific content, is subject to his will.

6

THE GATE OF HORN

6

THE GATE OF HORN

W E HAVE several times touched the edges of psychiatry, the therapeutic branch of psychology. Inevitably. The increasing interest of the novel in the depths and springs of the mind has led it to the disturbances of the mind that psychiatry deals with. Concurrently, the development of dynamic psychology, bringing with it the first systematic psychiatry, has strongly influenced fiction. Only one aspect of this immense subject is relevant to our purpose, a tendency of both fiction and psychiatry sometimes to invade each other's fields and to make insupportable demands of each other. Some novelists write as if they were bad psychiatrists and psychiatry shows some willingness to ask all novelists to be good ones.

And in fact it is rather the challenge of psychiatry than the claims of fiction that must be examined. Psychiatry itself, the disturbances with which it deals, the part they play in experience are all material for fiction. Novelists are free to use the content and points of view of psychiatry so far as they are able to understand them, which is not often to an impressive degree. Likewise psychiatry is a benevolence to fiction in so far as it may help novelists to understand them-

selves or others, or as it may enrich their art or their craftsmanship. Finally, psychiatry also works with symbols and
has given fiction a kind of shorthand which is readily understood by readers. Even here, however, we must go warily.
A novel that is a fictionalized study of the Oedipus relation
is on all fours with one that is a fictionalized study of Gres-
ham's Law. The novelist is to approach life directly, not by
way of any theory, even a psychiatric theory about motives
and emotions, and he is to write in the round what he finds
there. He deals with people, not with people as case histories, not as people illustrating abnormal psychology, and
he must deal with them of his own wisdom, not by rule of
even Freud's thumb. To dramatize the data of psychiatry
instead of people in pain is false art, and fiction's symbols
as well as its characters had better arise in wisdom than be
worked out by logarithms. They were, after all, art's symbols before they were psychiatry's.

Novels about psychiatry, however expertly they may be
documented, remain merely documentary fiction unless they
transcend their material. But the occasional novel of or
about psychiatry is less suspect than the one in which emotion and behavior are approached, interpreted, or portrayed
by means of psychiatric concepts. Such a novel is open to
criticism more serious than that based on the use of concepts from other disciplines. If a novelist deals mistakenly
with the material and concepts of, say, engineering, he will
expose himself to the derision of engineers but the fundamental value of his novel, the experience of his characters,
is not likely to be impaired. Whereas psychiatry deals with
the same substance as fiction, human emotion, human motives, and human behavior. It approaches them in its own
way, makes its own interpretations, applies its own methods.
If fiction chooses to abandon its native approach and to sub-

stitute the concepts of psychiatry, then psychiatry is justified in protesting when the borrowed approach leads to shallow, erroneous, or deceptive results. It can require a novelist who uses its tools to use them right.

But sometimes psychiatry seems unwilling merely to resist invasion of its domain. It shows an occasional tendency to demand that novelists limit themselves to the same kind of reports on human experience that psychiatry makes, accommodating them to the psychiatric understanding. In exuberant moments it even tends to bid fiction stay within the boundaries of psychiatric concept and interpretation. This tendency is of course a usurpation. It arises, I think, from an ambivalence in the way psychiatrists tend to think about novelists. On the one hand they are likely to accept a novelist's account of behavior and emotion as valid — to accept imaginary characters as suitable subjects for their own specialized study. On the other hand, they are likely to think of the novelist who wrote the account as a spellbound man.

That is, in one mood the psychiatrist is apt to accept a novelist as capable of making trustworthy observations of conscious and unconscious behavior, but in another mood is apt to regard him as a person expressing his own inner compulsions, in the last analysis an automatism. Each half of this dilemma has logical implications from which psychiatry cannot escape and which sometimes become explicit in what psychiatrists write about fiction. The occasional implication that the writing of fiction is neurotic behavior may be disregarded: some novelists are neurotics, some aren't. (And whenever someone rewrites *Degeneration*, someone else will always appear to rewrite *The Sanity of Art*.) More important is the evident implication that fiction should confine itself solely to reporting emotion and behavior, that it has no other legitimate function, and that its reporting must agree with psychiatry's on penalty of disallowance. Behind this there is usually some form of a thesis I have discussed earlier in this book, the thesis that fiction may further oppress with false ideas about life the human mind that is already sorely beset by illusion, unreal phantasy, and the assault which the unconscious makes on reason and control. Once more and from another source there comes a fiat that some kinds of novels are right and some wrong, this time linked with an assumption that the purpose of fiction is to help psychiatry reduce the power of unconscious forces in human life. In the end this asks novelists to be therapists, to take out a medical license and accept a code of fair practices based on the Hippocratic oath.

But this leaves out some of the fundamental purposes of fiction, which cannot accept a limitation from psychiatry any more than it can accept one from Buddhism or atomic physics. Fiction is of itself. It conducts its own natural history in obedience to its own laws. It is not psychiatry, is not in competition with it, is not under its sovereignty. It renders an entirely different service to the human spirit. I will not say that the service it renders is the lesser one.

*   *   *

The arts are seldom on a single plane or to a single end. Their significances are multiple — varying with what is asked of them — and stratified, yielded up according to the capacity of those who ask. Fiction's house has many mansions. We do not necessarily get from one novel what we get from others. There are trivial and serious novels, simple and complex, shallow and profound, novels to different ends, of different grain and flavor, of different mass. They have different significances at the same moment, and may move simultaneously on several planes of significance. They may serve different ends at the same moment, and the service they render to a reader may be multiple and stratified.

I have said that the literary form called fantasy is a permissive lie, that the reader assents to the lie when he picks up the book. I went on to say that the clearly false ideas frequently expressed in cheap fiction have their fangs drawn because the reader understands them to be a dream, one which he volunteered to dream. In Chapter VIII I will show that the effort of fiction is to get its particular illusion accepted as permanent and that sometimes, in a way, it succeeds. In contrast, the illusion of the drama is understood to be terminable. And the fantasies of the stage, even more openly than those of fiction, are permissive lies. They are dreams which the spectator is aware that he is dreaming. In one particular kind of stage fantasy, the musical drama, the process is voluntary, conscious — and co-operative. The dreamer gladly relinquishes the sense of reality by which he tests most literary effects in order to experience a specific pleasure, to enjoy this falsehood by way of his knowledge that it is false.

"Oh, Fortune, to my aching heart be kind!" the Chorus sings in *Patience* when Bunthorne has sold the tickets that will raffle him in aid of a deserving charity.

> *Oh, Fortune, to my aching heart be kind!*
> *Like us, thou art blindfolded but not blind!*
> *Just raise your bandage, thus, that you may see*
> *And give the prize, and give the prize to me.*

Time's brass knuckles have taught us that the prayer is made in vain. But it must be made — none of us can help making it repeatedly all his life — and there must be a place where it can be made in safety. The world of the Savoy operas, an exquisite form of the co-operative dream, is a sanctuary where such petitions, shameful outside the theater, may be made without shame and where they may be granted. The taxis that bring us to the door, all the hard surfaces we have been sorely taught to accept as reality, forbid us to listen for the soft note of the echoing voice of an old, old love, long dead. The by-experience-conquered part of us, which would be all of us if the world had been designed logically, accepts the prohibition and even comes to rejoice in it. But the echoing voice will not be stilled. Defying both sense and shame, it insists on whispering to the sorrowing heart "rejoice" — and it must be gratified or, like any Gilbertian lover, we die. There must be a place where Fortune does raise the bandage, where the old, old love, with remorseful thought opprest, sincerely doth repent, where bitter unavailing tears for one untimely dead may plead successfully for Iolanthe's boy.

The essence of this dramatic fantasy is that it becomes a dream you are aware of dreaming. It undeludedly acknowledges the omnipotence of the real world and its attendant logic — and proceeds to defy the reality and flout the logic. In this make-believe the everlasting and unendurable sentimentalities of mankind are given dignity while they are mocked, and the admission of their power assuages them.

I have mentioned the musical drama because the principle may be seen there with the greatest clarity. It operates, if less transparently, in trivial novels. The reality-principle is never completely victorious. Our wretched, shameful sentimentalities and pathetics go on smouldering. I do not know if it is foolish to seek to give them relief; I do know that nothing is strong enough to keep us from seeking to. In the actual world we have learned, if barely, not to lower our guard, not to mistake the wish for the reality.

What happens with the trivial novels is that we permit ourselves to lower our guard, knowing that for the moment, between the covers of the book, it is safe to do so. We accept
the reality but ease the frustration. The whirlpool of our
private phantasy is never still. We have seen that the aim of
phantasy is fulfillment, that since fulfillment in the real
world is impossible (or decidedly inconvenient) phantasy is
a turning-away from reality. The trivial, cheap, vulgar, sentimental novel — add any adjective that psychiatry or high-
brow condescension can provide — permits the fulfillment
that is the aim of phantasy. And in order to achieve the
fulfillment, we must remember, it organizes the phantasy
into artistic form; that is what produces the discharge of
phantasy. The cheap novel does not itself turn back to
reality but, after finishing it, the reader does. He closes the
book. When he closes it, he does not carry back with him
any species of delusion. We may dare to say instead that,
because the phantasy has been discharged, he has been
strenghtened for his mortal struggle with reality. He has
derived strength from the literature of dream — or, more
accurately here, from the literature of recognized dream. In
that mortal struggle, I think, sanity needs all the support it
can get. Who will have the temerity to refuse anyone the
support of even the humblest art?

All of us, that is, will get what we can from art. We will
take art on whatever plane we are prepared to take it, even
if that is only the pictorialized fiction of a comic strip.
Whatever the plane, it has dignity. Moreover, the same
bloodstream that nourishes the lowest planes of fiction gives
life to the highest planes. The forests felled to make wood-
pulp for fiction's permissive dreams are not felled in aid of
the meretriciously false. There is a kind of fiction that preceded what we now call novels and has resisted all righteous

insurrection, and we are forced to say that it is a complete misrepresentation of life — myth, folklore, fairy tales. It is false but it is not meretricious and it does not feed delusion. The apes hunkered round the novelist are able to distinguish the fairy tale from the reality and also from the kind of fiction that seeks to counterfeit reality — and may be counterfeiting it at the very moment while the apes are listening. All novels are fairy tales, whatever else they may be besides. The apes make the vital distinction — but they must listen.

Day by day in his consulting room the psychiatrist watches the little man climbing the beanstalk to find and kill the giant, the gorgeous coach changing to a mere pumpkin when the clock strikes, the princess sleeping till the prince comes to kiss her awake. Outside the consulting room, the psychiatrist well knows, one or the other of two things is going to happen. The thumbling, when he reaches the top of the beanstalk, is going to meet the giant and get his head bashed in, which is a victory for the reality-principle but very painful. Or else he is going to believe that he has met the giant and spitted him on his sword, which is delusion or at best neurosis. No doubt the function of psychiatry is to bring him to and through the first alternative in health. But the principal function of trivial fiction, and a basic function of all fiction, is to give him the second experience in safety — that is to say, in sanity.

None of us has ever killed a giant or kissed a princess awake and we know we never will. But, oh, yes, Lord, we all want to. Nothing this side of death can keep us from wanting to. In the mind's dark theater where the drama of fiction is staged we can be, for a little while, mightier at either than the Lord has let us be. That is why, never considering whether it is tawdry and not giving a damn if some consider it contemptible, people read the humblest fiction. We can kill the giant. And in precisely the same way on higher planes of fiction we can experience a moment of love or friendship or achievement purer and more intense than we have ever managed to feel by ourselves — but the substance remains the same as giant-killing. All that has happened on the higher plane is that it has been refined, the fairy story has been forged into accordance with the reality-principle — which is another adequate definition of fine fiction. Our dream has been made to conform to what we began by trying to escape. No doubt all this is heartbreaking, but it is final and it is a condition of all fiction. No matter on what plane the novel which meets this need exists, we ask of it first that the pattern be carried out, that it be finished symmetrically. It may be crude, absurd, or by unreal means, but if it gives us what we need we will abide by any cheapness, any vulgarity, in order to achieve the symbol. Give us the pattern working out, give us the outline coming complete, give us the symbol achieved, and we pay anything for it, any price that may be set.

*　　*　　*

It should be clear by now why the phrase "in safety" had kept recurring in this discussion. But the case for the defendant has only opened.

Unquestionably many novelists, even many great ones, are profoundly neurotic. There need be no surprise and, on behalf of fiction, no resentment. When the depths are disturbed they may the more readily yield up their secrets. Literary legend has William Butler Yeats advising James Joyce not to attempt fiction since he did not have enough chaos in him to make a world; the advice proved bad in this instance but fiction may or may not build worlds out of chaos. Writing a novel may sometimes be a way of keeping a neurosis in check. It may sometimes be an expression of a neurosis. It may even be a way of safely channeling a psychosis, a way of staying sane. If I am right, *The Mysterious Stranger* was Mark Twain's way of staying sane, and we need not go far back in history, or far from the office of any publisher, to find novels which suggest that they were written to encapsulate paranoia or some other cancer of the mind. A neursosis, even a psychosis, we are instructed, is a biological adaptation. It is an adjustment that the tortured organism makes in order to go on living. In a way, some novels may be just such an adaptation.

So far as I can see, this is a matter of indifference to the reader. He is concerned with what is in the novel, not how it got there. His concern with the novelist is with a man writing fiction, not with a mind in distress or disease. The deeply disturbed mind may speak for the fears and premonitions of fear in everyone, whether in doing so it distorts them, whether it distorts reality, whether in distorting reality it speaks from the destructiveness of unconscious forces. And it is to be remembered that psychiatry's eidolon of the personality completely adjusted to real things and completely at home in the world is just that, an eidolon, a Platonic Idea — exemplified by the organisms that live under the bark of trees, perhaps, or under stones at the bottom of streams, but not by organisms more complexly evolved. It is to be remembered further that there are realistic and justified fears as well as neurotic ones. It is to be remembered, finally, that any intelligence which did not face reality with some measure of loneliness, terror, and disgust would be half-witted or, under any definition known to psychiatry or the courts, insane. "The M.D.'s," a friend writes to me, "can maybe cure us of scarlet fever or pneumonia but they can't cure us of dying." He reminds me that the psychiatrist's Platonic Idea of the mind delivered from neurotic fear might approach reality with courage and confidence, but if it did not also approach it with a distrustful wariness based on terror and disgust it could not survive.

And also the deeply disturbed mind, because it has been honed and pointed by its disturbance, may return more accurate accounts of real things, real emotions, real behavior. It makes no difference to the reader of a novel which path the disturbed mind takes or whether it takes both. Following it down any path, the reader wins.

And the substance of giant-killing, in one of its transformations, rises higher to render another of fiction's indispensable services to the human spirit. We have seen that fiction sometimes procures the discharge of our phantasies in safety. But on any plane, even at its most mature, it also has the function of confirming fundamental phantasies which psychiatrists sometimes come close to asking it to dispel. Fiction is always, and especially at its most mature, something that gives us a second chance. Why, yes, I failed it once and forever. I botched the job. I was smaller, more craven, more base, more ignominious and humiliated than in the secrecy of my heart I can bear. But for a few hours, in the valor of better if equally defeated men, I can readjust the balance and appeal the sentence. For a few hours — but only in phantasy. Fiction is our license to meet disaster on more favorable terms than reality permits.

* * *

But who said that a mind deeply disturbed by reality is therefore necessarily neurotic? And who will say that fiction must approach reality with psychiatry as its guide? We may suppose that some novelists have been emancipated from the slavery of their own unconscious forces, disinfected and garnished, their minds laid open to the sunlight and the mountain air, scented with the perfume of pines. We may even suppose that some novelists have never needed this deliverance, never having been in such strict bondage that they could not deal rationally with the real world and rationally practise their trade, which counterfeits it. Gifted at scrutinizing themselves, gifted at comparing themselves with other people, able to deal truly with motive and emotion that issues from them, able to identify their own emotions in others and the emotions of others in themselves — prepared by all this, they set out to tell us what, they believe, the world is like. Let no one underrate the effectiveness of the instruments they bring to the effort, or discount in advance the validity of its results.

Such novelists do deliberately what certain others do involuntarily or inadvertently, and they do consciously what still others do only unconsciously as the result of something else. It does not matter in the least: in different ways various novelists produce representations of reality that, up to a point, will stand all the tests we can apply to reality except that of experiencing it. The effort begins in phantasy, which we have said is a turning-away from reality, but we have also said that the aim of phantasy is fulfillment. The push toward fulfillment can be so strong that it ends by turning back to reality.

Precisely here Freud himself located the function of art. Phantasy, he said, might be seen as beginning with the play of children, which he regarded as not in the least playful but deadly purposeful, and ending as the secret activity of adult minds which we have considered it. At the first step the phantasies of the artist are the same thing; he "is originally a man who turns from reality because he cannot come to terms with the demand for the renunciation of instinctual satisfaction as it is first made." But he is also a man who, by the very nature of his gift, reconciles the necessity of knowing reality with the necessity that is in bitter conflict with it, the necessity of finding pleasure. "He finds a way of return[ing] from this world of phantasy back to reality; with his special gifts he moulds his phantasies into a new kind of reality, and men concede them a justification as valuable reflections of actual life." They are, that is, valid — and Freud lists art higher in the scale than most servants of the reality-princilpe. Up to his capacity, a novelist may find and express the truth about human experience. To a degree, in a way necessarily tragic but in the end noble too, he may make true statements about real things.[1]

So that in the judgment of the greatest psychologist fiction is not invariably an evasion of reality but, at its will, can achieve reality. But I have cited Freud merely to quote Scripture, not because the testimony of any psychologist is needed. The way of art has always proved acceptable to

[1] This is the passage I referred to on page 64. Freud here states what he considers the fundamental purpose of art. Elsewhere he briefly discusses other uses that art makes of phantasy. My two direct quotations in this paragraph are from "Formulations Regarding the Two Principles of Mental Functioning," one of the "Papers on Metapsychology." I quote them because of their condensation but he says the same thing at greater length, more movingly, and with reference to modern culture in *Civilization and Its Discontents*. See also Chapter 23 of the first series of *Introductory Lectures*. It is a great pity that Freud never made an extended or even a separate statement of the place of art in his psychology. It has a fundamental place but he was a man of such wide culture and turned to art so naturally for idea and illustration that he took it for granted his readers would do the same. His ideas, however, can readily be traced in his books, notably *The Interpretation of Dreams, Three Essays on Sexuality,* and *The Future of an Illusion.* The fourth volume of *Collected Papers* contains several essays that bear on the subject here at issue, notably "The Uncanny," "The Relation of the Poet to Day-Dreaming," "The Occurrence in Dreams of Material from Fairy Tales," "The Theme of the Three Caskets," "The Moses of Michelangelo," and "A Childhood Recollection from *Dichtung und Wahrheit.*"

mankind. For one final quality of fiction is that sometimes it is able to say "This is what is" and people who take its word are not betrayed. It remains phantasy but it has become congruent with the real.

Let it go at that for a moment. We have seen that people are always asking fiction, What is this that is happening to me? What am I feeling? By what path did he travel? What is the key? For lack of what horseshoe nail is this defeat? The person who answers these questions truly can hardly be a defective and it does not matter what path he followed to the answer. At one phase of its orbit fiction says, "This happened," or "This is how this man is," or "This is how men are," or "This is the emotion" — says it and bids you let it stand as said. Take it or leave it: art has reported experience. The announcement is austere but at its best it is final. Man has declared his knowledge of man.

The orchestration of *The Guermantes Way* comes to climax in a passage where the Duke and Duchess de Guermantes are presently going to go to the Princess's ball. The thirty or forty pages of this scene are incomparably rich with allusions to the matter that has gone before in this and the two preceding novels. Time, the periods of *le temps perdu*, shimmers through it like the shadow that moves before breeze-driven ripples across a pond. Every item of this intricate contrivance is to the end that life itself shall open to a reader and inclose him. In the midst of a conversation that has included epochs of the Guermantes' history, half the titles and heredities of France, *Dreyfusisme*, the Duke's art gallery, Swann's photographs of medals of the Knights Templar, an embroidery of people and circumstance magnificently patterned, and a fugue in three voices about death — in the midst of this conversation the Duchess invites Swann to accompany her and the Duke on a visit to Italy next spring. Swann declines and is presently forced to explain that before spring he will be dead. The Duke is impatient to get to dinner, there is a flurry while the Duchess changes her black shoes for red ones, she and the Duke wave away as medical gossip the rude intrusion of a friend's death on a moment of social importance, and the door of the carriage bangs shut, leaving the dying man with the Duchess's invitation and the Duke's shout, "You'll live to bury us all." And the novel ends.

As fiction this is many things but first of all it is a declaration from which no appeal can be made. The thing happened. This is imagined experience but it is nevertheless the thing experienced. Here it is: make of it what you will but whatever you make of it you will be deriving from life. . . . We tell time by observed movements of the stars, which, we persuade ourselves, are real. But also telling time involves celestial and terrestrial meridians, which are imagined.

This is a scene in a great novel. But fiction of the better kind does the same thing repeatedly, is always doing it. The representation is valid: the phantasy is as acceptable as the reality. From now on the reader may refer to it as he might refer to any event in history or to something that happened in past time to him. It *has* happened to him. It has left its slight deposit on him, as a historical event in his life does. If only in a way, if only for a moment, a magical operation has transformed printed matter into life.

* * *

There is no longer any need, therefore, of talking about phantasy. This is vicarious experience but it is experience.

That, however, is only part of the magical operation. In a line of type the Duke remarks to Swann, who is dying, that the Duchess's delay will give both of them indigestion before tomorrow. The evocation of the moment for which that line of type stands has required a prolonged and amazingly complex arrangement of minute details. They are all to the point, they are all relevant. Everything that is not relevant has been cleared away. So the scene not only brings a true experience to be, and it not only lays bare the entirety of the people whose experience it is — it also states their significance. Fiction is to be read, I have said, with recognition and surprise. This, then, is not only what happened — it is also the meaning of what happened. A novelist has made a fictional representation of life. In doing so he has revealed to us more significance, it may be, than we could find in life by ourselves.

Novels increase the circumference of our experience. They telescope lifetimes into reading time and so open more lives to us than the span of our days. From those lives the débris has been cleared away, so that, up to the novelist's capacity and ours, we are persuaded that we understand them. I repeat that the illusion is brief and the deposit slight, but they stand. Part of what we know about man and his estate came to us through the gate that fiction opens. For a moment there has been a heightening: the flame has burned hotter and given more light. Whether it shines on life's horror, its mediocrity, or its fortitude, something has been added to us. At best any of us has little enough understanding or wisdom, and little enough rebellion against indignity, but a part of what we have comes from the fact that we have looked at a page and found people caught up in circumstance.

The magical operation goes farther. Not only psychiatry

strips away successive layers. To the shock of recognizing
the real thing and finding meaning in it, art adds another
shock for it brings us to the mist that lies beyond. If the
substance of fiction is so refined that we can coast the whole
shoreline of a life in a few hours, and explore the wilderness inland from the coast, it leads on to strangeness. If the
miniatures of fiction concentrate what is to be learned in
the land distant to Henry Thoreau, it concentrates too the
mystery all travelers come to know.

The mystery circumscribes such a scene as the one we
have taken from *The Guermantes Way,* which, I have said,
is the full experience. Or a not wholly satisfactory novel
flames with sudden magnificence when in *Lord Jim* Marlow
goes to Stein to inquire what wisdom there may be concerning Jim. The devices that produce the effect are much
simpler than those used in *The Guermantes Way,* though
fully as artful, and the substance of the scene is almost
penuriously sparse. There are only two men talking for a
few pages about another man. Yet there is no difference in
the reality. Both scenes are events so tense, so charged, that
one reads them as if with caught breath. The real thing
happens as you watch. The statement that a novelist makes
in Stein and in the Duke de Guermantes is of a man complete and wholly himself. But, more than that, both statements are made so finally that, the reader knows, they are
true not only of these two men but, somehow, of all others
as they find themselves otherwise enmeshed with life. Levels
of significance lie in strata, one below another. Life has not
only been revealed, it has been criticized and appraised . . .
under a strong light.

And yet in both scenes there is an effect which the movements of Stein about his lamplit room with its glass cases of
butterflies mirrors exactly. Talking, he moves in and out of

the light, into the shadows, into the dark, and comes back into the light. "His voice leaped up extraordinarily strong, as though away there in the dusk he had been inspired by some whisper of knowledge." The movement of all true fiction is on many planes at the same time, and it is in and out of the light, into and out of the dusk and dark. With it we touch the mystery and strangeness of all other lives and our own. Beyond the light there is a whisper of knowledge in the dusk.

But there is no need to labor the obvious or prolong a contention that, originating in a false premise, should never have been brought to court. Fiction can be held to no end but its own. We are content to base our judgment of the world as solidly on its imagined representations as on the real, if sometimes to our apprehension the less real, thing. We have all been enlarged and enriched by it. It has enabled all of us to live more abundantly.

That is to say that nothing within the competence of psychiatry is the novelist's job. If you hold him to psychiatry you will spoil a novelist without getting a therapist. And you will lose everything we have found, for which the right name may be warmth. A novelist works not to cure a patient but, if I may summarize everything we have seen, to persuade a reader that for a moment he is not alone.

Psychiatry has no binding claim on fiction. It should, perhaps, resolve its confusions and recognize that fiction's approach to reality, although altogether different from its own, is fully as valid and to an incommensurable end. That we are all tossed about by the stormy waters and that, whereas psychiatry is to conduct the shipwrecked to dry land, or at least to hold him up till he can breathe again, fiction is to let him know that someone is swimming by his side. Psychiatry undertakes to bring us at last to conform to the laws which the gods have made, but art permits us to defy the gods and say that their laws have no force. Psychiatry may show a man how, losing the battle, he can still stay sane. But art is man nerved to die sane in the war which, while he is fighting it, he knows he cannot win.

7

TOWARD
INHERENT FORM

TOWARD INHERENT FORM

W E HAVE FINISHED with novelists as men of feeling; from here on they are men of skill. Any further psychology I may have to venture on will be that of the reader's belief, with everything I have so far said taken for granted. The reader is Ruth Martin not as the pattern of need and motive we have too crudely traced but as she was first introduced, a woman who likes to read novels. The word "unconscious" cannot entirely disappear from this text. But when I use it now, I am afraid, it will usually be a dignified way of circling round the more indefinable aspects of a novelist's skill.

I have said that there is one critical absolute. If a reader leaves a novel unfinished, the highest court has issued a decree that cannot be appealed. It is a novel only so long as it is being read: the novelist's primary job is to keep the reader reading. He will go on reading as long as he is interested, which is to say as long as he believes. The primary job, then, is to persuade the reader that, subject to the special terms of the particular novel, what is happening on the page is an actual event. That the event is occurring to people who are formed and governed like the reader. That they behave in ways which he can accept as proper to them in the circumstances, which seem consistent with life and events as he understands them and harmonious with the special instances of life and events that the novel describes.

I have phrased it in this way to show what Conrad's famous definition omits, "to make you hear, to make you feel . . . before all to make you *see*." That is not the whole truth. It leaves out the inner logic of the thing heard, felt, and seen. What is more important, it leaves out the dynamic quality we have described, the engagement of the reader in that logic. More flatly, the task is to make you hear, feel, and see to the end that you will believe. It is to ally you with the events of the page and with the relation of the characters to them in such a way that for the moment their logic and emotion are binding on you.

This is craftsmanship and I am going to assume that ordinarily it is conscious and deliberate. Much of what is taken to be unconscious, or rather instinctive, in artistic skill is merely unformulated; the artist may be unable to say clearly (or at all) just what he has done or just why he did it, but into his doing it have gone criticism and wisdom, both highly conscious if not analyzed. Novelists vary in their analytical capacity from the lowest degree to the highest, and it would seem that either extreme is something of a handicap. If a writer cannot analyze his effects he may grossly misjudge them. But too much analytical ability may seduce him into equally serious ineffectiveness, excessive concentration on technical methods or on technical experiments for the sake of the experiment alone. Preoccupation with technique usually indicates weak creativeness, the slighting of it weak intelligence.

"Technique" is only a word used to name the means which a novelist employs in order to do what he has undertaken to do, in order to achieve in effective detail the purpose he has set himself in general. Properly a reader does not think of a novelist as a craftsman and is not aware of the technical procedures he responds to or is aware of them only in the vaguest outline. A novelist reading the work of another novelist feels an interest of the workshop, the interest of any workman in considering how he himself would have solved these problems and done this job. This professional interest, however, is antagonistic to the one which alone justifies the novel. The lay reader is the better off as he is the more completely free of it, as he experiences the effect without considering the means used to produce it.

Yet any reader's interest in any novel is secured and maintained by technical means. And, however unaware of them he may be, he constantly expresses what are, in effect, technical judgments, though happily naive ones. A reader who, on finishing *Forever Amber,* remarks that it is too long has expressed an opinion on technique and nothing else, for the just length of a novel is a purely technical consideration. He is still more technical when he objects to a novelist's use of coincidence or to his solving a problem of the novel in an implausible or unnatural way. When he criticizes the behavior of a character in one scene on the ground that it is inconsistent with what earlier scenes have shown the character to be, he may be accusing the novelist of dull perceptions or defective intelligence, but more often he is observing that one of the most intricate technical problems in the writing of fiction has not been solved.

These are technical judgments, though the reader does not so understand them. He reports the effect of fiction on him; he does not analyze the means by which the effect was obtained. He may tell you that Arnold Bennett is too thorough or too detailed; he does not consider which details would have sufficed or how thorough would be thorough enough. He may say that a given passage of Thomas Mann is long-winded or has no point; he does not determine where it should have stopped or how it missed its point or what point it missed. He may praise Hemingway's dialogue as natural without wondering what naturalness in dialogue consists of, or admire the cumulative horror in an episode of Faulkner's without thinking of the structure that upholds it. He is concerned only with what technique achieves.

But the writing of a novel involves the continual solution of technical problems. The novelist may deal with them critically according to theory or principle, empirically according to his past experience, or unthinkingly according to habit and feeling — but he must solve them. They are not his most important consideration but they are an everpresent one and they are one governing force in the relation between the novelist and the reader.

Having made a concession, I must qualify it. Craftsmanship is not a novelist's most important consideration but he must be an effective craftsman or he will not be a novelist at all. He must have skill enough, and that minimum is not only the final ingredient, the *sine qua non*, it bulks larger than most readers are aware, than many critics believe, than some writers admit. The worth of a novel depends on who the novelist is, on how deeply he feels the life he deals with. We will always choose the novelist who is a superior person but a second-rate technician over the one who is a first-rate technician but a second-rate person. Nevertheless the person's effectiveness as a novelist is so strictly a function of skill that only greatness of mind or spirit, or great inner urgency, can transcend serious lack of skill. Greatness of mind or spirit, great inner urgency, great sensitiveness to life or beauty or nobility or despair never yet made a novelist by itself. The forms of fiction must be imposed on the materials of fiction before its content can be communicated. A novel is not a thing in itself. It is not a novel until it is read and only craftsmanship can get it read. When it is just at or just above the minimum, anyone's first dissatisfaction always means a regret that the novelist did not have more skill.

I have said that I believe Thomas Wolfe a bad novelist and that there was probably no help for him, he probably could never have written otherwise than he did. One may disagree with both judgments and yet understand that if Wolfe had been more able to give his material form he would have been a better novelist than he was. Nature apparently meant to give England a great novelist following the First War but the egg divided mitotically and produced mirror-image twins, Aldous Huxley all intelligence and skill, D. H. Lawrence all feeling and little form. Or take Theodore Dreiser. He is unlikely to outlast the present generation of college teachers of literature, who learned from H. L. Mencken to think of him as a symbol of vitality returning to American fiction after a period of bloodlessness. We have been told repeatedly that an obstinate groping for life and an equally obstinate honesty in reporting it transcend the fearful clumsiness with which he wrote. I doubt it; I doubt if he has any importance except a historical one. Perhaps his dead and deadly prose could be accepted as a convention but from page to page the simplest conduct of his fiction is so inept that he seems to write in technical clichés. His principal champion today, in succession to Mencken, is James T. Farrell. Well, it is possible to remember the exuberant experiments with technical devices in *Young Lonigan*. We would be better off today if Mr. Farrell had refined some of them and kept them on his workbench, instead of settling into a method that relies on weight and mass for its effects.

Technique, the skill of fiction, is empirical: there are no

rules. I am about to discuss something different, principles, but they can never be more than tentative. To the chagrin of theory, all the arts subordinate everything else to effectiveness. The tests of technique are pragmatic: does it work? If it does, it is right. A reader is to read believingly and toward the novelist's intended end. Whatever may hold and enhance that belief toward that end is right. If an effect is achieved powerfully it may radiate belief to passages in which no application of derived principles seems possible. The deliberate flouting of principles that elsewhere are the guaranty of his success is, in fact, part of a skillful novelist's skill. And no principle is universally applicable. Passages that would horrify you if they were in Proust are sometimes the highest achievement of Dickens, who was also a great novelist. But, after allowing all reservations, we may say confidently enough that the reader's belief depends primarily on the novelist's technical procedures.

*   *   *

There are fashions in kinds of novels and fashions in ways of writing them. No type or style or method is immortal. There are always those who mistake a new preference of the most people, or the most-literary people, for a belatedly discovered but absolute law of fiction, and who therefore declare that this is the right kind of novel and that hereafter no other kind can be written. When *Ulysses* appeared, a wholly subjective novel with stratified symbolisms and intricate psychological mechanisms, such critics told us that Joyce had made the writing of any other kind of novel impossible, or at least absurd. A smaller number now assert that, at any rate, he did so with *Finnegans Wake*, which would appear to have made novels like *Ulysses* absurd, or at least rudimentary. Following the publication of *Ulysses* many imitations and modulations of it were written, and a brisk if somewhat esoteric fashion got under way. It did not last long and one concludes that Joyce has given instruments to the art of fiction, not limits or necessary conditions. Though many novelists use those instruments for brief passages and occasional effects, few now care to use them for Joyce's purposes or to the exclusion of other instruments.

A few years after *Ulysses* Mr. Hemingway's *The Sun Also Rises* evoked on a smaller scale the same assertions of universality and finality. Except for occasional passages in which Mr. Hemingway was patently remembering Joyce, it was wholly different in kind and method. Whereas Joyce was as subjective as possible, Hemingway was as objective as possible. The greater part of the characters' behavior in *Ulysses* consisted of thought-processes, and all of it was governed by energies and patterns of the unconscious mind. That of the characters in *The Sun Also Rises* neither exhibited nor implied any thought-process whatever but appeared to be a form of conditioned reflex. Leopold Bloom was a series of free-associations; Lady Ashley was a tropism. Yet some critics who had recently been convinced that fiction had not really begun until Joyce now concluded that it had begun over with Hemingway. The usual number of imitators agreed with them, and since the imitable part of a novelist is his technique, there was a rash of novels in which neither thought-process nor vocabulary got very far beyond a grunt. It would appear that Mr. Hemingway as well as Joyce failed to fix the metes and bounds of fiction for all time. He brilliantly renewed an instrument of fiction and widened its scope on behalf of all novelists. But though fashion produced quantities of small Hemingways, who were harder to take than minor Joyces, the limitations of his method were easily ascertainable. Certain young novelists

seem now to be making a cult of repudiating him. They
are impelled to insert in their novels irrelevant derision of
him, as for a while he habitually derided novelists who had
the misfortune to write outside his admiration or to be less
frightened by ideas.

Small or larger shifts in fashion are a commonplace of
the literary scene, and so are the critical imperatives that go
with them. We may recall that the "group-novel" as prac-
tised by Mr. Dos Passos, say, or M. Romains was once to
make other kinds of novels obsolete. In fact, it killed the
poison-ivy twice, for after *avant-garde* thinking in deckle-
edged magazines abandoned it for finer truths the revolutionaries of a fashion then called the proletarian movement
proclaimed it the only form through which social significance could be imparted to fiction. As this is written, there
is a flurry about what I can only describe as allegory-and-a-
half. Novelists have been stimulated by the sudden lifting
of a taboo that had held for a long time. They have been
sanctioned to write seriously about religious experience —
these sanctions are reflexes of fashion in other fields of
thought — and some of them have found it hard to do so
without the device of personification used in old morality
plays. A character is not only Jack Robinson but Evil or
Gluttony as well. Novelists intent on the exposition of non-
religious abstractions have also seized on the device, and the
quarterlies are beginning to beat non-personified fiction to
death with it. But it is certain to make only a short run. It
is self-limited because ultimately self-contradictory; the novelist who uses it is writing against his own interest.

These matters belong to the literary folkways, and usually
to the critical genera of them. Though they may be widespread and temporarily very influential, they break up in
spray. The heterogeneity of the art of fiction prohibits im-

peratives. *Ulysses, The Sun Also Rises, The Big Money, The Sixth of October,* and *Joseph and His Brethren,* which I have alluded to here are all novels, but an imperative that could quadrate them would be a little astonishing. *Tarzan of the Apes* is also a novel and so are *Against the Grain, Black Beauty, The Red and the Black, Looking Backward, Adventures of Huckleberry Finn, The Water Babies, Farewell My Lovely, The Golden Bowl, Pierre, The War Between the Worlds, Nausea,* and *Uncle Tom's Cabin.* Such a list of titles only begins to suggest the spread of fiction but what imperative can comprehend them all?

Our concern with folkways and fashion is only to point out that they have had an important part in the history of fiction. Looking back over that history, however, one sees other developments which were not the result of fashion and which have continued through a variety of fashions. They have fluctuated, they have not got so far without interruption or regression, and it would be rash to think of them as immutable. But they look like attempts of an impure art to purify itself as much as may be by determining its own relevant methods. For fiction is an impure art in the exact sense in which sculpture is a pure one, or if you prefer, in which poetry is a pure one.

The movies borrowed from other arts on the way to finding methods implicit in their medium. Their narrative methods came from both fiction and the drama. In a primordial movie the scene is likely to be from the stage and the sequence of scenes from the novel, but from the beginning the camera's almost unlimited freedom of space not only permitted but required a sweep of movement that changed the dramatization of scenes and the determination of their sequence. A new kind of narrative method was implicit in the medium. (In the same way visual symbols and visual condensations implicitly cinematic replaced literary ones. A film's allusions and recapitulations are unlike those of the stage or the novel.) The medium sets conditions for storytelling radically different from the conditions of other mediums. Translation from one medium to another is so difficult that a story changes some of its essentials, frequently all of them, on the way through the necessary alterations in narrative.

When the movies became talkies a regression to narrative methods of the stage occurred — natural enough but against progress — and an evolution shorter than the original but very similar followed. A new condition had been imposed on screen narrative. The radio appears not to have found inherent narrative methods as yet. It turned directly to the stage and practically all radio storytelling is still essentially theatrical, though this imposes severe and, one believes, unnecessary limitations. But the radio drama is necessarily blind and so stage techniques were not adequate or wholly appropriate. Innumerable musical devices and other instruments of sound have buttressed the spoken drama. They have established conventions but they have hardly achieved so much as a useful symbolism, and the infinite possibilities of suggestion, anticipation, and intensification open to the storyteller in fiction or on the stage or screen remain beyond the reach of radio. To escape the limitations of the blind drama, the radio invented the weird known as the Narrator, who is a novelist lifted from his novel. Typically radio drama alternates stage scenes played in the dark with material out of fiction filtered through the Narrator. The larger part of his material is summary, for the exigency of time is greater in radio than in any other medium, but much of it is also a tortured substitute for visualization. There has been little experimentation with non-theatrical narrative, and radio has not found implicit methods. Paradoxically, though it tries to dramatize practically all of its materials with methods taken from the theater, it is nearer to fiction than to the stage, and since when hard problems arise it flows from the scene into rhapsody, it is probably nearest to poetry, bad poetry.

A comparable selection and evolution occurred in fiction. We may say arbitrarily that early in the eighteenth century the novel began to be a unified work of art: it began to have a structure whose parts supported one another and formed a whole that produced an intended artistic effect. The divergence from the traditional prose narratives that had preceded it was sharp but of course there was no break. A medieval romance consists of a series of episodes coupled to one another like freight cars, given no more coherence than the reappearance of characters or a vaguely consecutive theme can supply, and only occasionally and incompletely dramatized. Its characters are both static and lifeless; they have names but they remain anonymous. It has no particular point of view and it moves in no particular direction, by no particular route. It might be broken off nearly anywhere for the convenience of the publisher, for the episodes are not preparing an end.

Come down to *Don Quixote* (1605). Here the episodes are more pointed of themselves and, usually, much more fully dramatized. A satirical purpose gives the book uniform tissue if not unity, and its characters are not mere designations used to keep the narrative moving forward but, many of them, figures observed in life and intended to be individuals in fiction. But there is only a rudimentary situation at the beginning from which events flow, events create no particular pattern, and they do not act to produce a necessary end. The episodes are simply added on, with neither logic nor necessity from within the book, which might very well be published in independent sections. In fact it was so published. When the great success of Part One suggested that a Part Two would be a good idea, nothing stood in the way of Cervantes' writing one or a reader's accepting it. Part One had not come to an end but only to a termination. There was nothing in it that prohibited its being indefinitely extended, as the medieval romances usually were. And if there is no inner, self-determining logic of events in *Don Quixote,* it is equally innocent of the inner logic and necessity of character developing through events and interacting with them.

By the end of another century, with Defoe and especially with the four novelists who the textbooks usually say established the form of the novel, fundamental alterations have been made. Disregarding their immediate predecessors, we may say that in the work of these men the novel becomes what it had not been before, an organism, and has an anatomy, physiology, and metabolism of its own. If in *Don Quixote* episodes were more fully dramatized than in the various King Arthur cycles, they are still more fully dramatized in *Moll Flanders,* and much more so in *Tom Jones.* It is equally important that they are dramatized toward a foreseen end and, in the other four if not indeed in Defoe, are dramatized with the devices of the theater as closely as prose fiction can approximate them. And the fact that they are dramatized *toward an end* has necessitated a coherent inner sequence or succession. Episodes develop as the result of preceding episodes and combine with them to make further episodes necessary: a logic of events has been revealed. Moreover, the episodes originate in the interplay of characters as individuals with the situation in which they are placed. This involves motive as motive simply does not exist in the Arthurian cycles or even as late as the Elizabethan romances and *Don Quixote*. Difficult as the fact may be for the winded reader to keep in mind *Clarissa Harlowe* does move toward an end necessitated by the particularized situation in which the characters are placed, and does move toward it as a result of individual character responding to circumstance. The end is far away, hundreds of pages over the hill, but terms have been so set that there can be no terminating the novel till it is reached and no carrying it on thereafter. *Tom Jones* has an extremely intricate pattern of events and *Tristram Shandy* an extremely intricate pattern of motives, but in both novels event and character shape each other and so create the patterns. Within the pattern, the novelist is following the truth of fiction, discarding irrelevance for inevitability, and sustaining the movement of the novel by means of energies that arise within the novel. It would be unsafe to say that any succeeding novel has been held to its own terms more faithfully than *Tom Jones*. At any rate, by the time it was written the novel existed as a new form. The books of these men are novels as we call books novels today. A hundred years earlier there had been no books that could be called novels in our contemporary meaning of the word.

This, I have said, represents a sharp divergence from prose fiction as it had previously been written, but not a break. All novels are stories and people have been writing prose stories as long as there has been literary prose. The most revolutionary change in technique that fiction has ever experienced came long before stories were ever written. Much earlier than Tegumai Bopulai, some gifted Primitive who, O Best Beloved, lived cavily in a Cave, changed the "I" of the narrative of imaginary events with which he compensated for his timidity at hunting mammoths to the "he" that

permitted him to compensate on a truly majestic scale, as
the Hero or a god. No one has done so much for fiction
since. The eighteenth-century novelists continued to make
use of this genius's innovation and of his predecessors' methods as well. Novelists are still using them — are still using
methods and expedients from the earliest fiction. But they
are using them in modifications required by the form that
the eighteenth-century novelists developed.

The new form discarded some methods of its predecessors.
It did not feel free, for instance, to interpolate unmotivated
lyric poems in the process of a scene. It was chary of inter-
polation. The story within a story is with us still but the monstrous cabbage it derives from is gone forever. The story
within a story within a story within a story, a narrative
juggling act with four or five narrators inclosing within as
many sets of quotation marks first-person accounts supposed
to be verbatim.[1] It is just to say that the rejection of such
interpolations shows a determination to avoid irrelevance
and an awareness that its implausibility endangered the illusion. So does the rejection of the *Euphues* strain, verbal
virtuosity for its own sake alone. The emphasis is on "for
its own sake alone." Virtuosity of style has remained an
indispensable instrument of fiction, and there is still something roughly equivalent to the *Euphues* strain. It recurs
periodically throughout *Ulysses*, for instance, and becomes
the medium in which two of the major episodes are ren-

1 As I have pointed out, there have been interruptions and reversals.
Smollett, whom I am treating here as one of the prime innovators, sometimes got snarled in this device. It recurs during the next few decades and
again just before the great novelists of the mid-nineteenth century — but
always in a much simpler form. Such coils and spiderwebs as are found in
the *Arabian Nights*, for instance, became inconceivable in the novel as soon
as the novel was differentiated as a form.

dered.[2] But Ulysses shows what has happened. Verbal virtuosity has been brought within the novel and made to serve
the purposes of the novel; it is functional, not accessory or
extrinsic.

The new form, then, has declared against irrelevance and
the non-functional — and much of the later development of
the novel must be seen as a refinement of the principle thus
established. Equally important, perhaps more important, is
that the direct rendition of event becomes the usual instead
of an occasional narrative method. The blight of indirect
discourse which makes the romances anesthetic to a modern
reader from page to page and whose defect not even Defoe
had fully understood, though mostly he avoided it, is reduced to what it has since remained, a connective device for
saving time and space, to be used sparingly, briefly, and in
the awareness that a serious risk is being taken.

*Then Arderay swore that his foe had done wrong to
the daughter of the King, and Amis made oath that he
lied. Thereupon, incontinent they drove together, and
with mighty strokes strove one against the other from
the hour of tierce till it was nones. And at nones Arderay fell within the lists; and Amis struck off his head.*

*The King lamented that Arderay was dead, but re-
joiced that his daughter was proved clean from stain.
He gave the Princess to Amis for dame, and with her,
for dowry, a mighty sum in gold and silver, and a city*

2 The stylistic parodies at the Lying-In Hospital and the catechism at
Bloom's house. But, though I am (I trust) a complete Joycean up to
Finnegans Wake — through which the reader may follow the *Euphues* strain
at his pleasure — I am not convinced that the device is made altogether
good in either passage. If I were cornered and forced to make a flat judgment, I should say that, esthetically, Joyce does not fully justify it either in
effect or by demonstration that no other device will do as well.

near the sea where they might dwell. So Amis rejoiced
greatly in his bride; and returned as quickly as he might
to the castle where he had hidden Amile, his com-
panion. . . .

That is from a version of *The Friendship of Amis and*
Amile. It will remind us how powerful is the desire of
people to be told stories of imaginary events, since the audience who loved the romances were content with just such
static statements that something had happened. And this is
the usual narrative statement of the romances for several
centuries, a statement that something had happened made by
an impersonal narrator, as here, or made in the first or third
person in the same indirect discourse. Only occasionally
does the narrative become direct, presenting the thing as
happening while we watch. In this passage there are a formal oath impugning a woman's virtue, an oath in denial, a
combat, a death, a beheading, a marriage and a dower, a
honeymoon, and a journey. Not only are they all in indirect
discourse but they are all at the same length, of the same
undeveloped simplicity, of the same emotional tone and
value, of the same emphasis. All have the same value: each
counts five points. . . . I need not remind you how they
would be done in *Tom Jones.* Quite certainly the fight,
the beheading, and the honeymoon would take precedence
over the others, and the rest would be developed according
to a proportion determined by the end in view. All would
be dramatized as direct event occurring before the reader's
eyes.

Not only Fielding, who began as a playwright, but the
three I have named with him habitually dramatized scenes
and they did so much more in the manner of the stage than
fiction had done before them. All four, but especially Field-

ing, used devices of dramatization taken directly from the theater. The result was a composite, produced by blending methods of fiction and the stage, and it was new to fiction, but the point is that the new form had borrowed a method from the stage and converted it to its own purposes. In the same way it borrowed from the essay, a more vigorous form in the eighteenth century than it has ever been since, ways of perceiving and reporting character, ways of uncovering motive, ways of sharing the writer's observations with the reader, and even characteristic types of the essay itself as a unit.

I mean by sophistication merely the opposite of naïveté when I say that, with the new form which has been called a novel ever since, fiction became much more sophisticated than it had been even in Defoe. In technique it was far more sophisticated than *Don Quixote* or, say the stories of the *Decameron*. But methods in part adapted from other literary forms were artistically impure. One characteristic shown in the development of the novel from that time on has been a fairly steady transformation of its technical methods that has made them, in the same sense, more sophisticated. And one way of looking at this transformation and sophistication is to see them as a search for methods and devices implicit in the novel as a differentiated form of art, a search for implicit technique.

Other fairly steady developments have worked to the same end. The novel has steadily widened the areas of experience it will deal with. It has widened its boundaries to inclose ever more subjects, themes, and activities. And if it has widened its objective content, just as steadily it has increased its subjective interests, exploring the mind as thoroughly as the exterior world. Both developments have required increasing complexity and subtlety of technique. The techniques of the novel have progressed, fairly steadily, in the direction away from naïveté. But also the reciprocal relationship between novel and reader has reinforced the same process. Readers have steadily grown more sophisticated and have steadily demanded more of the novelist.

8

THE ILLUSION

8

THE ILLUSION

ALL STORIES are drama. All dramas take place in theaters. All theaters are dark and the darkest theater is the one where the drama of fiction is staged: it has no light at all except on the novelist's word. Finally, in view of what has already been said in this discussion, it is a pleasant accident that the most famous theater in literature is first introduced to us as a den. For Jowett translates as "den" the word which presently becomes "cave" in Plato's allegory.

"Behold," Socrates says to Glaucon, whose voice is the antiphony:

Behold human beings living in an underground den, which has a mouth towards the light and reaching all along the den. Here they have been from their childhood. [They] have their legs and necks so chained that they cannot move, and can only see before them, being prevented by the chains from turning round their heads. Above and behind them a fire is blazing at a distance. Between the fire and the prisoners there is a raised way. You will see, if you look, a low wall built along the way, like the screen which marionette players

177

have in front of them, over which they show the pup-pets.

I see.

And do you see, I said, men passing along the wall, carrying all sorts of vessels, and statues and figures of animals made of wood and stone and various materials, which appear over the wall? Some of them are talking, others silent.

You have shown me a strange image, and they are strange prisoners.

Like ourselves, I replied . . . and of the objects which are being carried . . . they would only see the shadows? [Which the fire throws on the wall they face.]

Yes, he said.

And suppose further that the prison had an echo which came from the other side, would they not be sure to fancy when one of the passers-by spoke that the voice which they heard came from the passing shadow?

No question, he replied.

To them, I said, the truth would be literally nothing but the shadows of the images.

Socrates develops his figure to establish a hierarchy of knowledge and show the soul mounting toward the eternal forms. But we need go no further than the illusion of the strange prisoners that the images they see are real people and that the voices echoed in the cave are the speech of those people. All storytelling deals with these strange images; the effort of storytellers is to create just this illusion in the minds of their audience. Our job now is to define the illusion of fiction. How does it differ from the illusions of other kinds of storytelling? [1]

1 Dr. Beata Rank has remarked that Plato's allegory is also a striking metaphorical description of psychoanalysis.

All stories are told. A dramatist tells his by means of actors, who speak his lines and perform the actions implied by them. He has at his disposal the resources of stage scenery, backdrops and similar visual helps, and actual objects such as furniture, telephones, automobiles, or anything else that can be brought on the stage. He can use the resources of lighting to create literal effects of light, or to suggest things that he cannot reproduce or simulate on the stage, or to influence the emotional content of his scenes. He has many other mechanical implements that can be used literally, as when actual water falls on a scene as rain, or suggestively, as when an offstage wind machine produces a sound which is identified as that of a gale. He tells his story in a period of between two and three hours. He may break it up into such scenes as suit his purpose but there is a limit to these, for it is hard to establish the reality of more than a dozen or fifteen in three hours.

The limitations a dramatist works under are evident. Like all artists, he will work better as he accepts their severity; the more resistant the medium, the finer the effect. The limits set by the time at his disposal confine him to the crises of his story, requiring him to condense almost to the vanishing point the preliminaries, the course of development, and the explanation of how these crises happened to come about. (All of which are usually integral material in a novel.) In fact he will try to make the crisis explain itself and imply its origin and development as it works out. The time-limit also restricts the lapse of time he may deal with. Most individual scenes suggest that they last longer than they do by the clock, but the number of separate periods represented can be no greater than the number of scenes.[2] A break between scenes

2 This in general, although of course in fantasies or by use of some such device as the dream of a character (a story within a story, scenes within a scene) the number may be increased.

may represent as long a time-lapse as the dramatist pleases but if there are several long lapses — a year, a decade, a generation — they will tend to get in his way for he has more condensations to make, more recapitulations of what has happened and what has changed during the breaks, and his three hours are running out.

The fixed space of an inclosed stage just off a city street also sets determining conditions. A dramatist cannot have, say, an actual river, volcano, or skyscraper on the stage. A canvas hummock spouting sparks would burlesque his intent and he can only suggest that such things are present or near by, calling on the stage manager to help out with lighting and sound-effects and such connotive objects as may be put on view to bolster the illusion. Much ingenuity is expended on making the available space more flexible, so that, for instance, actors may walk out of one scene and into another without interruption. Finally, there is no way for a dramatist to tell his story from inside a character's mind. Many expedients are used to overcome this limitation, from the soliloquies of Elizabethan drama to Mr. O'Neill's doppelgängers and on to the ectoplasmic personifications of the everlasting *avant-garde*. They succeed to a point if they are established as conventions with sufficient authority, but that does not happen often for few dramatists are up to it. When it does happen it is still under great strain, for the stage has no way of representing the insubstantial except by the literal. It is always better when it treats the insubstantial by suggestion.

Literalness, in fact, is not only a defining condition of the stage but its tyranny, and the drama repeatedly tries to escape from it in order to enhance the illusion. Dramatic fantasy faces a threat that never relaxes, for an actual Peter Pan swinging through the air does so on a wire. If the illusion's hold on the spectator is not firm, then his awareness of the wire will kill it stone-cold dead in the market. Fantasy makes herculean efforts to support its illusion with machinery, but multiplying the means also multiplies the possibility that the machinery may be seen working. Fantasy, indeed, runs fewer risks when it abandons machinery and on a simple or a bare stage the dramatist's language and the actor's voices do the job — when the spectator is led to complete the illusion by himself. The terms of the theater are that Puck had best only promise us to put a girdle round about the earth in forty minutes; if he tried to fake it under a blue spot we should be troubled by skepticism. But the principle thus uncovered in fantasy defines a condition to which the drama that represents life is also subject. There is a tension between the representing thing and the actual thing it represents. The ordinary scene-by-scene conduct of a play is circumscribed by the fact that its content is to be imagined as actual but is represented by living actors who move through a mimic, not the actual, event. The dramatic illusion stems from that fact, which determines its nature, its limitations, and its power.

I suppose that the illusion of the stage is the most powerful of all fictions. The spectator for whom the illusion holds good is a spectator of the event itself. He is there in present time at the moment when it happens. Here is heartbreak, fear, suspense, desperation actually occurring. He is also a participant for identification has drawn him inside the event, he is an actor in it and the heartbreak has become his. The directness of the emotion gives it an immediate intensity that no other fiction can hope to have. But the conditions that make the illusion powerful impose limits on it.

For one thing, both the dramatist and the spectator are at the mercy of the third party who comes between them, the actor. Again, the conditions under which the illusion is produced tend to set a term to its duration. The very intensity, I mean, subtly undermines the ultimate effect. The golden half-second of the theater at its most powerful, the half-second of the caught breath, of the audience straining forward in their chairs, is so greatly desired by both audience and dramatist that it tends to become the end in view. It is no derogation of the theater to say that the nature of its illusion makes it choose the theatrical, the momentarily effective, at whatever price must be paid. In the heightened suggestibility of a crowd assembled in a dark hall, the theater trades on a will to believe that has mostly relinquished the faculty of criticism. The effort is to produce an emotion so strong that it will fully discharge itself — the katharsis we have read so much about. If it produces that, the theater is not much concerned thereafter. It does not retard the movement of a scene, as a reader frequently does when reading a novel so that he may examine its validity, and it does not play the scene again, as the reader of a novel may when he feels a doubt. Momentary effectiveness is incomparably more important than belief after curtainfall. When the critical judgment of the spectator reasserts itself, the theater is not concerned if, thinking things over, he finds some flaws.

That is, the truth of human experience and the theatrically effective may exist together and when they do the drama makes the same report on life that the novel does. But when the drama must choose between them it must always choose the theatrical. The golden half-second, the katharsis, must dominate. So we are accustomed to ask and receive from the theater less permanent enlargement of our experience, less depth and subtlety of understanding, than from fiction. Only at its best does the drama compete with the novel in finalities, and it can be at its best only very seldom. It requires greatness — Shakespeare, Ibsen, Shaw, whom you will — to effect on the stage the congruence with life and the validity of experience that we expect from the novel on planes considerably below greatness. The illusion of the stage does not ordinarily seek to go along with us when we leave the theater and we do not ask it to. Ordinarily what we remember of a play is not the characters as human beings nor a richness of experience that came to us by way of them but a high moment, the intense pleasure they gave us.

Other conditions of the theater work out to the same result, the transience of the illusion. The enthralled spectator, though he is engaged in the action more directly than a novelist can engage him, is more passive than the reader of a novel. He resumes activity when the curtain falls on the third act; the illusion has already struck a reef when he stands up. This was after all a *play*, it has happened in a playhouse; that it was make-believe is italicized by the mere clatter of folding chairs and the talk of one's fellow illusionists. The actual blows in against the carry-over of belief with the honking of taxis in the street. . . . Well, though splendid, it was a dream. Though I may carry with me a feeling of having been fulfilled, the release of emotion roused and purified and purged, I am now awake.

And for the audience as well as the dramatist there is the tyranny of the literal. It was mimicry; we invoked it in order to succumb but it must now be understood as mimicry. These were characters in the drama and heartbreak and death did happen to them before our eyes, but they are only actors after all. They do not go along with us beyond the marquee, they do not masquerade as ourselves when we turn homeward at eleven-thirty in the rain. The curtain has fallen on them. Precisely that is the consummation of our desire.

Here was a heartbreak as poignant as any we have ever

suffered. But when the curtain breaks off the dream we leave the theater knowing that behind it they are already shifting scenery for tomorrow's repetition. Downstairs the shattered hope and the bitter death are scrubbing off illusion's greasepaint and preparing to go out for supper and a glass of beer. The deaths of our own beloved are forever and no curtain falls on our own heartbreak. They are forever: they go on with us. But within the theater's enchanted walls they are terminable. The novel's effort is to make us understand more clearly just how and why it has come about that the beautiful Bertha is tied to the railroad tracks — and to reconcile us to the fate of mortals while the Empire State Express thunders toward her. But deep in us it is entirely otherwise with the theater, which allows us to grieve for her without a lasting wound. It has an *absit omen,* an *Unberufen!* that exempts us from Bertha's pain. See, the Empire State Express is only painted canvas, its thunder was only a bellows that a union stagehand was cranking in the wings. Bertha herself, though cut cleanly through, will presently rise and walk offstage with her betrayer. It seems so, the theater whispers just audibly to our inward ear, but be not troubled overmuch, for though it seems it is not so. Fate is three hours long: you will wake when the curtain falls. That is the fullness of the theater's healing, which we cannot do without. But the effort of fiction is that the curtain shall not be rung down, the illusion is not to end.

The movies ape Plato's strange images. Here are truly the appearances of appearances. If actors come between the dramatist and his audience, a further remove conditions the illusion of the screen, for one sees not the actors but facsimiles of them registered on a salt of silver. The screen, however, escapes from the limitations of space that restrict the stage. Whereas the dramatist will be fully laden with a dozen or fifteen changes of scene, the scenario writer can use scores. The camera's movement is fluid and can accompany the action as the scene changes, can carry the scene itself through any desirable extent of space. It can also bring Rockefeller Center or anything else upon the stage. At the director's will it can produce the volcano or the river that the dramatist can only suggest, either genuine ones or simulacra which photography makes indistinguishable from them. It has many more implements for assisting fantasy, as well as realism, than the stage has. It also has more conventions for seeming to tell its stories from within a character's mind, but they all have the defect of their stage counterparts, that they are mechanical conventions. One doubts if they are ever as effective.

That the illusion of the screen is completely acceptable is attested by the millions of people who go to the movies every day, but one can hardly doubt that it is less powerful and more transitory than that of the stage. Again, fantasy reveals one of the basic reasons. Unlimited space, complete flexibility, full freedom of time within the fixed time-limit, lighting effects impossible to the stage, sweeping and complex movement, the innumerable and versatile controls that photographic processes make possible — all these serve the imagination but display an even stronger slavery to the literal. The screen can give us any cloud-cuckoo-land the author may ask it to, but the clouds will be photographs of actual steam and the cuckoos will be actual birds or facsimiles magnified till as physical realities they are more galling than birds. In the one great American play it is enough for angels to wear on their backs small pieces of crinoline that will become wings for the audience. It cannot be doubted that on the screen wings would be cut to size and feathered, if not indeed scaled to an engineer's calculations of lifting-power per square foot of surface. We must avoid the easy sneer of elevated minds, we must not attribute this to weakness, vulgarity, or timidity of imagination. Nothing happens to a fine literary imagination when it is given full freedom to produce its effects — nothing, except that the wealth of literal possibilities makes dependence on the literal all but inevitable. The imagination cannot escape from the literal but at best can only refine it.

But what happens? There is that just-audible whispering to the inward ear. Underneath awareness, the temporarily believing mind reserves a doubt: immensely complicating the machinery only establishes more firmly that it is machines. And if this is true of screen fantasy, it is true in some degree of every other movie effect and form. The abundance of literal objects and literal expedients, inherent in the medium, greatly reduces the need for suggestion. The screen has its own implements of suggestion and they can be very fine, but they are shallower and more limited and there is much less need for them. The medium is softer — less resistant. The director can reproduce, and because his medium is what it is he must reproduce, what the dramatist can only suggest. And this in turn increases the passivity of the spectator. "This man, with lime and rough-cast, doth present Wall, that vile Wall which did these lovers sunder." When the dramatist so acknowledges the limitations of his medium, he issues a challenge which the spectator is honor-bound to accept. So challenged, he will erect by his own belief a wall that is insubstantial but vilely sunders the lovers. But the movies give him masonry to look at, and so he has no work to do.

Finally, all the influences of the stage that anesthetize the spectator's critical faculty are present, usually in greater strength, in the movie house. Of the consequences the most important one is that the awakening comes more quickly and abruptly after the last fadeout. While it lasted it was a weaker dream and now it is over for good. We may remember that an effect was produced on us but we do not remember for very long what the effect was. We cannot go back to it and it does not try to accompany us.

What I have said so far has been defining the illusion of fiction by difference. There remains an illusion of the theater that brings us closer. Let us approach it on a tangent, by way of a related psychological effect.

For three hours Orsino and Sebastian, Olivia and Viola, Malvolio and Sir Toby Belch have played their Illyrian idyll. It is a drama impossible anywhere except in the poetic comedy and achieved only in this and a few more of Shakespeare's plays and a small handful of plays by some of his contemporaries. Suspended in a shimmering solvent for which there is no name, it is fantasy and reality and farce, convention and pretence and mockery. No one cares what it is, except that it is delight, and no one can say what it is . . . until the end. When the last distempers have been cured, the last misunderstandings and contrivances resolved, the last pairings attained, the characters walk off stage — or, as we would do it today, the curtains close. Then Feste, the clown, comes on — comes through the curtains. Today we would have the temerity to enhance the moment with a wholly darkened house and a single spotlight focused on him. He sings a song, "The rain it raineth every day," and we would dim the spotlight while he sang till with the last verse he would be singing in the dark. There is no longer any doubt. This is the insubstantial fabric of our vision, an unreality enveloping both the reality and the fantasy that it brings alike into question and gently impels on into mystery. The magician has added a spell to a charm.

Surely it is for a similar reason that one of the great novels of the nineteenth century ends with an assertion that, once the magic has been worked, its effect will be permanent. Becky is at Bath of Cheltenham and her name is on all the Charity Lists, Amelia and her William, George, Jenny, the *History of the Punjaub* — everything has been brought to the intended end. And then, "Ah," Thackeray writes as the final paragraph, "Ah, *Vanitas Vanitatum!* which of us is happy in this world? Which of us has his desire? or having it, is satisfied? — come children, let us shut up the box and the puppets, for our play is played out."

And we shall presently see, only superb confidence in his art could justify Thackeray in thus shocking the reader at the end of the novel with a reminder that what he has taken to be life was only words after all. It is a confidence that the illusion can stand even the revelation of its unreality, that it will indeed go along with the reader. But the allusion to the puppet show is not an accident. And it is not by accident that Socrates compares the stage from which his strange images are projected with the stage of a marionette show. Both are acknowledging the uncanny, the certainly magical, dominion that wooden dolls hung from strings have always exerted over the imagination of men. And Thackeray is acknowledging that the art of the puppet show comes closer to his own than any other.

Soon after his adventures in Montesino's Cave, which would not have been altogether out of place in Plato's den, Don Quixote de la Mancha comes to an inn. Presently an itinerant puppetmaster arrives too, with his company and equipment. (Pleasantly enough, he is also a magician.) And that evening he sets up his theater and performs a True History of "how Don Gayferos deliver'd his Wife Melisandra, that was a prisoner among the Moors." His technique is to say the least eccentric but it subjugates the knight. After desperate adventures the Christian lovers escape but an alarm is raised and a number of Moors on horseback furiously pursue them. The peril is greater and more urgent than Don Quixote can abide. He rises from his chair, shouts defiance at the Moors — "Forbear, ye base-born Rascals!" — and, drawing his sword, slashes the theater and its actors to bits. He cannot be stopped, though with a prophetic reminiscence of Thackeray the puppetmaster protests, "These are no real Moors that you cut and hack so, but poor harmless Puppets made of Pasteboard." It will not do. The Don knows they are Moors and when at last the realities are restored Sancho Panza swears that "he had never seen his Master in such a Rage before." . . . The scene is a variant of a joke that has faithfully served fiction through the generations and was probably worn shiny before Cervantes. It is the Rustic at the Play, Fielding's rustic, Mark Twain's rustic, *The New Yorker's* rustic. But also it is the magical operation of the puppet show.

On the surface, few things could be so improbable. This is a theater but only in miniature. The stage is a few feet high, a few feet wider. The voices echoed (behind a masking curtain) from Plato's wall may be a single voice and at most are only two or three. The figures are "made of Pasteboard," or wood, or pottery, or pewter, or metal — inert, roughly carved, painted impressionistically or in burlesque. Confined within their handful of lighted space, they walk a plane that is patently air, and they walk with spasmodic jerks unlike any human motion. All their movements are inhuman. Their horses are unequine, their dogs uncanine. Foot-high manikins swimming in space rather than walking a stage, sometimes entangled in the strings they hang from, sometimes out of time with music meant to accompany them, always staggering away from the contrived voices that are attributed to them — believe that these things are people who feel and act while we watch? It is clearly absurd, clearly impossible.

But it happens, and the clue may be that we believe because it is impossible. Perhaps what is wrong with Peter Pan is not the wire he swings from but the fact that he swings from it as a living actor. Perhaps the wire is right apart from the living actor and the living actor is right apart from the wire. At any rate the curtain has been raised on the puppet stage for only a few minutes when we are as subjugated as Don Quixote was. There is nothing wrong with the movements of these dolls now; they are natural, proper, accepted. Voices have lost their falsity and these are people talking to one another as you and I would talk in the same circumstances. The foot-high doll on a ten-foot stage has grown to be a man as tall as you walking the sane and actual dimensions of the world. . . . "Really and truly, Gentlemen," the Don says, "I vow and protest before ye all that hear me, that all that was acted here seem'd to be really transacted *ipso facto* as it appear'd."

The illusion is at least as old as the stage and possibly older. Puppets were used by primitive peoples (American Indian tribes among them) whose theater had not developed beyond the ritualization of religious ceremonies. For most spectators it is as powerful as the illusion of the stage; for some, I dare say, it is more powerful. But think how strange and paradoxical the illusion is. On the stage a living person transmits the author's intent; on the screen it is a photographic image lifelike in everything except that it has no life. But puppets are patently lifeless and incapable of animation. Their voices are openly contrived, their movements a convention. Something like an act of will must occur when we accept them as walking and talking and believe that the sawdust heart feels pain. But it is not will. The secret, I think, is contained in the word "passive" we have already had to use. The illusion of the stage was stronger than that of the screen, I said, because (in part) the spectator had to do more for himself. He was less passive than the spectator of a movie, for whom almost everything is done. At a puppet show the very inertness and barrenness force him to do far more; the puppets are mere symbols and he can participate *only* by imaginatively acting on the suggestions they provide. They come alive because he works in faith and works hard. He builds the illusion for himself . . . at the direction of the dramatist.

To come to my point at last, the analogy leads straight to the heart of fiction. The reader of a novel builds the illusion for himself at the direction of the novelist, and builds it in much the same way as the spectator at a puppet show does. But though the puppet show has brought us to the far frontier of the drama, we cross over to something different when we reach fiction. Up to now there has always been some mimicry of character and event but now there is none. There are no entities, nothing is actually happening. There are no actors, no photographs of actors, no dolls; there are only words printed on a page. The reader is not present at the event, for there is no event. The novelist must persuade him that an event is occurring, that he is present at it, and that what in the theater happens in mimicry before his eyes is happening at a place which exists only by consent of his imagination. When the persuasion succeeds, the illusion of fiction is established.

The condition of that illusion should now be clear. That there is no event, no mimicry of an event, entirely changes the requirements the novelist must meet. So does the absence of actors to effect his intent — but if this lays new requirements on him we may say at once that it also frees him from handicaps that the dramatist must accept. He deals directly with the reader; no one comes between them. Moreover, there is no one to twist his purpose askew under inspiration or interpretation, or to betray it by incompetence. A dozen actors playing Hamlet will enact a dozen different characters, and all of them will spread still wider the inescapable refraction that the spectator makes of the dramatist's Hamlet. The dramatist is at the mercy of even a good actor; he and the illusion too are at the mercy of a poor one. The strength required may vary with the sensitiveness of people's noses but for anybody a single whiff of ham is enough. If inferior acting forces on him even a momentary awareness that this is not a man suffering the pangs of dispriz'd love but only George Spelvin in a crêpe beard and some funny-pants reading lines, there follows a shrugged shoulder or a muttered "Oh, Hell!" Once an "Oh, Hell!" has been felt the illusion can never fully recover. There are never enough competent actors in the world. There are seldom enough of them at liberty to furnish out a single company. Any member of the company can destroy the illusion at any moment.

The novelist must forfeit something even more important than actors and mimicry of events: immediacy. In all drama, the event occurs in present time with the spectator on the scene. He is there when it happens. But the novel is imprisoned in past time. The event has already happened when the reader hears about it. This is true even if the novel is dated in the year 2000 and is written in the present tense. The reader cannot see it happening, he can only be told about it in retrospect, when it has become immutable, when it can in no wise be affected by anything he may feel about it. He knows that it has happened, but the effort is always to make him believe, in spite of sense and logic, that it is happening now.

Here is a powerful deterrent to belief. The strain put on a reader's credulity can be seen nakedly in mystery stories, or stories of the marvelous or supernatural, told in the first person which must end with the death of the narrator. The imaginary person with whom we are identified sits penning the last lines of his account of the events that have made his death inevitable. He brings everything to judgment, accounts for everything, ties the last knots, blocks the last remaining exits. In a moment now the pursuer will catch up with him or the indescribable beast will claw through the tar-paper walls. He writes, in effect: When I have blotted this sentence I will go up to the deck and leap into the sea, or I will open the door and with the love of my children warm in my heart I will face the Thing. Even if the novelist leaves it at that, as he is usually wise to do, he has assaulted belief with a bludgeon. Whatever motive kindliness is willing to ascribe to the character for so odd a literary impulse at such a time, the novelist has invoked the future to eke out what is already past, and this flouts a reader's logic. The character is speaking of the future but he has been dead for some time when he is read and the future has already become the past. Or perhaps the narrator does not end with that statement of his fortitude but has a moment still, while the claws are scratching at the wall, to add another paragraph. This record, he says, will be found by more fortunate men in a quieter, happier hour (perhaps when the space ship has been perfected and a return to the Earth is possible), and they will understand many things — but the thing they have got to understand for the sake of the novelist is that the narrator did indeed die. This beats belief over the head not only with a future added to the past but with a second period of past time different from the first. Or the narrator may drop out, having kept his promise to leap over the rail into the Gulf Stream, and the novelist takes over and thrusts in a new character, the pursuer or the commander of the rescue party, who finishes the book with a statement that he found this pitiful document and a left shoe which showed the marks of teeth. The future has been left out and this is only a double past but the post mortem discoverer of the relics gives it an even more serious concussion.

In any of these endings, the logic that is forever working in a reader's mind, whether or not he is aware of it, has discounted the effect. Sometimes the discount rate is so high that the illusion becomes non-negotiable. He followed the story with belief because he seemed to be present at the event. Now he has been coarsely reminded that he was not. It seemed present but all along it was the past.

This is a crude illustration. But the same logical skepticism hovers above the margin of the reader's mind no matter what novel he is reading; it is as much a part of him as his eagerness to believe. It is what must be put to sleep. There is no way of reporting an event to a reader except as past. It can be seen only in retrospect, the emotion can be felt only in retrospect. What he deals with is actually not a shadow on the wall but a memory that one was cast there, a reminiscence after the fact. And this is the greatest severity of the medium — for the event must *not* be after the fact, the reader must be there when it happens, he must seem to see the actual shadow on the wall. So that a constant tension of fiction is to convert a statement of past time into a perception of the immediate present. The illusion has other components as well but the validity of everything else depends on this one. To be sure fiction has established the current immediacy of its past as a convention which is accepted and thereafter disregarded. But its illusion depends on this disregard and will perish at the hands of anything that brings the paradox to the reader's attention. The foremost effort of the novelist is to make the past this present moment.

Well, fiction has no objective mimicry of events, it has no actors to effect the writer's intent, and it is locked in past time. But the medium has unique attributes that compensate. There are no limitations whatever on space: the novelist may and usually does use hundreds of different scenes and settings. He may transport us anywhere with a word or two, and may use half a dozen different locales in a chapter, a page, or even a paragraph. This is a tremendously important freedom, but his freedom from time-limitations is even more important. He can cover generations or centuries with a wave of his hand and without damage to the illusion, whereas even the movies must observe limits that an implicit logic sets, and he can weave back and forth between periods of time at his will. And he can achieve an effect of time that no other medium can even suggest: he can work simultaneously, in the same context, with two or several different periods of time and the reader will be present in them all.

Nor does the question of length trouble a novelist; the novel may be as long as it need be. A stage play usually runs two and a half hours and must then stop. Mr. O'Neill can double or triple that length but exhaustion of the company if not the audience will eventually bring even him to a stop. A movie is usually ninety minutes long, though the massed genius of Hollywood can stretch one through a whole evening. Within these limits the writer of a play or a movie must tell his story. But a novel has no imposed length. Its story is to be told as proper telling may determine, and the novelist consults only his art. If he needs a hundred or five hundred pages more, very well. The result is a richness of incident and a multiplicity of effects impossible in any kind of drama. The movie based on *Gone With the Wind* ran twice as long as an average feature picture but it left out nearly everything that gave the novel individuality.

It left out a good deal more than that. For we have now reached two fundamental characteristics of the novel. I have pointed out that the stories which a dramatist tells consist mainly of their own crises, that he condenses or suggests or implies the components and the long course of developments that produced the crises. A novel is concerned primarily with exactly those components and that course of development: it tells the parts of the story that a play leaves out. Ordinarily, novelists find that the big moments will take care of themselves, that their skill is mostly to be expended on the evolving process. The novel deals with the necessity, that is, and not solely with its climax. It may even disregard the climax: frequently the finest effect of fiction is to be secured by leading up to the crisis and then leaping over it and picking up the story at a later time. And this scrupulousness to show the evolving process, the course of necessity, is the first and perhaps the most important reason why the illusion persists. If fiction leaves some slight permanent deposit on a reader's mind, if its people and events tend to go along with him after he has closed the book, this effect stems from the reader's long and close association with them which no other medium can give him.

Finally, the novel does directly what the drama can do only indirectly and only in small part: it works within the mind of a character as naturally as outside it. More than that, it works within the minds of as many characters as the novelist may choose to enter. In all forms of the drama thought and feeling are objectified as behavior and, in order to be experienced, must be inferred. The theater's devices for escaping this limitation are literal and clumsy; they can succeed only to a slight degree, rarely, and with a rigorously limited effect. But the mind and the emotions are wholly open to a novelist, who at his pleasure can give us either the effect of emotion or the emotion itself as it is experienced. Fiction holds the interior world in fee simple.

And yet all this is words printed on paper. At the base, none of it is more than a statement made by the novelist which the reader accepts and converts into an illusion. It is of primary importance to my reader here that he understand the word "statement" as I have just used it to mean the process, for I shall presently be saying that statement as mere announcement will not do, that it must be a dramatized statement. But my point is that the illusion of fiction has attributes that might justify us in calling it a hallucination, for it arises from printed words which the novelist has written and which by means of his skill and the reader's active belief become not merely a stage and actors, but living people, the true event, the motive, and the emotion. The rest of this book will be concerned with showing how.

We may repeat what Glaucon said. The reader of a novel is a strange prisoner and the shadows moving on a wall that is only his mind are strange images.

The critical absolute I have set up is the extreme. A novelist has indeed failed entirely if his reader gives up with the novel unfinished. That does happen and I cherish an incident that occurred years ago. I had taken to a friend of mine a new novel then and since much praised by discriminating readers. The calm of a summer afternoon, on the porch of a cottage near the shore of a Vermont lake was suddenly shattered. My friend stood up, threw the book into the lake, and shouted in passionate denunciation, "The man is a fool." The man was no fool but my friend's outrage showed that in at least one passage he was an unskilled novelist. Even so, here was an involuntary tribute to the illusion of fiction, for it showed what a reader had tacitly but confidently expected. But our interest is not the complete destruction of the illusion but the insufficiencies of technical skill that diminish or impair it.

Instead of hurling the book into a lake, the reader feels a vague dissatisfaction. His attention wanders from the novel to the world outside his window. Or he slips from the fictitious scene he has been reading to a more compelling scene in a reverie of his own. Or he "skips" — he lets this scene go and flips pages looking for another one that will convince him. His interest in the novel begins to be replaced by a feeling of discomfort which he does not relate to either the story or the characters who compose it but which resembles his annoyance when he hears a familiar song sung off key. At a moment of intensity in the novel, instead of responding with intensified emotions of his own, he is unmoved. Or worse still, he feels a kind of antagonism or superiority or distaste. He finishes the book and reports to a friend that it is implausible, unconvincing, weak, clumsy, inept, or stupid — you wouldn't like it, don't waste your time on it.

Now readers differ, materials vary in inherent interest, and there are accidents of interest and such exterior factors as timeliness and purpose. But whatever allowance must be made for such matters, the reader's dissatisfaction is to be understood as primarily the novelist's failure to keep him reading with belief. The novelist's failure to maintain the illusion. His job is to exercise the skill of novel-writing effectively — "to ally you with the events of the page and with the relation of the characters to them in such a way that for the moment their logic and emotion are binding on you." He is to set the puppets moving and talking and draw you into the scene that does not exist so that you will accept it without demur.

His most valuable asset is the reader's faith and charity, the will to believe. For a moment disregard the long analysis we have made of Ruth Martin's expectation and put the matter on simple economic grounds. She has paid three dollars for the novel at a bookstore; mere practical good sense will take her out to meet the novelist believingly. So economic determinism gives a novelist some leeway, especially at the beginning. (Most of his privileges are confined to the early portions of the book.) Implicit in this goodwill too is the reader's permission to add to the usual conventions of fiction the special conventions of this particular novel, which will use up a varying amount of time and space. (To anticipate: the way in which a novelist writes dialogue is in part a convention of his own; so is his process of revealing the basic situation; so is his combination of methods.) Especially in the early portions of the novel, that is, the reader is most co-operative and docile, will most uncritically accept the novelist's leading. But the will to believe persists throughout, so long as the novelist does not frustrate it. The reader wants to believe: he wants the illusion to succeed. That is why he began to read the novel.

Let us call this favorable predisposition the reader's tolerance or toleration. Up to a point the novelist may rely on it and there are times when he has to rely on it as on the mercy of heaven. But it has limits. The believing mind is also a critical mind, and the desire to believe makes a reader

all the more resentful of whatever may interfere with belief. Moreover, there is time for the critical mind to assert
itself, as there is not in the theater. The reader may pause
and follow a doubt back to its cause and convert doubt to
certainty. The limits of toleration will be the wider as the
novelist has been the more expert in periods when belief
was not endangered: a strong illusion will establish a margin
of belief, a drawing-account, that will help in a passage
where the illusion must necessarily grow weaker. But the
limits must not be transgressed.

Come back to the vague dissatisfaction. A reader has been
reading with acceptance and belief. That means that the
relationship between him and the novelist has been satisfactory so far, which in turn means that technique has been
accomplishing its ends. Then, suddenly or gradually, his
engagement with the logic and emotion of the novel is impaired. What he is reading has lost some of its validity. It
has become doubtful, mystifying, opaque, or (and this is
worse) untrustworthy. He feels that something has gone
wrong with it. He may feel no active rejection but merely a
kind of resistance. He may endure it and go on, in the hope
that things will right themselves, but for the moment the
novel is ineffective. The flow has been interrupted, the
reader has slipped out or partly out of his engagement. (A
moment of hesitation too short to produce resistance is
clearly the same kind of thing.) The illusion has been
broken. If it has been broken for only a moment, the danger is nevertheless dire: total failure is in one pan of the
balance. What the reader now feels is not produced of the
novel; on the contrary, it has been occasioned by the novel.

And there was no reason exterior to the novelist. He has
used up the drawing-account, his skill has lapsed. The hesitation, the doubt, the resistance are on the margin of the

reader's mind, but the failure is from the core of fiction. The novel has broken out of its medium and the illusion on which everything else depends has vanished. The effect is that of the spectator at a play who has suddenly noticed the greasepaint and the ham.

9

THE INVISIBLE
NOVELIST

THE INVISIBLE NOVELIST

I N THE UNITED STATES puppet shows are so often given for children or for rapt souls who think them precious that an adult of unperturbed tastes cannot easily find one in the pure state. Tony Sarg's repertory included a production called *Don Quixote* that was built round the few episodes which, as Mr. Cabell once said, everyone is familiar with since they occur early in Part One. (Unhappily it did not involve a puppet show within a puppet show, perhaps because the Don's assault on the pasteboard Moors is in Part Two.) Since Mr. Sarg was a master of his art the performance was enchanting. But at the end he did a shocking thing.

The puppets hung suspended in their last tableau. The stage was fully lighted and it was as big as the world. One's pleasure still ran clear; the illusion was untouched. But suddenly from behind the backdrop that so truly suggested a landscape in Spain an enormous foot appeared. A leg followed, a leg the size of an oak log. Then Mr. Sarg in his awful entirety was before us, a giant bent double who smiled and waved a vast hand in answer to the children's cries. The illusion had been so strong that for a moment he was as big as Og the king of Bashan, who slept in an iron bedstead nine cubits long. But he beckoned the realities in with both arms and abruptly was just a life-sized man, and Don Quixote and Dulcinea and their companions, lately alive, were now small, ridiculous dolls, the poor puppets that Cervantes' puppetmaster had called them in the novel.

One disliked Mr. Sarg. For the surprise of children, whom we may treat here as the readers of novels who have the simplest hearts, he had sinned against his art. There had been Spain, castles, the bemused knight, his mistress, his squire, and ho! such bugs and goblins finally drowned in laughter as would make any theater alive. But now there was just a litter of miniature stage lumber, some hanged figures, and disgust. The producer of the illusion had destroyed it by stepping into it.

*   *   *

When Henry Fielding wanted to put into *Tom Jones* some of his ideas about the credibility of the marvelous, he put them in straight, without reference to the story of his novel and in his own person. He wrote Chapter I of Book VIII, a gentleman's essay by Henry Fielding, just such an essay as under the name of Sir Alexander Drawcansir he might have published in his newspaper, *The Covent Garden Journal*. There is a passage in *Anthony Adverse* which discusses an aspect of the same subject, but Mr. Hervey Allen, the novelist, did not write an essay in his own person: he presented the ideas as a meditation of Anthony's. This device, the presentation of the author's ideas by means of a character, was not a modern novelty; within a few years after *Tom Jones*, Sterne had Mr. Shandy present ideas about the marvelous in a monologue. But there is a difference. Mr. Allen was forced to express his ideas about the marvelous through the mechanism of the novel, whereas Sterne was not forced to.

Thackeray's passages in *Vanity Fair* on the waste and suffering of war are not independent essays but a natural outgrowth of the novel's action and they are in tune with the emotions of the characters. They are closer to the story that Thackeray was writing than Fielding's essay was to his story. But they are not fused with the story — they are separate from it. Mr. Hemingway's feeling about war is exactly the same as Thackeray's but it does not appear as such in *For Whom the Bell Tolls,* and it cannot be separated from the novel. Mr. Hemingway himself is not present in the novel. As the puppetmaster he may move the characters about as he likes and put into their mouths such words and sentiments as he chooses, so long as the reader accepts them as the words and actions of the puppets. But he may not appear on the stage in his own person.

Between Fielding's time and ours the art of fiction has developed a sentiment or convention which holds: that an essay is one kind of thing and a novel another kind of thing, that a mixture of kinds is improper (to be understood as ineffective), and especially that the interposition of the novelist in person is discordant. Certainly the sentiment is not universal; there are many readers who do not share it and some novelists who do not observe it. But as a psychological rather than an esthetic principle it is binding on most readers and most novelists. We may say that it is one of the determining principles of modern fiction and one of the refinements, or purifications, that fiction has achieved on the way to its implicit methods. Interpolated essays or apostrophes by the novelist are of course a blatant violation of the principle, but its greatest importance is rather in its subtlest applications. The momentary hesitation of the reader which we have undertaken to explain arises most often because the novelist has departed from the principle so slightly that he is not aware of having done so.

But all stories are told and as I have said the uniqueness of the novel is that it is related: it is told by the novelist, without being projected through actors on a stage or a screen. How can a novelist relate his fiction without appearing in his own person? How, especially, can he do so under the requirement that he must make past time appear to be present time?

Sometimes a dramatist introduces between the scenes of a play a robed and masked or otherwise stylized figure who narrates to the audience action which cannot take place on the stage but which the audience must know about because it bears on what does take place there. This expository device, whose legitimacy is one of the perennial debates of dramatic criticism, usually bores the audience painfully.[1] The audience has so far witnessed the action of the play; it has been present on the spot. It has seen the French ambassadors deliver the tennis balls to King Henry, and has heard the King's anger break out in a declaration of war. Action and emotion have been rendered directly. But when the Chorus, on an empty stage, describes a conspiracy of three corrupted men that is to have an effect on the play, it does not see the conspirators or hear them conspiring. Consequently, it is less anxious about the King's success. It saw the presentation of the tennis balls, it heard the declaration of war, but it learns about the conspiracy at second hand.

As I have pointed out, the novelist must always be per-

---

[1] Variants of the device are used, most often in the prayerful theater, to make comments on the action, to proclaim that the pit is part of the stage and the audience are actors in the illusion, or to suggest a vast and windy symbolism too inexact to be forged into dialogue, action, and emotion. At the extreme of this, the theater gets caught shedding its skin.

forming the function of this robed, anonymous figure. What is first-hand on the stage can only be second-hand in fiction. The audience sees but the reader must be told. And he can be told only about the immutable: the play is present time, the novel past time presented in retrospect. The novelist as Chorus relates an event now ended, set in its final form forever, but he must persuade us that something whose issue we know is already settled is nevertheless continuous with our perception of it, the outcome still in doubt. He must deal with Molly Bloom's erotic reverie of this morning at a separation as complete as that of a historian who is translating an inscription by Octavius Caesar on a pediment in Rome.

The illusion is of the present and we made a start toward understanding how it is produced when we glanced at the different narrative methods of stage, screen, and radio. The narrative methods of fiction are determined by a convention implicit in the medium, a pretense that the novelist has and has had nothing to do with what is happening. The pretense may be simple or elaborately contrived, sometimes it is transparently thin, but it is part of all fiction's narratives, and as the novel has developed it has steadily tended toward the aboslute. What makes the reader uncomfortable when he encounters such interpositions of the author as I have mentioned is the fact that they call attention to exactly the function of the novelist which ordinarily he takes the greatest care to conceal. An apostrophe on war by Thackeray in his own person brings him on the stage in robe and mask as Chorus. So he abruptly reminds the reader that he has been hidden in the wings all along, that Dobbin, Amelia, and Becky Sharp, after all, have not been living of their own right but only jerking to the strings he pulled.

As we move away from the animism of children such a re-

minder becomes increasingly fatal to the illusion of fiction.
You can tell a child a story in your own person and he will
disregard you entirely, with a faith in the events themselves
so lively that every beanstalk is a practicable ladder to the
sky. The primary effects of fiction are on exactly that plane,
the effects that are called a story. Basically they are as simple
as a fairy tale but it must be remembered that they are
eternal effects, that they are the roots of fiction. If a novelist
has a good enough story — if the events are absorbing
enough, vivid or powerful or arresting, for the maintenance
of his illusion — he need have little else and especially he
need have little technical skill beyond that of narrative. If
the story is good enough, the reader will show a tolerance
for inner illogicalities, contradictions, and disparities, and
even for emptiness, that contradicts everything the theorist
of technique asserts.

Let me say here what I will elaborate later on, that one
kind of fiction tries to make the foliage spring directly from
the roots. It tries, that is, to make the events contain, or at
least suggest, all the dimensions of thought and emotion that
give it significance to the reader. For two generations that
kind of fiction has exerted a strong influence on most other
kinds. At its purest, it creates the maximum tension between content and form.

But the moment you ask a story to have logic, the moment
you require that its events be related to one another, you
forsake the naïveté of a listening child. You have limited
the area of illusion and you have set conditions which the
novelist must meet. And you have reached a state of mind
that resents Thackeray's speaking for himself in his novel.
. . . I repeat that these restrictions and requirements must
not be thought of as a reader's conscious perceptions. Such
an objection as he feels is ordinarily well within what I have

called his tolerance. He is a little bored by the passage, he hurries through it, he skips over it — which is to say, he gets on to fiction that will once more move in its own terms. But his tolerance can be exhausted as well by a sum of small strains as by a single severe one.

The first step, therefore, is to get the Chorus into the play and devise means of keeping it there. The event which is seen at second hand will seem much more readily to be seen at first hand if it is related not by the puppetmaster but by someone who takes part in it or who has an emotional stake in it. "Then Arderay swore that his foe had done wrong to the daughter of the King, and Amis made oath that he lied." This is the Chorus in its most elementary and objectionable form relating an event. If the novelist has Amis relate it in any of the conventions that permit him to, or if he relates it by means of Amis from within the event itself, then the reader's perception will be from within the story, not outside. Amis is an actor in the event; the King's daughter has an emotional stake in it and though she is a spectator of the event she is inside the story; there are various ways of leading the reader to perceive the event through her. The effects of the methods will be different, and the novelist will choose according to the effect he desires, but with any of them the illusion will be stronger than in an unattached relation by the Chorus. The point of view of the story will be within the story.

"Point of view" is a textbook phrase. We are forced to use such terms to designate processes but they have no virtue of their own. Actually, I suppose, "means of perception" would be more accurate here, for the principle is that the reader perceives the story, its events and meanings, from within the story. What is required is a means of getting him inside the story that will also serve as a fixed point by which he may

thereafter orient what goes on. Usually the device is a character about whom authoritative statements can be made or
who can speak authoritatively for himself.

I have attributed to the first novelist an elementary and
inevitable device, a narrator who speaks in his own person
but is a character in the story. He is an "I" who relates it
with the authority that comes from having taken part in it.
This is a natural narrative method and it is dramatic. "Amis
made oath that he lied," is impersonal, it is a statement in
indirect discourse, and it is clearly at second hand. If you
change it to, "I said, 'By the body of Christ, you lie,' " you
have dramatized it, brought it into direct discourse, and made
it seem to be at first hand. As will soon appear, however,
though this is direct discourse, it is still not the direct rendition of event. But it is much nearer to it than the simple
narrative statement it has replaced, and it is immensely more
vivid.

This use of a character as a narrative "I" is a common
method in stories of vigorous, hurried, or somewhat implausible action. It is frequently used in detective stories,
for instance, whether the "I" is the principal character, as
with Mr. Raymond Chandler's Philip Marlowe, or a less
important one whose technical function is to convey the activities of the principal character, as with Dr. Watson or Mr.
Rex Stout's Archie Goodwin. (My reader will see at once
that effects are open to each method that are impossible to
the other. Marlowe cannot admire himself as Archie admires Nero Wolfe, for instance; and the reader must be in
possession of all the information that Marlowe has but Nero
Wolfe can have information that Archie has not got and so
it can be naturally withheld from the reader.) It is the commonest method in stories of the fantastic or the supernatural; a reader is more willing to accept an improbable
event if someone who was there at the time assures him that

it occurred. (*Is* occurring.) It is useful when the values of the story require the reader to be kept in ignorance of forces that are operating beyond the immediate scene: there is psychological plausibility in his knowing no more and understanding no further than the narrator. Furthermore, it enables the novelist to convey any information to the reader or make any comments he may choose to, for he need only make information or comment natural to the narrator in the circumstances. In proportion as the narrator is a meditative, analytical, or inquisitive person, it permits any kind of speculation and makes it legitimate by investing it with emotions derived from the story.

A common axiom in Mr. Somerset Maugham's novels is that we cannot know the personality and the true motives of other people, that we can only speculate about them. It is therefore entirely proper for the "I" who is so often his narrator to speculate about the motives of other characters. And it is a first-rate effect of fiction when this speculation by a character gets itself accepted as the certainty which the novelist has but makes his narrator impugn. The complicated double "I" of Conrad's narrator plus his Marlow creates the ether of doubt in which alone the tentative, half-frustrated psychological probing that is the essence of his art could exist. In James's "Turn of the Screw," the unnamed "I" who introduces the story achieves a comparable effect. Besides handily dramatizing the expository preliminaries which without him would be inert, he provides the reader with a point of orientation that makes the desired uncertainty inevitable as soon as the governess, a second "I," begins to tell her story. James used a personal narrator in many short novels and short stories. The method enabled him to make extremely fine differentiations of feeling and extreme attenuations of doubt and belief. His "I" could be naturally preoccupied with bewilderment about the motives of other characters, a bewilderment that is sometimes the principal substance of the story. No other narrative method could sustain bewilderment so long without accessory substance. Only an "I" for whom bewilderment is for the time being the core of experience could make it the core of a reader's interest.

The most complex and versatile "I" in fiction is the never-named narrator in *Remembrance of Things Past*.[2] In Proust's hands the method achieves effects that were new to the novel, of a kind never before achieved in any literary form. Our purpose does not require us to describe them but two observations are pertinent. The narrator's auto-analysis, which again is the ether in which the great work exists, would not be possible with any other technique, for its culminating value is his awareness of his self-analysis together with his appraisal of it. And also the "I" repeatedly

2 This is the statement usually made in the texts. Actually he is named at least twice, if once only by indirection, in Chapter I of *The Captive*. "As soon as she [Albertine] was able to speak she said: 'My ——' or 'My dearest ——' followed by my Christian name, which if we give the narrator the same name as the author of this book, would be, 'My Marcel' or 'My dearest Marcel.'" And 116 pages later Albertine says, "The ideas you get into your head! What a Marcel! What a Marcel!" Here we may notice that in a letter written while *Swann's Way* was still in manuscript and a publisher had not been found, Proust spoke of "the character who narrates, who calls himself 'I' (and who is not I)."

Proust did not, I believe, give *The Captive* a final revision. It is reasonable to suppose that if he had done so he would have worked over both of these passages till he had found a satisfactory way of not naming the "I," for to do so violates his very stringent discipline. He would probably also have smoothed out an awkwardness in Chapter II. There has been a party at the Verdurins'. One of the intense scenes in the long process of their break with Charlus has taken place at it. The narrator, "I," has been present during most of it. Then M. Verdurin and his wife are left alone and talk about Charlus and others who were present at the party. Probably no reader would ever have noticed the discrepancy, for by now the method has been established so long and so memorably that it seems to be inclosing everything. But for the only time (so far as I am aware) Proust becomes self-conscious about the fact that, after all, there was no one to overhear this dialogue and report it. So he is at pains to explain that "I" heard about it some years later.

drops out for short or long passages and a different narrative method is used. We are asked to assume that the "I"
has so identified himself with Swann or whoever else is con-
veying the story that he is reproducing out of sympathy what
had happened. But once this convention by assumption has
been hinted, Proust retires the "I" out of sight.

There are, that is, effects which an "I" cannot achieve
and ends of fiction which he cannot serve. If the reader
must be *certain* about the motives, thoughts, or entirely
private experience of any character other than the narrator,
an "I" will not do. He was not along when Swann was med-
itating in solitude or when he was in bed with Odette. With
whatever perspicuity he may speculate about such occasions,
he is debarred when the end in view requires us to know
exactly. Nor can he be used when the novelist must deal
with the content of more minds than one. It is natural for
a person to tell you what he thinks and feels, and so a reader
accepts what a character says he thinks and feels. But when
someone tells you what another person thinks or feels he
can, like yourself, only guess at it by interpreting speech
and expression and behavior in the light of what he knows.
Consequently, an "I" who undertakes to tell the reader what
is going on in the mind of another character, no matter how
preternaturally sensitive and sympathetic he may be, risks a
disbelief that will destroy the illusion. He is within the illusion so long as he presents it as a guess or a hypothesis, and
sometimes the reader may be induced to forget that it is no
more, but when he represents it as certainty he is outside
the illusion and the effect is gone. The unformulated skepticism that is always hovering at the margin of the reader's
mind pounces and rejects. So the novelist is constrained to
use some means of perception, some substitute for the
Chorus, other than an "I."

But we must face a hard fact, that a personal narrator, an

"I," must always be, if only shadowily, something of a Chorus or expositor. He is within the logic and belief of fiction, for he is engaged with the events of the novel and affected by its emotions. Since that is true, there are many areas of fiction where it does not matter in the least that he is also an agent in the second-hand presentation of fiction. But there are other areas and occupations where the illusion requires that there be no such agency — requires the apparent elimination of all expository, interpretive, or summarizing instruments which relay the event to the reader. Most of them occur as the direct rendition of thought and emotion, which as I have said is a unique ability of fiction. No other literary form presents the behavior of imaginary characters in terms that are both psychological and dramatic. At the point where the device of the first-person narrative breaks down and the elimination of expository agencies is required, we reach the most complex convention of fiction. It is the convention which removes not merely the fourth wall of a room, as the stage convention does, but a section of the human skull as well, and enables the reader to believe that he perceives what is going on inside.

*   *   *

When you tell a friend an amusing incident of your vacation or, with more art, an anecdote about the traveling salesman and the farmer's daughter, your instinctive method is one which a novelist is usually at pains to avoid. You relate what you did, break off to explain what your wife thought about it, abandon her to describe what the traffic cop was doing before you reached the corner, and leave him to bring in the amusing misconceptions of the bystanders. You do the same with the farmer, his daughter, and the traveling salesman. You are careful to make clear what was in the minds of all of them, for the flavor of the story comes from their saying one thing while thinking something else. You are the narrator, and it is your privilege to take any position in space that pleases you, to occupy several in succession or even at one time, and to move in and out of the minds of all your characters as convenience may suggest.

Such a method suffices for a dinner-table story but it creates resistance when used in fiction. The imaginary world of a novel is always at some variance with the common sense world of the reader's experience but must never challenge its axioms. No one can be in more than one place at a time or learn what is going on elsewhere by any but natural means of communication. The novelist's abrupt shift of scene from Raleigh in Virginia to Elizabeth in England, or from John in this room to Mary in the next one, is as unaxiomatic as a magic carpet. The reader is willing to travel those distances between one scene and the next but he is not willing to have one place superimposed on another place in the same scene, even though they may be separated by only a few inches. He cannot even look at both John and Mary simultaneously; both optics and psychology forbid. When he is asked to do so, the puppet strings become visible and the illusion has been impaired. Again, though in a subtler way, the novelist has come upon the stage.[3]

The reader's tolerance establishes an area of indifference

[3] I avoid technical terms as much as possible but it is time to make two definitions. I use the word *scene* to mean direct, dramatized narrative — action, dialogue, immediate emotion, etc. — as opposed to indirect discourse, summary, and other kinds of static substance that will presently be described. I use the phrase *a scene* as it is used in the stage directions of Restoration drama: to mean a passage of direct dramatized discourse during which neither the setting nor the number of characters whom the reader sees changes. A scene ends and another one begins when a character exits, a new character enters, or the setting changes to another place.

within which this principle may be safely disregarded. That area becomes progressively smaller as fiction turns from physical action to thought and emotion. No one can be directly aware of any thoughts and emotions as such except his own. One can read his own mind but can get at the minds of companions only imaginatively, by interpreting what they do and say. When the reader comes on a group of characters in a novel, he must make his perception of the group coincide with that of one member of it. The novelist would severely strain his belief by asking him to see the group first as one member does, and then, a moment later, as another one does. Among the least effective scenes in fiction are those in which the means of perception, the channel of thought and emotion, changes as the speakers in the dialogue change. The novelist who tells you what Mary said, what she thought as she said it, what John thought as he heard it, and what he then said in answer — is employing a device guaranteed to defeat his intention. The reader's marginal skepticism is at once alerted. He grants that if he were Mary and said what she says here he might well think as she does, and he could certainly hear what John replies. But so long as he was Mary he would not know what John was thinking. When he is told directly instead of being led to infer it, he protests. He cannot be in two minds at once, nor can he shift from one to the other when both are present.

He [Jimmy] saw in Ed's way of calling his vocation a "job" a desire to express modesty about something Ed was secretly very proud of, and this hypocrisy, as Jimmy felt it to be, irritated him. He sensed that Ed was distressed by the mocking use of the words "saving souls," and understood that they had a grave and precious meaning in Ed's mind, part of that complicated explicable whole which had robbed him of Ed.

"Saving souls," he repeated maliciously, *"and practicing humility."*

He hit the nail on the head. Of the many things which troubled Ed, want of humility was dominant. [The means of perception has shifted from Jimmy. This is a statement by the author, though by implication it may pass as in Ed's mind.]

"We are trained to strive for humility," he said carefully, *listening to the tone of his own voice which he tried to invest with candor and modesty, and aware that he was trying, that neither candor nor modesty were genuine, and ashamed that it was so. [We are within Ed's mind.]*

"You talk of it as if it's something you can get, like going into a store and buying yourself a new suit."

Which again hit the nail on the head. It was exactly what Ed often became doubtful about, whether it could be acquired. Would he ever be deemed worthy to be thus blessed?

"That's why you want to be a priest. To feel superior. You think you're superior. And that one," Jimmy jerked his head at Mack viciously, *"He thinks he's superior too." [We are back with Jimmy.]*

"Me, superior!" Mack was dumbfounded. *His mouth hanging open, the spoon heaped with ice cream poised in mid-air, he started. The thought had never entered his honest head. [This is alternately by means of Mack, the third mind we have entered, and by statement of the author.]*

He suddenly turned and addressed Ed:

"It's no use talking to him. He just won't give a guy credit. If a guy makes good at a job, he says the job **is**

easy, and if a guy tries to live decent, he calls him a coward, says he runs away from life. Mom, I'd like another cup of coffee."

"Why, Mack, of course," his mother cried, grateful for the interruption. [*This is Mom, the fourth means of the reader's perception.*]

She had not dared stop the argument since Ed was taking part in it. She had sat there on pins and needles, casting frantic glances at her husband for advice but poor Joe had never quite got over the shock of being father to a future priest. [*Inferentially a fifth mind?*] *Now, in answer to her anxious glances, he made a gesture signifying "Let well enough alone," and started on his dessert.*[4]

A principle of psychological plausibility operates against such a passage, and probably one of optical validity as well. The narrative method more frequently used than others to satisfy their requirements is the fixation in one character of the point of view from which the reader observes the scene. The scene unfolds as this character experiences it, and his understanding of it provides the first step in the reader's understanding of it, if not further steps. (The principle leaves the novelist free to call on another character to perform the same function when a new scene begins, if he chooses to, or to use the same one throughout.) The character so chosen is the medium by which the scene, with all its implications and significance, is transmitted to the reader. He is the means of perception, the reader's eyes and ears and the fulcrum of his judgment if not, as may happen, the lever as well. The relation of this character to the events of the scene, or to its principal emotions, may be anything from that of an observant bystander to that of the central

4 From *The Story of Mrs. Murphy* by Natalie Anderson Scott.

figure. But he is the novelist's deputy as an expositor and the reader's means of engagement with the novel.

At the simplest he is a mere conveyor. He need have little more personality than is required for acceptable reporting. Yet all the material of the immediate scene, whether straight physical action or the subtlest and most secret emotions, must be transmitted and translated by means of what he does, feels, knows, perceives, and understands. Therefore the greater the demands of the scene, the greater will be the need for him to have personality, and the more complex will be the reader's relationship to him. One of the richnesses of fiction depends on the fact that as a character he has individuality. No matter what the events are and who the other characters are, he has attitudes of his own toward them, and so his personality adds another dimension to the scene. There is the event itself, there is the other character as he really is (that is, as the reader ultimately makes him out to be) — and also there are both the event and the other character or characters as understood by the one through whom the reader sees them, as colored by his sympathies and prejudices, the extent of his understanding of this scene and of life in general, the defects of his intelligence, the emotion he is feeling, the eccentricities or insufficiencies of his nature. So he provides refraction and parallax, which enable the novelist to control the effect on the reader, since the reader makes use of his awareness that they exist. His deviations or known errors furnish another bearing to help the reader steer a true course. Thus the reader always has at least a dual relationship to the character whose eyes and mind he is using. In part he identifies himself with the character, as he shares his perceptions, and in part uses him impersonally as a point of orientation. The duality or multiplicity of this relationship is one of the properties unique to fiction and it creates one of the additional levels of significance, beyond that of the immediate fact, on which a skillfully written novel may move simultaneously.

*   *   *

By restricting the means of perception to one character, the novelist accepts severe limitations of his freedom. There are many characters in his novel and they are all necessary for the effect he set out to produce. The simplest of the corollaries that follow is remarkably complex: he must so manipulate the character in whom the perception is fixed that the story will flow freely, the understanding of the reader will be precisely what he wants it to be, and everything will seem as natural and unforced as if the character had the omniscience which the novelist has but dare not visibly use. This implies skill in contriving to have the character in the right place at the right time for the right reason. What is more important, it implies having the character see, feel, understand, speculate, meditate, guess, be mistaken, be deceived, be correct, in precisely the right way to precisely the right degree. All this must be done in character, though it is at the behest of the novelist. He must control every item of the scene but must control it in terms of the character. If John is allowed to see something which not he but someone else would have seen, the illusion is marred. If he is allowed to feel an emotion that he would not have felt, it is destroyed.

John is a fallible human being with his own personal limitations but he acts in place of the novelist, who is omniscient and infallible. At almost every moment while the novelist is working through John, more must be done than John is by nature qualified to do. The more complex a novel is, and especially the more subjective its material is,

the more John tends to become (we hope without the reader's noticing it) an astonishingly observant, thoughtful, in-
tuitive, and philosophical person. The path ends in Henry
James's third-person onlooker who is even more sensitive to
the experience of others than his first-person narrator. This
onlooker is so concerned with the emotions of his friends
and so attuned to them that he almost becomes the heroine
he is reporting. Only the thinnest identity of his own, an
identity forever being restored at the point where it was
about to merge with Isabel, keeps him interpreting what he
feels rather than expressing it for her — and reminds us that
we are seeing her through him. Henry James is at the end
of the path — so far — but most novels go some distance
down it. Much of the spadework in any novel is John seeming to present his own emotions but presenting them in such
a way that actually he is interpreting Isabel's. He is acting
for the author and he does so because if the author interpreted Isabel himself, the machinery would again show beneath the flies. The reader has been cajoled into accepting
an interpretation because it is apparently made at first hand.
It is expressed through a character who is within the novel.

And Kate in these days, was altogether in the phase
of forgiving her [Milly] so much bliss; in the phase
moreover of believing that, should they continue to go
on together, she would abide in that generosity. She
had, at such a point as this, no suspicion of a rift within
the lute — by which we mean not only none of any-
thing's coming between them, but none of any definite
flaw in so much clearness of quality. [In this last sen-
tence the puppet master appears on stage.] Yet, all the
same, if Milly, at Mrs. Lowder's banquet, had described
herself to Lord Mark as kindly used by the young
woman on the other side because of some faintly-felt

*special propriety in it, so there really did match with
this, privately, on the young woman's part, a feeling
not analyzed but divided, a latent impression that Mil-
dred Theale was not, after all, a person to change
places, to change even chances with. Kate, verily, would
perhaps not quite have known what she meant by this
reservation, and she came near naming it only when
she said to herself that, rich as Milly was, one probably wouldn't — which was singular — ever hate her for
it. The handsome girl had, with herself, these felicities
and crudities: it wasn't obscure to her that, without
some very particular reason to help it, it might have
proved a test of one's philosophy not to be irritated by
a mistress of millions, or whatever they were, who, as
a girl might have been, like herself, only vague and
fatally female. . . .*

The passage is from *The Wings of the Dove*. Coming on
such a fragment out of its context a reader might be unable
to determine which character is reporting the other. More
likely, however, the minute registration of Kate would make
him suppose that he was seeing matters through Kate's eyes.
But actually it is Milly who is reporting for the novelist.

The novelist's relationship to this prime character must
be noted. As we have seen, the validity of the "I did," "I
thought," "I felt," of a simple adventure story comes from
their being within the fiction. The "he did," "he thought,"
"he felt," of any novel are flagrantly expository, but they
come inside the fiction because the expositor relinquishes
the omniscience of the novelist and the reader accepts the
limitation of perception to a single character. Clearly there
are degrees of the novelist's retirement into that character.
He is only a little way in when he reports, by way of John,

what John did, said, and thought and then discusses those data objectively. He has been further absorbed when what John said and did comes into relationship with the discussion of John and dominates it in personal terms. He has all but disappeared when it turns out that not John himself but Isabel by means of John is the burden of the scene, the point both of rendition and of discussion.

These stages — there are many more than the three I have differentiated — move in a common direction: toward the presentation of John, or even of Isabel through him, directly in terms of himself alone. Toward, that is, the immediate expression of thought and emotion. The illusion sought after is an illusion that behavior, thought, and emotion are being rendered directly. If not at the moment of their occurrence, as on the stage, then at least without being transmitted through any medium or along any channel or perception.

That illusion can never be complete. There must always be an expositor. But completeness is approximated when the novelist appears to drop out entirely and nothing seems to be related, when he works within character rather than by means of character. He puts not only the means of perception inside the fiction but the perception itself. He makes the act of perception, that is, not something reported or assisted but something in process of occurring.

IO

DYNAMICS

10

DYNAMICS

I T WILL BE instructive to look closely at several short
passages from *Ulysses*. The first is the beginning of the
novel.

*Stately, plump Buck Mulligan came from the stair-
head, bearing a bowl of lather on which a mirror and
a razor lay crossed. A yellow dressinggown, ungirdled,
was sustained gently behind him by the mild morning
air. He held the bowl aloft and intoned:*
  — Introibo ad altare Dei!
  *Halted, he peered down the dark winding stairs and
called up coarsely:*
  — Come up, Kinch. Come up, you fearful Jesuit.
  *Solemnly he came forward and mounted the round
gunrest. He faced about and blessed gravely thrice the
tower, the surrounding country and the awakening
mountains. . . .*

With the next sentence Stephen Dedalus comes up the
stairs, and with the second one he becomes the point of approach to the scene, the means of perception. It is through
him and in the second sentence, for instance, that we see
Buck Mulligan's hair, "grained and hued like pale oak."

Thereafter, the novel is transmitted through Stephen until, fifty pages later, Leopold Bloom is brought on the stage and the perception shifts to him. But observe that in this opening passage, though Buck Mulligan is seen to come out on the platform, no one sees him. We do not perceive the scene through him. He could himself see the mirror and razor crossed on the bowl, feel the dressing gown float behind him, and be aware of his coarseness when he calls down the stairs and his solemnity when he mounts the gunrest — but actually we are not admitted to his mind, we observe him from without. He is asserted: dramatically in that he is shown in action, but nevertheless expositorily in that the novelist tells the reader about him.

This is presentation at second hand, with no attempt to conceal the expository function. Theoretically there should be a slight hitch or awkwardness when the presentation shifts to the perceptions of Stephen, but actually there is none. The reader is still neutral, waiting for the means of perception to be established; if the shift were to occur a page or two farther on he might feel the slight, implicit awkwardness. The fact to be observed here, however, is that the scene becomes more alive as soon as we begin to see it by way of Stephen. It is now inside the novel: it is presented to us as Stephen experiences it, and its vividness is increased by his participation in it. By feeling and thinking about Buck Mulligan he vitalizes the reader's perception of Mulligan as well as his perception of Stephen. The refraction of one character through another makes both more alive.

The sentence, "Halted, he peered down the dark winding stairs and called up coarsely," is a statement by the novelist about Buck Mulligan from outside. Let us now look at a paragraph that comes two pages later. Mulligan has taunted Stephen about his refusal to pray for his dying mother (and has thus introduced thematic material that will become increasingly important). The first sentence reads, "Stephen, an elbow rested on the jagged granite, leaned his palm against his brow and gazed at the fraying edge of his shiny black coatsleeve." This differs from the sentence just quoted in that, though it is a statement about Stephen as the other is a statement about Mulligan, it is made by way of Stephen's own perceptions, The paragraph goes on:

Pain, that was not yet the pain of love, fretted his heart. Silently, in a dream she had come to him after her death, her wasted body within its loose brown graveclothes giving off an odour of wax and rosewood, her breath, that had bent upon him, mute and reproachful, a faint odour of wasted ashes.

The statement is not quite the same as that of the opening sentence of the paragraph but it is closely allied. It is a statement not of Stephen's behavior but of his feeling and remembrance — of his emotions and his obsessive phantasy of his mother's death. But it is still made after the fact, in summary or synopsis, on the novelist's authority and in his words. It is the content of Stephen's mind but it is reported by the novelist. It is, if you like, both inside and outside, both thought and exposition. We understand Stephen from within, and so share his feeling and phantasy, but we are still directed to do so by the novelist, who summarizes and states by way of Stephen. He does not directly present what Stephen thinks. This is the commonest method of representing thought and emotion in fiction, at least in modern fiction; it is the usual convention.

We may say that Tony Sarg is fully concealed behind the puppet stage. The reader does not see him and in fact is not aware of him at all. But a closer scrutiny than a reader is likely to give the passage shows that the puppets are still being worked by strings — and it is fiction's past time that reveals they are. Or put it in terms of Plato's allegory. The wall that is built along the raised way conceals from sight the people who are carrying the images which make the shadows on the wall, but they are still being carried. But fiction can intensify its illusion by concealing the puppet strings altogether, appearing to dispose entirely of those who carry the images, and bring the scene into the immediate moment.

Some hours later than the scene on the tower with which *Ulysses* opens, Stephen is walking along the seashore, after teaching his class and talking with Mr. Deasy. Impressions of the outer world mingle in his mind with philosophical and literary reflections, with memories of his parents and family, with fragmentary scenes remembered from his student days, and with many other associations — a flow and configuration of thought in which we have already begun to perceive something of a pattern. He passes the carcass of a drowned dog, which acquires emotional significance from events we have already witnessed. Then a live dog runs toward him, stops, and runs back. It reminds Stephen of an earlier occasion when a dog terrified him and impels him to think of various men who were brave whereas he seems cowardly in contrast to them. We need not explain here the associations his mind makes as it moves on from these heroes. But observe the way in which his thoughts are presented:

> *The man that was drowned nine days ago off Maiden's rock. They are waiting for him now. The truth, spit it out. I would want to. I would try. I am not a strong swimmer. Water cold soft. When I put my face into it in the basin at Clongowes. Can't see! Who's behind me? Out, quickly, quickly! Do you see the tide flowing quickly in on all sides, sheeting the lows of*

*sand and quickly, shellcocoacolored? If I had land
under my feet. I want his life still to be his, mine to be
mine. A drowning man. His human eyes scream to me
out of horror of his death. I . . . With him, together
down. . . . I could not save her. Waters: bitter death:
lost.*

*A woman and a man. I see her skirties. Pinned up,
I bet.*

*Their dog ambled about a bank of dwindling sand,
trotting, sniffing on all sides. Looking for something
lost in a past life.*

(The marks of elision are in Joyce's text and stand for
ellipses in Stephen's thinking; they do not mean that I have
deleted anything.)

Here there is (seemingly) no exposition, summary, or
representation by the novelist. Everything is presented at
the moment when it appears in Stephen's consciousness.
There is, to be sure, a kind of translation, since we are so
deep in the mind that some of this thinking would not
actually be formulated in words, and since some other parts
of it are not inevitable to Stephen's mind but are present
there only because the reader needs them. The phantasy
of the drowning man's eyes would surely be visual; Stephen
would see the image, not describe it to himself. The memory of his own fear of drowning would be emotion unformulated in words. And he would not think, "A woman and a
man. I see her skirties." He would be aware of the figures
and would simply see the skirties, without telling himself
that he was seeing them. But, granting that some things are
formulated in words which in actual thought would remain
unformulated, the passage is a transcription of what passes
through Stephen's mind.

He sees, he reflects, he forms conclusions. Memories rise

out of the past, he responds to them with fear and pain, conditioned associations follow. In one place ("Out, quickly, quickly!") thought as such disappears altogether and, so far as words can represent it, there is a mingling of pure reflex and pure feeling. *The reader is present at the moment of occurrence.* He is not as deeply submerged in the mind as it is possible to be — see later passages of *Ulysses* and the sleeping mind of *Finnegans Wake.* He is not deeply submerged for very long, for perception of the exterior world keeps breaking in and with the sentence before the last one quoted it is momentarily restored altogether. But he is entirely inside the mind. He is not looking into it by courtesy of the novelist, as he was in "Pain, that was not yet the pain of love, fretted his heart." He is looking out from within it and by means of it. He has the same relation to events that Stephen's mind has. The novelist has withdrawn altogether. There is no novelist: there are only Stephen's thought and feeling, and the reader's coterminous perception of them.

I have pointed out a transition from exterior and impersonal statement to interior statement which is made in various degrees of subjectivity. It will do no harm to look at a concentration of these things in a single passage. It occurs at the beginning of the second section of*Ulysses.* (To some degree the problems posed by the beginning of a novel are posed again at the beginning of its lesser divisions.)

Mr. Leopold Bloom ate with relish the inner organs of beasts and fowls. He liked thick giblet soup, nutty gizzards, a stuffed roast heart, liver slices fried with crustcrumbs, fried hencod's roes. Most of all he liked grilled mutton kidneys which gave to his palate a fine tang of faintly scented urine. [This is almost like the

*first statement about Buck Mulligan, but observe that
it is on the way toward the first statement about Stephen
Dedalus.]*

*Kidneys were in his mind as he moved about the
kitchen softly, righting her breakfast things on the
humpy tray. Gelid light and air were in the kitchen
but out of doors gentle summer morning everywhere.
Made him feel a bit peckish. [This paragraph has
brought us inside Bloom's mind but it still consists of
statements by the novelist after the fact. The last sentence is on the verge of direct rendition.]*

The coals were reddening.

*Another slice of bread and butter: three, four: right.
She didn't like her plate full. Right. He turned from
the tray, lifted the kettle off the hob and set it side-
ways on the fire. It sat there, dull and squat, its spout
stuck out. Cup of tea soon. Good. Mouth dry. The
cat walked stiffly round a leg of the table with tail on
high.*

The last paragraph contains direct rendition, though in
different degrees of subjectivity. Perhaps the fourth and last
sentences are completely within Bloom's mind only by attraction, by force of the fact that the rest of it has been —
like the dog in the last paragraph of the previous quotation.

Finally, we may quote some lines (any lines would do)
from Molly Bloom's interior soliloquy at the end of the
book. Other passages are more completely subjective than
the soliloquy — because they express the deepest planes of
the mind — but none could be more immediate. The event
and reader's perception of it are simultaneous.

*. . . that frock from the B March Paris and the coral
necklace the straits shining I could see over to Morocco*

*almost the bay of Tangier white and the Atlas moun-
tains with snow on it and the straits like a river so clear
Harry Molly Darling I was thinking of him on the sea
all the time after at mass when my petticoat began to
slip down at the elevation weeks and weeks I kept the
handkerchief under my pillow for the smell of him
there was no decent perfume to be got in that Gibraltar
only that cheap peau despagne that faded and left a
stink on you more than anything else I wanted to give
him a memento he gave me that clumsy Claddagh ring
for luck that I gave Gardner going to South Africa
where those Boers killed him with their war and fever
but they were well beaten all the same as if it brought
its bad luck with it like an opal or pearl must have been
pure 16 carat gold because it was very heavy I can see
his face clean shave Frseeeeeeeeeeeeeeeeeeeefrong that
train again weeping tone once in the dead deaead days beyond recall close my eyes breath my lips forward kiss
sad look eyes open piano ere oer the world the mists began I hate that istsbeg comes loves sweet ssooooooong
Ill let that out full when I get in front of the footlights
again Kathleen Kearney and her lot of squealers Miss
This Miss That Miss Theother lot of sparrowfarts skit-
ting round talking about politics they know as much
about as my backside anything in the world to make
themselves someway interesting Irish homemade beau-
ties soldiers daughter am I ay and whose are you boot-
makers and publicans. . . .*

*   *   *

We have seen some of the ways in which perception is
conveyed or achieved. We must now turn to certain attributes of the thing perceived. For if a novelist is compelled

to accommodate the presentation of his material to the logic and limitations of the point of view from which the reader sees it, he is also compelled to respect limitations implicit in the material and to meet conditions that govern its use. Some of his material needs only to be written down in order to be fiction. Some of it cannot become fiction no matter what is done to it. Some of it must undergo processes of conversion or transformation. Much of the resistance of the reader which we undertook to explain comes from the novelist's offering him material which is not properly fiction at all or which has not been completely converted into fiction from its original state.

It has been natural to speak here of a scene as moving, to remark that some things may interrupt its progress, and to observe that others give it motion. For a fundamentally important attribute of fiction is movement. Easily recognizable when it is present, immediately missed when it is not, it cannot be easily defined. For the movement of fiction is not so simple as that of music, where tones follow one another in a time-sequence, or that of the movies, where movement in space is added to the succession of images in time. It is always a complex movement, for various kinds of motion are usually occurring together. And to tell the truth it is sometimes a doubly metaphorical movement, since some of the things that produce the movement of fiction cannot be said to be themselves in motion. Furthermore, it is often movement only in the response of the reader and sometimes, at its most difficult, it consists of a unique relationship between the fiction and the reader. But we must make at least a rough analysis, for a common mistake of novelists is to treat the material of a dynamic art as if it were a static one.

Examining the scene itself, we can distinguish three kinds of primary movement. It may move in space, it may move in time, and (less obviously) it may move by being emotional, by producing emotion, or by intensifying emotion. (Of course it may move in all three dimensions at once, and may also have other qualities of movement which can be called secondary.) When stately, plump Buck Mulligan comes from the stairhead, his dressing gown floats behind him, he raises the bowl, he speaks, he goes to the stairway, looks down, and speaks again. All his actions are, in the terms of fiction, equivalent to physical movement on the stage or screen. We follow them as we should follow them in a theater or, if we were present, on the tower itself. In the later, more subjective passage the same kind of movement occurs: "Their dog ambled about a bank of dwindling sand, trotting, sniffing on all sides." Less directly recorded, it occurs in "Do you see the tide flowing quickly in on all sides, sheeting the low of sands quickly shellcocoacolored?" and in Molly Bloom's "the straits shining I could see over to Morocco almost" and "at mass when my petticoat began to slip down at the elevation." If my reader is sufficiently well acquainted with Molly's soliloquy he will recognize that the single word "kiss" in my quotation from it is the same sort of thing. All this is simply physical movement in space. It needs no further description, and it is the same whether the hero of the amateur's short story raises an eyebrow or an antique villain pushes toward the buzzsaw the carrier on which he has bound the helpless and innocent Bertha whose virtue has frustrated his lust. It is motion in space, within the scene itself. Its primary effect is to keep the reader's visual image of the scene in motion. Conrad's "to make you see" can be translated as to make you see the shadow moving across the wall.

It is not at once apparent that what Buck Mulligan says is also dynamic, but let us recast the sentences. "He held the bowl aloft and intoned the opening words of the In-

troibo of the Mass." And, "He peered down the dark winding stairs and told Stephen to come up." Buck Mulligan's
personal movements are still rendered directly but what he
says has reverted to "Then Arderay swore that his foe had
done wrong to the daughter of the King." It has been put
in indirect discourse. "Told Stephen to come up" is reported, summarized, stated. But " 'Come up, Kinch. Come
up, you fearful Jesuit.' " reaches the reader in the process
of occurring. It is in motion, whereas the statement in indirect discourse is static. Allowing for a reservation to be
made later, we may say that dialogue is movement whereas
a summary or statement of it is not.

*   *   *

The characters of a novel are not always moving about the
stage or talking to one another. What is movement in fiction when they are not?

(Sometimes, alas, they provide movement when we should
prefer them quiet. An unskillful novelist's characters are
apt to twitch a lot. "For a long moment he looked at her, his
eyes unwavering. She saw a muscle quiver under his sleeve.
He looked away, picked up his highball, frowned at it, set
it down, stared at his hands. They became fists and the
knuckles whitened, then were again the sensitive, groping
hands she knew so well. One eyebrow rose, half-quizzical,
half-weary. Now his forehead creased. His shoulder hunched
convulsively. She saw that he was trembling. . . .")

When we approach the question from its converse, several kinds of inert material, material that lacks movement,
come to mind. The commonest is what the textbooks call
description. College students used to be — sometimes they
still are — required to distinguish descriptive writing as a
separate literary genre, which it is not. Description for its
own sake does not exist in prose literature. Even in the

loose techniques of the earlier novel descriptive passages had, at least vaguely, a functional purpose, and a sustained development of fiction has been to confine them to it more strictly. Today it would not be excessive to say that any description which has not been converted to other uses of fiction is amateurish. And yet there is that necessity Conrad pointed out, "to make you see." The reader must be made to visualize at least something, if he is to create the rest for himself.

Here again the margin of toleration will vary from reader to reader. But certainly the leisurely set-pieces of almost any novel before about 1850 are intolerable today; if the modern reader encounters one, he simply skips it. To begin a novel by introducing the traditional solitary horseman riding across the middle distance at evenfall and then go on for twenty pages writing beautifully about the glamour of the landscape would be to make sure that no readers would be left by page twenty and only a few by the bottom of page one. Novels could begin and go on in that way when Mrs. Radcliffe was writing, or Scott. They cannot begin that way today and I doubt if anyone but a student under compulsion now reads such passages when he turns to Scott. A volunteer reader begins with chapter two, and when he comes to similar passages later in the text he skips them and picks up the novel where it begins moving again. Does he take without protest the once-celebrated first chapter of *The Return of the Native?* I doubt it. When I was in college my teachers said that such passages "set the mood" of the scene or "created atmosphere." But what is a mood, what is atmosphere, apart from someone who is feeling it? These passages may be written in fine prose, they may contain topographical or botanical information of great erudition, they may speculate profoundly about the mystery of life, but they are not fiction in its own terms. They do not move as fiction must move if it is to be read with satisfaction. They are not part of the process of the scene, they are not engaged with the emotions of the characters.

Not only the elaborate set-pieces of description are suspect. The incidental paragraphs and even phrases in which a novelist sets the stage and gives the scene spatial existence risk marring the illusion and rousing a reader's resistance. A novelist is constantly tempted to be a scene painter, an interior decorator, and a dressmaker, to show himself an artist in color and line, and especially to display some unique ability to find what he thinks of as significant detail. Amateurs yield to this temptation but it is a short way to disorder, lifelessness, and irritation. Willa Cather once made a plea for a kind of novel in which accessory detail would be entirely avoided — the "furniture" of the page, the incidental and valueless litter of physical or personal trivia with which the scene is frequently encumbered. The tendency of modern fiction has been to evolve that kind of novel, though not precisely in the way she argued for. For furniture is valueless only while it is inert; it may become dynamic and therefore valuable by acquiring emotional meaning in the novel.

The problem is complicated by the reader's necessities. The scene must exist for him and cannot do so unless it has reality in space, some kind of geographical or architectural or personal validity. He must have some way of visualizing characters against background; he cannot accept disembodied voices speaking in a void. A scene cannot often be only a dialogue for him and no extended scene can ever be only that. There must be something for him to see; more important still, there must be something for him to feel in an environment. But he will balk if he is offered too much, and what he is offered must be of a special kind.

Thus, at the simplest level, descriptions of characters are precarious. An FBI agent may be able to form a visual image of a suspect from the data typed on a card at head-quarters, but he is a specialist and the general reader is not. A novelist who tells you that Emmy Lou stands five feet two, weighs a hundred and four pounds, is twenty-six inches round the waist, and wears size six shoes with three-inch heels, has on a wrap-around skirt of green with yellow braid bordering large oblong pockets, wears a dotted kerchief tied under her chin, and has hair that looks like minted gold when the sun shines on it, eyes like valley mist of an Octo-ber morning, and knees like full moons carved of marble but dimpled as if an angel had kissed the stone — has not created an impression but destroyed one. If you were to meet Emmy Lou you would observe at best only one or two of these details at first glance and would require time to take the rest of them in, if in fact you ever noticed them. In fiction such data are neutral, and hence an impediment, until the three-inch heels or the misty eyes acquire emo-tional import for one of the characters. Similarly, an enumeration of objectcs in a landscape or a room requires the reader to notice more than he would be aware of if he were present on the scene. The eye sees and the mind re-cords only a few objects at first glance; time and especially interest are required if the rest of them are to be noticed. A reader who is asked to piece together an unnatural number of details is antagonized. When a novelist regards them as important he is wise to convey them a little at a time, indi-rectly so far as possible, and as a product of the action or emotion of the scene itself.

One kind of descriptive detail frequently insisted on in

fiction is either tautological or altogether irrelevant. When Mark Twain composed an appendix of various kinds of weather bulletins and asked the reader to distribute them through the novel according to his taste, he was announcing a sound principle. Unless the weather, the calendar, and the time of day have a bearing on the action or emotion of the scene they do not matter, and notation of them is a kind of offense. Similarly with the noise and color of the crowd, the process of the seasons, the heavenly bodies, the sound of rain by night, the thousand offstage and background items that dangerously unbar the door to the novelist's poetic impulses. Similarly with items which the reader takes as axiomatic. He does not need to be told that grass is green or the sky blue, he will believe that characters are dressed appropriately and make natural gestures unless he is told otherwise, and he will understand that when they go from one place to another they pass over what lies between.

But even when the novelist has accommodated his descriptive details to the reader's need of visual impressions and to his logical and psychological requirements, he has still not done enough with them. Though reduced to a minimum and selected by functional tests, they remain inert so long as they are merely informative to the reader. They are another kind of exposition; they suspend the movement of the scene and remind the reader of the machinery. But if they are given meaning or emotional significance for the characters, then, besides informing the reader, they acquire movement and come inside the scene. They are, that is, transformed from description as such to experience. As components of the lives of the characters, they increase the reader's perception and judgment of the characters.

A celebrated passage from *The Red Badge of Courage,* a mannered and carefully calculated novel, will show this principle in operation. Henry Fleming, the boy whose emotions in battle are the subject of the book, has fled from the firing line and for some time has been in the company of a wounded man, who has just died.

> *He now sprang to his feet and, going closer, gazed upon the pastelike face. The mouth was open and the teeth showed in a laugh.*
>
> *As the flap of the blue jacket fell away from the body, he could see that the side looked as if it had been chewed by wolves.*
>
> *The youth turned, with sudden, livid rage, toward the battlefield. He shook his fist. He seemed about to deliver a philippic.*
>
> *"Hell —"*
>
> *The red sun was pasted in the sky like a wafer.*

Down to the last line the descriptive material is fused with the action of the scene and cannot be separated from the developing narrative. Its descriptive force is derived from the fact that it is part of the narrative, that it reveals both how "he" perceives the scene and how he responds to it. "Pastelike," "showed in a laugh," "had been chewed by wolves," subjectively depict Henry Fleming while they present the scene, and so engage the reader with both. The last line is a simile so vivid that it has become a fixture in anthologies, but it would be irritating and anticlimactic if it were merely a striking detail interpolated here for its own sake. Instead, while the image informs and assists the reader, it simultaneously expresses Henry's sudden recognition of the external world at a moment of intense feeling after the panic of flight and the horror of his companion's death. It is shaped by his flight and horror. It expresses his emotion fully as much as it describes the scene. It carries the reader farther along in his perception of Henry Fleming. The inertness of descriptive detail has been overcome by making it render an emotion within the scene.

That sentence of Stephen Crane's is at one technical extreme. Another extreme that achieves the same result may be seen in Joyce's "Glittereyed, his rufous skull close to his greencapped desklamp sought the face, bearded amid darkgreener shadow, an ollav, holyeyed." The skull and eyes of John Eglington are being seen by Stephen Dedalus and the presentation is saturated with the melancholy and resentment of Stephen's present mood. The sentence has the technical function of presenting John Eglington to the reader but its descriptive function is blended with an emotional one. It moves on the momentum of Stephen's emotion and carries the reader with it, farther along.

The descriptive touches that are present on nearly every page of a novel usually lie well within such extremes. But the principle holds: to be effective they must be important to the characters. Description that has not been fused with the fiction is always a threat to the attention and belief of the reader. But the information and the sensory assistance which description is intended to provide may be indispensable to the reader. Character in action and dialogue is seldom enough for him very long; he must set the fiction as he perceives it in a frame of physical and personal reference. A skillful novelist governs himself by these limitations and solves the dilemma by keeping his descriptive details well within the reader's tolerance, and by contriving, whenever possible, to make them not items of information and assistance alone but also part of the emotional movement of the novel.

*   *   *

Description sometimes shades into a kind of summary or

analysis of character made for the reader's benefit. Something important is about to happen to Francesca — love,
suffering, fright, a meeting that will change her life, a succession of events that will be pivotal in her experience —
and the reader must know beforehand just what constellation of motives, traits, and earlier experience makes it inevitable for her to act as he will presently see her act. Or
something has happened and Francesca has acted in response
to it, and certain aspects of her resulting state of mind must
be made clear to the reader, who otherwise may be puzzled
or may think that she is being portrayed inaccurately. So
for a space the novelist abandons all his other objectives in
order to explain Francesca.

Whenever he does so he retards the movement of fiction.
The nature of the offense should now be clear: any explanation is expository, no matter how completely it may be
phrased in terms of the character. In fact, the more completely it is so phrased, the more likely it is to reveal the
author's hands on the puppet strings. The effect is like the
awkwardness in the theater when an actor comes down to
the footlights and soliloquizes about his own motives, a
device possible to dramatists today only when they are writing farce or fantasy. The modern audience rejects Iago's
explanation of his own villainy; the modern reader tends to
be uncomfortable when the novelist explains it for him.

Many gradations could be shown but two must suffice. A
passage from *The Brothers Karamazov* will show this "character work" at only a slight remove from pure description.
The physical appearance of Dmitri Fyodorovitch has just
been described; the passage goes on with a generalized
characterization:

> *Even when he was excited and talking irritably, his*
> *eyes somehow did not follow his mood, but betrayed*

something else, sometimes quite incongruous with what was passing. "It's hard to tell what he's thinking," those who talked to him sometimes declared. People who saw something pensive and sullen in his eyes were startled by his sudden laugh, which bore witness to mirthful and light-hearted thoughts at the very time when his eyes were so gloomy. . . .

This is not the appearance of Dmitri's eyes in the immediate scene but an item of his customary appearance set down here to help prepare the reader to understand and accept his later behavior. Nearly any chapter of Henry James will show a considerable extension and attenuation of the same sort of thing. The following is from *The Portrait of a Lady*:

Isabel might have believed it and not have been far from the truth. He thought a great deal about her; she was constantly present to his mind. At a time when his thoughts had been a good deal of a burden to him her sudden arrival, which promised nothing and was an open-handed gift of fate, had refreshed and quickened them, given them wings and something to fly for. Poor Ralph had been for so many years steeped in melancholy; his outlook, habitually sombre, lay under the shadow of a deeper cloud. He had grown anxious about his father, whose gout, hitherto confined to his legs, had begun to ascend into regions more vital. The old man had been gravely ill in the spring and the doctors had whispered to Ralph that another attack would be less easy to deal with. Just now he appeared disburdened of pain, but Ralph could not rid himself of a suspicion that this was a subterfuge of the enemy, who was waiting to take him off his guard. . . .

This is only the beginning of a long passage that is packed

with the same kind of information, definition, qualification, and analysis. It is intended to differentiate the various components of Ralph's character and present mood, and to reveal all the intricate relationships, subtle modifications, and precise shades and degrees of feeling that will eventually make him act in a certain way and respond in a certain way to the actions of others. But such analysis (and the simpler kind shown in the quotation from Dostoievsky) lays a heavy burden on the reader. All this minute differentiation is aimed at something to happen hereafter, it is not something happening now. It is a statement at second hand and a statement, further, made not for any value of its own but for its bearing on something else that is still to come. It is inert, not the thing occurring, not the event, not the emotion being felt. If continued too long — as it frequently is in the last novels of Henry James — it will bog the reader in a motionless morass of supplementary detail from which the thing supplemented, the reality of fiction, is entirely absent.

Notice that no one makes the observation about Dmitri's eyes while the reader is at hand. It is a generalized observation, a summary of observations, made as a statement by the novelist. Similarly, the illness of Ralph's father occurred last spring and the renewal of it that is currently disturbing Ralph is still to come; summary statement has been called on to do even more, and the reader has been asked to submit to more. How much, in fact, have we learned about either Dmitri or Ralph? How likely is it that we will bear in mind either the simple summary of Dostoievsky or the complex one of James, when the events for whose sake only they were written actually occur? Repetitions of this sort of thing may indeed lay down a deposit that will be useful to the reader when the event does occur, but also they may exhaust him before he reaches it. At any rate, we are a long

way from the odor of cheap perfume in Molly Bloom's
soliloquy.

Nevertheless, such differentiation, definition, analysis, and
summary — or their equivalent — are indispensable. The
dilemma is unavoidable and a novelist must grapple with
it on nearly every page. Every passage of analysis or character work he writes is a possible threat to his effect for it
halts the movement of fiction, and he must write it in full
realization of the risk he runs. If he extends it too far he
will damage the illusion and forfeit some of the reader's
acceptance. How far he can safely prolong it will depend on
his skill. There are always the resources of rhetoric; they
are in fact an ever-present help whenever he must take any
kind of technical risk. He can allay a reader's apprehension
or postpone the moment of irritation by cunning and ver-
satility of style. Like any other perilous moment, this is a
time to draw the reader's attention to the excellence of his
prose. Epigrams have hidden many a palmed card. He can
do something more by making his analytical passages short
and by rigorously relating them to the scene, so that they
will seem not to depart from it. But his most dependable
resource is to transform them so far as they can be transformed: to make them not only analytically informative but
also, simultaneously, part of the primary movement of the
scene. Such analysis as that quoted from Henry James cannot be completely transformed, and some use of it without
transformation is frequently unavoidable, but the usual result is a compromise. The novelist avoids using such material when that is possible; elsewhere he operates on it by
main force to disguise the expository element or to attach it
at least feebly to the actual scene.

Of similar material in the drama George M. Cohan used
to say, "Don't tell 'em — show 'em." The aphorism is even

more binding on a novelist, whose effort is to tell as little as the circumstances permit, to show what he has decided is essential, and to make what is shown suggest the rest.

One method of fiction undertakes to avoid analysis altogether by transferring it from the novel to the reader. In Hemingway, for instance, what the characters do and say is so rigorously selected and forms such a revealing system in itself that the reader is compelled to derive the motives behind it from the action itself. The emotions of Jake and Lady Ashley in *The Sun Also Rises* are never analyzed nor even stated, but they could behave as they do only because they felt the emotions which the reader has been led to attribute to them. Much modern fiction thus tries to force the reader to analyze the behavior of the characters in order to understand their motives. The method has obvious limitations. It can be made effective for any character in short passages, or for transitory emotions or uncomplicated motives. But it can be effective throughout long passages or an entire novel only with characters whose inner lives — motives, ideas, affections, doubts, impulses, inhibitions, compulsions — are simple, elementary, and limited. The soldiers, revolutionaries, gunmen, expatriate drunks, bull-fighters, and contemporary Neanderthals of Hemingway can be rendered completely in this way, for their emotions are simple and lead directly to their behavior. But if the method were used with Henry James's Ralph and Isabel, the result would read like a collaboration between Hemingway and James Thurber. With such characters, of course, it is possible to avoid analysis entirely with the direct rendition of perception and emotion, some appropriate modification of the flowing consciousness of *Ulysses*. This expedient, however, is limited by its length and mass, its infinite detail, and will be falsified if it is reduced too much. A method that requires eight hundred pages to render partially the events of less than twenty-four hours in the lives of three characters, must be used sparingly in a novel about twenty people that covers half a century.

A skillful novelist relies on an appropriate combination of various methods, according to the needs of his book, and on the reader's margin of toleration, which he tries to increase by all means at his command. In some passages he will avoid analysis by using a behavioristic technique, in others he will use some form of direct rendition or free association. He will analyze forthrightly or by means of some artifice when he cannot avoid doing so. When he does, he will break up the analysis with other details as a subterfuge to keep the scene in motion, make the characters analyze one another for him where that can be done convincingly, attaching as many items of his analysis as he can to the movement of the scene, making one item imply as many more as possible.

Most of all he will utilize the ability of fiction to move on more than one plane at a time. Symbolic action analyzes itself, and is besides a great concentrator. And simple carpentry is just as useful. Handsome Harry's cruelty to the beautiful Bertha in a climactic scene does not require analysis if the reader has seen Harry pulling off the wings of a fly on page 50 and if similarly revealing acts have followed at intervals. At a higher level of fiction than Harry and Bertha such anticipation and preparation become a basic method. A complex emotion, an action that results from mixed motives, is immediately understood if its constituents have appeared earlier, in a simpler form, as part of the natural progress of the novel. The reader understands the working-out of energies if he has been familiarized with their pattern and development. If he has enough concrete items to make a foundation, he does not require the guidance of a blueprint in order to understand their meaning.

II

SUBSTANCE AND TIME

II

SUBSTANCE AND TIME

THE BOUNDARIES of fiction are so vague that no one has succeeded in defining them. We should not be surprised if sometimes one of its constituents, or more than one, is stressed at the expense of others, or if material beyond the boundaries, whatever they may be, is sometimes given the semblance of fiction. Nearly any theme or subject matter, nearly any idea, however abstract, may be given illustrative force by asserting it as the experience of imaginary characters, or by showing that it will explain such behavior. The most modest talent suffices to cast a theory about planetary motion, the future of the welfare state, the collapse of civilization, or the toxicity of filtrable viruses in the form of a parable in which Gerald is the Repentant Communist, Natalie the Crisis of the Western World, and the child Eloise the Aberrations in the Orbit of Neptune. Our time has been fecund in such fiction. Think of a single theme, revolt. Against how many social, political, economic, religious, suburban, ethical, educational, or industrial forces have lifeless characters rebelled in novels you have read?

Many of the muckraking novels of the early nineteen-twenties were simple parables of the coarse businessman and

the sensitive intellectual. Practically all the novels of what
we strangely called the proletarian movement were simple
parables of the sensitive intellectual, solidarity, and the great
red dawn. Many novels of all periods and movements are
simple parables. For it is much easier to give ideas the semblance of fiction than it is to transmute what the mind and
heart have learned about their meaning into fiction that will
have the validity of experience for a reader. But practically
all novels, whether fables as elementary as the sermons of
the *Gesta Romanorum,* or explorations of unconscious symbolism, have to be set not only in the familiar sensory world
that our descriptive passages undertook to suggest but also
in a matrix of practical affairs. The characters are beset and
conditioned by the ordinary operation of business, transpor-
tation, religion, medicine, politics, and a myriad other
forces and activities that impinge on everyone. The exact
manner of that besetting and conditioning may become extremely important in a novel.

Every novelist must therefore frequently supply information. If the life of John or Isabel is involved with the Prot-
estant Episcopal Church, the Municipal Hospital, or the
Springville Stamping Mill, the reader will frequently have
to understand something connected with the ritual for the
Burial of the Dead or the conduct of vestry meetings, the
routine of the pathology laboratory or the regulations for
the use of sedatives, or the operation of overhead cranes.
The Jack Harkaway type of novel is little more than a fictionalized account of processes in the manufacture of steel.
The sociological novel is frequently just a fictionalized in-
vestigation of a trade, profession, or social class. A species
of kindly intellectual patronage has frequently produced
the novel of social anthropology, a fictionalized study of how
the clam diggers, the rural Georgians, the Baptists, the mi-
gratory harvest hands, or the Nisei truck gardeners conduct

their society, make exogamous marriages, and propitiate their deities. But even in the most wrought and involved novel, if it anywhere touches on clam-digging or steel manufacture, information must be supplied. The information is sometimes central in the reader's understanding of the drama and the drama may pivot on it. But fiction no longer admits the loose techniques that sanctioned digests of information or expository essays to which the reader might refer the experience of his characters.

I have space for only a single illustration and it will be convenient to examine the specialized information with which historical novels must deal. A century ago Cooper was free to interleave his novels with long expositions of frontier life and economy, treatises on the importance of climate and geography, summaries of historical events, analyses of military campaigns and critiques of strategy, discourses on woodscraft or piracy or navigation or absentee landlordism. Many of these interpolated passages are excellent in themselves: an editor could easily select from Cooper's novels an anthology on sea-fighting, frontier social conditions, or the history of New York that would have the authority of a source book. Furthermore, many of them are indispensable to an understanding of the novels. The action of *The Pioneers,* for instance, is bewildering and even inexplicable if you read it, as a modern reader usually does, without reading the historical commentary that is scattered through it.

But the modern reader skips the commentary. We have seen that he skips it for two reasons: such passages are outside, not inside, the fiction, and they are inert, not dynamic.

Mary Johnston's novels are some three quarters of a century later. They contain a certain amount of such untransformed historical material, but the percentage is a great deal smaller than in Cooper. Miss Johnston faced the same necessity of informing the reader about historical forces and circumstances that bore on the lives of the characters but, this small residuum excepted, the techniques of fiction would no longer sanction her to inform him at her convenience or in her own person. She inserted little historical information in the pure state. She acted on the principle to which all of our inquiries have led us: she dramatized it in the form of behavior and emotion. Nevertheless the modern reader feels dissatisfied with much of her fiction, and the reasons for his discomfort illuminate the whole problem of information.

Take Miss Johnston's *The Long Roll,* whose principal subject is the Shenandoah Valley campaigns of Stonewall Jackson's army. She treats those campaigns so minutely that the book constitutes a reliable military history of them. Nevertheless it is a novel, and though she must constantly provide purely military information for the reader, she usually does so by narrating events in the lives of her characters. There are two principal groups of them, a group of civilians behind the lines and a group of officers and soldiers in the army. In what happens to these people and in what they think and feel about it, in the story itself, we can follow the main lines of the military history. But she is not content with the main lines of that history, nor even with the privilege (now no longer willingly granted to historical novelists) of having a principal character fortunately and attentively present at the scene of every important military action. She must get it all in: all the skirmishes, all the departments of the army, all the services of supply and reorganization and intelligence, all the facets of civilian life that war affects. So she employs a curious, free-floating device. Holding to her principle of dramatization, she covers the whole battle or retreat with scenes of action and emotion, but she can do so only by dramatizing many of them in the persons of strangers. She moves from flank to flank and from front to rear not because the lives of her characters require her to, but merely in order to get the battle fully reported. The reader finds himself present at forays, charges, counter-charges, and scouting expeditions which have no relation to the experiences of the characters — they have human partici-pants, to be sure, but these are alien and sometimes even unidentified in the novel, they are mere surging items of Confederate valor acting out scenes so that the reader will see it all. Or, fresh from a scene that is a proper part of the story, he finds himself transported across Virginia to a cabin and some people whom he has not seen before and will not see again, simply because the history requires a further specimen of the gallantry and self-sacrifice of Confederate womanhood.

Now such scenes as these are in the terms I have used movement, action, and drama, but they are singularly irri-tating to a reader. No contemporary historical novelist would dare take such liberties. In, for instance, Mr. Guthrie's *The Big Sky* an astonishing bulk of historical data is con-veyed but every item of it bears directly on the action of the characters and is so welded to the action that it becomes integral. If I may say that between *The Pioneers* and *The Long Roll* fiction decided that historical information must be conveyed only as drama, it is clear that between *The Long Roll* and *The Big Sky* it decided that historical infor-mation must be conveyed as relevant drama. To transform information into action is not enough; it must be further worked upon till it is part of the essential action of the novel.

Stated thus broadly, the principle seems to apply to the management of all information. Few novelists nowadays insert any kind of information in chunks or untransformed. Nearly everyone manages it as he manages description and analysis; he treats it as an accessory which he must contrive to give the movement of fiction. But many a novelist fails to carry the process to the point where the reader will accept it without noticing what is happening. Many a scene is one of convenience — that is, written not to the end that it may further the story but so that the characters can discuss the intricacies of diplomatic procedures, the use of streptomycin in virus diseases, the theory of thought-transference, or the failure of nations to respond to historical challenge — wholly for the information of the reader, as an assist to understanding the novel. There are few more irritating scenes in fiction. What is wrong with them is simply that, though the necessary information they convey has been cast in the form of fiction, it has not been fused with the story. Though it is fiction, it is not part of the essential fiction.

*   *   *

In the later novels of Sherwood Anderson a characteristic kind of passage becomes increasingly common. I refer not to the communal disrobing scenes so fully criticized in Mr. Hemingway's *Torrents of Spring* but to the Whitmanesque soliloquies on birth, blood fellowship, the soul's groping for brotherhood, the pain of the mind's failure to heed its own deepest promptings, the solitude in which human life is imprisoned — on a large number of vague but passionately developed themes. Most readers find them not only unintelligible but actively and offensively dull. They have troubled a number of critics, who have devised various systems of analysis to rationalize them, but their real insufficiency is immediately revealed when they are examined technically. Such passages are anomalies. They are rich with emotion, in fact they consist of nothing but emotion, and as such they are material out of which fiction is made. But fiction has not been made of them. The emotion as it appears is not the emotion of the characters but that of the author himself. It is relevant only to him, not to the people he is writing about nor the relationships in which they are placed. Fiction comes to a dead stop and Anderson feels passionately and with great eloquence before our eyes.

Thomas Wolfe's *Of Time and the River* has frequently been compared to *Moby-Dick*. A truer comparison would mention Melville's *Pierre,* which is similarly sown with long passages of unshaped emotion. At that period Melville frequently could not complete the process of creative transformation and was content to substitute rhetoric for fiction, which is what Wolfe did at his worst.

> *But this was the reason why these things could never be forgotten — because we are so lost, so naked, and so lonely in America. Immense and cruel skies bend over us, and all of us are driven on forever and we have no home. Therefore, it is not the slow, the punctual sanded drip of the unnumbered days that we remember best, the ash of time; nor is it the huge monotone of the lost years, the unswerving schedules of the lost life and well-known faces, that we remember best. It is a face seen once and lost forever in a crowd, an eye that looked, a face that smiled and vanished on a passing train, it is a prescience of snow upon a certain night, the laughter of a woman in a summer street long years ago, it is the memory of a single moon seen at the pine's dark edge in old October — and all of our lives is written in the twisting of a leaf upon a bough, a door that opened, and a stone.*
>
> *For America has a thousand lights and weathers and we walk the streets, we walk the streets forever, we walk the streets of life alone.*
>
> *It is the place of the howling winds, the hurrying of*

the leaves in old October, the hard clean falling to the earth of acorns. The place of the storm-tossed moaning of the wintry mountainside, where the young men cry out in their throats and feel the savage vigor, the rude strong energies; the place also where the trains cross rivers.

This sort of thing recurs periodically in the novel. For instance:

And finally, in that dark jungle of the night, through all the visions, memories, and enchanted weavings of the timeless and eternal spell of time, the moment of forever — there are two horsemen, riding, riding, riding in the night.

Who are they? Oh, we know them with our life and they will ride across the land, the moon-haunted passage of our lives forever. Their names are Death and Pity, and we know their face: our brother and our father ride ever beside us in the dream-enchanted spell and vista of the night; the hooves level time beside the rhythms of the train.

Horsed on the black and moon-maned steeds of fury, cloaked in the dark of night, the spell of time, dream-pale, eternal, they are rushing on across the haunted land, the moon-enchanted wilderness, and their hooves make level thunder with the train.[1]

[1] Quite apart from the point my text discusses, I cannot forbear remarking that this is fearfully bad writing. That the first of the passages I quote has been reprinted in various anthologies supposed to exemplify the best writing of our time, and that it is referred to seriously and even analyzed for beauty and subtlety of style in critical treatments of Wolfe only make the standards of American criticism seem more amazing. I have remarked that many critics of fiction work under the handicap of not being able to think of novels from within, but surely the first obligation of a critic is to understand what prose is. The prose of these passages is inept, crude, trite, sprawling. It is as sophomoric as the emotions it more or less eructates; in

In such passages the affairs of the Gant family have evaporated and Wolfe in his own person is pulsating with superhuman — or supersyntactical — ecstasy and pain. What is wrong with them and the many similar ones is not their intensity — intensity is always welcome in a novel — but the fact that they are in Wolfe's own person. That his novel deals with the imaginary Gant family is something of a legal fiction, but the reader requires the pretense to be maintained. Once he picks up the novel he is concerned solely with the Gant family; he is not indifferent but actively hostile to Wolfe's feelings, however they might move him if they were in a non-fictional context.

It is sometimes said in praise of such passages — which are a mildew on much fiction, though not often fiction which is taken so seriously as Anderson's and Wolfe's — that they are poetic. But fiction is fiction and poetry is poetry, and each is most itself in its methods. When the methods are blended you get something different from both and much less important than either. Both call on the same psychic resources, but fiction has to use the substance in its own way and shape it to its own purposes or the result will be disaster. Emotion in the raw can be an attribute only of the characters whose lives are engaged with one another inside the illusion. When it remains an attribute of the author it has not yet become fiction.

A passage of description that is intended to give the scene reality, a passage of analysis that is intended to interpret the behavior of characters, or a passage of exposition that is intended to give significance to the action, is fiction clumsily written. Nevertheless it is written in terms of the novel; its meaning, however imperfectly conveyed, is a meaning of

fact, only a sophomore singularly gifted with vagueness could write so badly. Just why should we waste time on a critic's imperatives about the social and esthetic obligations of fiction when he admires such stuff as this?

the novel, not of something outside it. But passages of emotion which have not been transformed, whose reference and relevance are not of the characters but of the novelist, are only a stage on the way to fiction, a stage that is still short of it. The same objection may be made to them as to the clumsily handled passages: they halt the movement of fiction as effectively as if pages from the telephone book had been inserted in a death scene and they destroy the illusion by bringing the novelist out of the wings. But the objection to the clumsily handled passages is to the handling only, the material in itself is acceptable. You have seen the novelist manipulating the strings and that is deplorable, but at least the puppets were giving the show. Whereas when the novelist is heaving with emotion of his own, when he is walking the streets forever in the hurrying leaves of old October or is horsed on the moon-maned steeds of fury in the dream-pale spell of time, he has become the show and there are no longer any puppets.

Technical analysis therefore is meaningless. All one can say is that the novelist has mistaken his medium or fallen short of it. He is writing something that resembles Old Testament rhapsody but differs from it in not having the living core. He most certainly is not writing fiction. Perhaps his material might eventually prove to have the highest usefulness for fiction, but before it can become fiction it must be submitted to processes that have been discussed in the first half of this book. It must stay longer in the tanning bath or the rising pan, it must be leavened — or whatever metaphor will suggest that a transformation must occur before it can acquire form. The essential thing has not yet been done to it.

*   *   *

The heaviest burden that the movement of fiction is required to carry is that of idea. Many times both the purpose and the significance of a novel are the idea it embodies. So long as the novel does embody it, there is no danger — so long as the idea becomes the reader's deduction from the lives of the characters. But when we speak of "the novel of ideas" we are headed toward the outer boundary of fiction, whose native stuff is experience. Thinking, the intellectual function of the mind, is certainly experience and may be the most adventurous and meaningful part of individual life. But in novels thinking as such frequently fails to become fiction, and certainly intellectual experience is extremely difficult to render in the terms of fiction. One's own thought may have any or all the qualities of drama, and for all of us to follow the course of another's thinking may be as absorbing as drama, but to dramatize either thought or thinking in fiction is an enterprise so difficult that it usually fails. The novel must be a drama but idea is the most obdurate stuff it can deal with. If fiction is uneasy when only one character is on the stage, it is anxious when he is there as a thinker and palsied when he is there as thinking or idea. Moreover, what I may call the scene of discussion, the scene which consists of characters arguing or developing or refining ideas, is so precarious that it suggests a repugnance perhaps implicit in the novel. It is direct and dramatized, it is given the primary movements of dialogue and such accessory movement as the writer can arrange with the expedients of technique. But it lays on fiction a strain that is always severe and usually fatal. We will agree that *The Brothers Karamazov* is a great novel, but has it ever had a reader who was not sometimes on the edge of desperation from its debates?

I have said that fiction came to insist that an essay is one kind of thing and a novel another kind of thing. Its wariness of intellection implies that the kind of thing a novel is prevents it from being a treatise, a platonic dialogue, or anything else whose primary function is to transmit ideas. A "novel of ideas" is so nearly a contradiction in terms that only with difficulty can it be kept a novel and only by considerable power and skill can it be made a good one.

I have mentioned the compendium of information cast in the form of fiction that becomes a simple parable. There are similar parables of idea, dogma, thesis, theme. They are fiction's morality plays a little heightened, and for the most part we should be better pleased to take their tuition straight, to read about mankind halfway up the precipice in such a literary form as Mr. Toynbee's, where we are not distracted by a contrived love affair between mouthpieces of doctrine or such an adventitious interruption as the illness of an ideational child. In *The Brothers Karamazov* Ivan has the grace to make the Grand Inquisitor passage a dramatic poem but there are passages where equally tremendous ideas are only Ivan dissecting them for someone. But even this differentiation is not enough. The tremendous ideas of *Remembrance of Things Past* are behind the novel, not in it. A reader may make of them what he will after he has finished — but what is before him is Swann, the Guermantes, and Charlus.

This is to say that basic ideas, ideas as such, become alive for fiction as they may be momentous in the lives of characters — and that to give them momentousness is as hard a job as a novelist can undertake. In *Darkness at Noon,* for instance, it is done by making imprisonment, integrity, the breaking point of men, the destruction of personality, and death itself pivot on the ideas at issue. The ideas are absorbed in the characters. In Mr. Graham Greene's *The Heart of the Matter* not only death but damnation hangs on the idea, and again the idea is not discoverable as such for we are merged with it in the suffering of people. A novel is no more idea than it is theme and no more theme than it is exposition: a novel is people.

The commonest problem, however, is not basic ideas, whether they are wholly absorbed in novels or left with the kiln marks of parable showing on them. It is the progress of scene when the content of scene centers on thought, whether the discussion of idea or the process of thinking untinctured by feeling. The illustration of idea, no matter how completely dramatized, remains irrelevant until the ideas illustrated have been given central importance in the lives of the characters, and even then there remains the considerably more difficult job of making them important for the reader. Characters fiercely clashing over an abstraction are still tepid in a reader's mind until they are linked with destiny, unless they are charged with more than thought. It would seem that they cannot be given a high charge, even when wrought into the central movement of fiction and made the pivot of the characters' experience, for very long at a time. Mr. Lionel Trilling's *The Middle of the Journey* may be taken as typical. It is a brilliant and moving novel in which the highest value is the ideas. It successfully solves the difficult problem, and in repeated passages the ideas themselves are the focus and movement of the scene. But Mr. Trilling was more than sedulous. He not only dealt with characters who were passionate about ideas, thus transfusing intellectuality with the blood of fiction to begin with, and not only provided a principal character recovering from an almost fatal illness who as a result of experience and circumstance could plausibly be preoccupied with ideas, and not only played the theme and variations of his principal idea in the careers of his characters. He also kept at hand death, the threat and fear of death, the break-up of friendship, terror and suspense and pursuit, lovemaking and invol-

untary homicide. Before the momentum of any passage
could run out in metaphysics or economics he meshed it
again with rapidly moving story.[2]

As for the paragraph by paragraph treatment of thinking
by characters, it is like exposition and analysis: to some
degree unavoidable and always a threat to the illusion. Characters must think for their own sake as well as the reader's
but any extended treatment of idea as such will be expository and inert. In a skillfully written novel cerebration is
held to the practicable minimum and made rigorously relevant. It is subjected to every reagent that will give it significance in the scene and every expedient that will make it
move.

*   *   *

I have said that a unique richness of fiction is its ability
to exist simultaneously on many levels of significance. The
stories of the stage and screen readily utilize several planes;
narrative of any kind may do so. The number increases
whenever the stories achieve symbolic action but, for the
reasons I have examined, the stage becomes deeply symbolical only when a great dramatist is writing. Moreover,
the dramatist is confined by the comparative inelasticity of
time as he must deal with it. The stage and screen are
under other limitations as well from which the novel is
entirely free. The medium frees the novelist, up to the
limit of his skill, to work simultaneously with as many strata
of significance as he can perceive in experience or may
choose to deal with.

2 Mr. Trilling has a number of literary personalities, one of whom functions as a schematic critic. As such he is required to make imperatives for
literature and decide which kinds of novels are right and which wrong.
Shortly after the publication of *The Middle of the Journey* he went the
way of most novelists who practice criticism: he found that the safe course
for fiction hereafter would be to specialize in novels like Lionel Trilling's.

In no aspect of novel-writing are the novelist's endowment and his craftsmanship more inseparably linked than here. We may say that his talent is to perceive and create significances but he is the more expert as he may create them one above another in the same space. The economy of fiction asks an item of material to serve more than one function if it can, to disclose more than the immediate meaning if it can, to say what it says in such a way that it will say more. In what we have called the process of creation, one thinks, awareness of significances is reciprocal with the ability to impose on them the forms that will reveal them. But the principal technical conditions that make richness possible in a novel are the writer's freedom to use several or many narrative methods as his purpose may require, his freedom to fragment his story as he may see fit, and his complete freedom in the use of time. The last is a twofold freedom, in time as sequence and time as perception.

Take a theoretical illustration. In a scene of moderate length what happens will, we hope, be interesting in itself. A quandary is resolved, or there is an emotional passage between characters, or something as concrete as a collision of automobiles occurs. They have an intrinsic claim on the reader but he will also see them as necessary in this particular novel: they are an outgrowth of what has gone before. He sees them as an expression of characters at this moment, conditioned by earlier moments which he has seen. He feels the emotion in the same way, as itself now and in reference to what has made it inevitable now. Moreover, since he is remembering the earlier moments and their sequence, he sees and feels the colorations and he differentiates them. And this differentiation is multiple, for a number of characters are on the stage and each of them has his individual necessity. Here then is a collision, a humiliation, a

kiss: it is interesting as such but also it is the act of individual characters, and of characters as necessity, and of
events that have had their part in making it inevitable. This
thing happened as the interplay of character and circumstance, present and past. It happened because in the particular set of circumstances it had to happen; the characters
act thus because of what they have come to be.

Furthermore, the scene has moved in its own terms and
it has also moved forward. It has laid down a deposit that
adds to the necessity of what is still to come, alike in event
and emotion. The reader is seeing and feeling it in reference to the future, to the working-out of circumstance and
the destiny of the characters. At the same time he is seeing
it in reference to himself. The event may be true and the
emotion genuine in regard to him as well as the characters.
Action and emotion may enhance his own experience, or
illuminate it, or explain it. They may even a little heighten
his feeling for his own destiny. A still deeper reach may
make them symbolic of mankind — man's lot as well as the
individual reader's.

Perhaps the technical clue here is the additional dimensions created by the developing relationships of part to part
as the novel progresses. Or consider some of the functions
that dialogue serves.

At its simplest an exchange of speeches covering a page or
so may be merely a narrative method: a mechanism for con-
veying the physical and psychological action of a scene.
Even on this plane, however, it must serve other functions
as well. It must maintain the reader's belief, his acceptance
of it as human speech. It is not human speech, of course. It
lacks the assistance of intonation, vocal emphasis, facial expression, gesture, the minute physical accompaniment that
amplifies speech. It cannot permit itself the parentheses, in-

terruptions, digressions, and agreeable pointlessness of
speech. It is always purposeful and to the point, to an immediate point and a series of additional ones.

Actually, the dialogue of fiction is the novelist's own convention, no matter how vividly it may seem to be reproducing speech. If he establishes the convention early and
with authority, he need only adhere to it from then on. But
also dialogue is the part of any scene that is never written
well enough. Every novelist knows that he could always
improve it. It could be made more condensed, more packed,
more revealing, more evocative of character, more charged
with the emotion, more lively, smoother to the ear, of greater
impact and subtlety. In every novel you read the passages
of dialogue have been retouched oftener than anything else,
and still the author's first reading of an advance copy was
made uncomfortable by the twitch of his fingers to repair
them.

Furthermore, while dialogue is carrying the movement of
the scene, it must also differentiate the speakers. A reader
who is aware that "the characters all talk alike," has lost
his belief. Without the use of obvious tags or mannerisms,
the speeches of the various characters must be made identifying — shaded with individual rhythms, individual syntaxes,
individual idioms and condensations and ellipses. In compe-
tently written novels passages of considerable length may
consist entirely of dialogue in which the reader can identify
the speakers by their words alone.

All this is at the primary level; there are many others.
Dialogue is the most precise and versatile of a novelist's
tools. It leads into character and in fact is the principal
means by which the reader is made to understand character.
It is also, as we have seen, the handiest way to make the
scene carry the descriptive aids, the analysis, the informa-

tion that the scene requires. And it can never be for its own
sake alone; even an epigram, even a wisecrack, is not within
the scene unless it is functional. As dialogue advances and
intensifies the action, it may be disclosing another forward
motion in past time, as it is disclosing character and adding
to it. And it determines the balance between what is told
and what is implied. It is a direct means of holding the
reader to precisely the awareness, the knowledge, or the
understanding that the novelist's purpose requires, and it
is a direct means of suggesting more than is conveyed.

Here, then, are various dimensions, of character, emotion,
and meaning in which a skillfully written scene may move.
The number is increased by the progress from scene to scene,
for the significance of any part discloses significance in its
relationship to what has gone before and implies significance in relation to what must come hereafter. Fiction grows
richer as these relationships are created, and as any page is
given additional reference to what has preceded it. Economy requires the novelist to give every incident and emotion as many links as possible with its predecessors.

*   *   *

His ability to do so is facilitated by his freedom to treat
time as he may see fit. We need mention only two uses of
time that add dimensions to fiction. One comes from the
fact that the novelist may give the chronology of his story
any pattern that will produce the effect he wants, the other
from the fact that the mind is able to treat all periods of past
time as if they were one and as if that one were coexistent
with the present.

A natural form of the novel is the fictional autobiography,
David Copperfield or *Henry Esmond*. In his old age or after
a decisive turn in his life, the principal character describes

the strange path by which he has traveled, perhaps beginning with his birth, as in the former, or with his early boyhood as (after some displacement of periods) in the latter. A fictional biography is the same thing recounted in the third person. Perhaps equally natural is the novel of "the affair," which assembles all the forces that combined to produce a given outcome and, usually opening when they begin to bear on one another, follows them through till they are resolved. The natural way to tell either story is, as the King directed Alice, to begin at the beginning, go on to the end, and then stop. To give the events of the novel the straight chronological sequence in which they actually occurred.

But any event may be recounted in retrospect, at any point later than its occurrence, when it comes to bear on the present course of the story. Reaching the battle of Ramillies in his chronological sequence, Henry Esmond may skip over it for the time being and then return to it later on, when something that issued from it becomes directly important. He then narrates the events that led to his participation in the battle, carries the action through the battle, and takes it as far forward as the purpose of this parenthesis may require. The forward movement of the story in time is halted, and a forward progress earlier than the stage the principal one has reached gets under way. This also may be interrupted and a new beginning made, either earlier than the beginning of the parenthetical sequence or later than its beginning but earlier than the point it has reached when the interruption is made. These parenthetical and antecedent sequences may be made very complex, piled one upon another or even fragmented so that the parts can be arranged in various stratifications. I do not need to remark that complex rearrangements require great skill.

Look at the phenomenon first as movement. Each parenthetical sequence is moving forward of its own momentum — and it is moving in two dimensions. On the immediate page it is carrying the main progress of the novel toward the eventual end; at the same time it is moving toward the point which the principal movement of the novel had reached when it was interrupted. It is important to understand that a backward movement accompanies the dual (or multiple) movement. This backward motion can be more clearly seen in a comparable but less extrinsic device, when a single scene which has begun some distance toward its end discloses what happened in the omitted part while it moves straightforwardly toward its end. Essentially the same thing happens subtly and in a different way as part of the uninterrupted progress of a scene when the action and the emotions, in themselves and as part of the forward progress, reveal situations, events, emotions, behavior hitherto unknown to the reader but necessarily a part of what is going on now. Within all these devices separate periods of time are orchestrated according to the novel's needs.

But these orchestrated times provide additional dimensions. They are ineffective unless the reader correlates them and is aware how their concurrent additions to the novel increase his understanding. They are made to the sole end of enhancing the effect: for greater emphasis or power, for such primary values as suspense or climax, for fuller explanation, for the solution (or the partial solution) of any of the mysteries that a novel involves. Or for delicate *rubato* effects: the complication or dissection of character, the complication or dissection of motives or behavior or relationships, the modulation of character or emotion or motive, the interplay of theme and variations. It does not matter here why they are used — my point is that the novel is using many dimensions, alike of story and of significance. They increase light, they increase impact, and they increase meaning.

It will be useful to examine in detail a specimen of this narrative fragmentation. Nobody writing in the United States today uses the technique more skillfully that John P. Marquand. Let us look at *B. F.'s Daughter*. It concerns three principal characters, Polly Fulton, her husband Tom Brett, and Bob Tasmin who was once her fiancé; but her father, B. F., though he is seldom on the stage is also a determining force throughout the novel.

The book opens in December, 1944. Polly Fulton Brett travels to her country house and returns to New York the same night, when she learns of her father's illness. The time-lapse is less than two days but there is considerable reminiscence that brings in earlier times. (Three chapters.)

One month later on Guam Bob Tasmin learns of B. F.'s death (which had occurred almost at once after Polly returned to New York.) The story moves forward till he starts toward headquarters, when he is launched on a series of reminiscences, each involving vital action in the story, of various earlier times:

The summer of 1916, when Bob first met B. F., after the Fultons had moved to an aristocratic summer resort called Gray's Point. (Chapter 7.)

The summer of 1920, when Bob, now sixteen, goes on a motor trip with B. F. to New Hampshire.

During this episode Bob's reminiscence moves forward to a scene with Polly in New York. The date is not sure but it is probably 1929.

Back to Gray's Point, at the end of the motor trip of 1920. But the story comes on up to 1944 again because Bob relates these associations to the present. (Chapter 8.)

The story now moves forward from Bob's arrival at headquarters, but there are brief allusions to earlier periods in Bob's brief, disjointed memories of Polly. (Chapters 9 and 10.)

"At just about this time" the story moves back to Polly in the United States. She goes to Washington, where her husband Tom has a war job. We see that there is bitter tension between them. It launches Polly on just such an exploration of past time as we have just been through with Bob Tasmin. (Chapter 13.)

No date but Polly is ten years old. She visits her father's home in New Hampshire. (He was making a visit to it when he took Bob there in 1920.)

December 1944. She talks with B. F. before he dies about the visit which she has just remembered.

An undated scene out of Polly's adolescence.

Various times. Polly is remembering derogatory comments of Tom's about the place at Gray's Point.

A time when Polly was "a little girl." She runs away from B. F.'s home in New Hampshire.

An undated series of scenes during her adolescence when she was at boarding school.

1926. The earliest hint of her romance with Bob. We can now date earlier undated scenes for we learn that Polly is fifteen.

The spring of 1930. Various episodes involving Polly, Bob Tasmin, his father, and B. F. (Chapters 15 and 16.)

The winter of 1930. Bob plans to take Polly to a party in Greenwich Village.

Here the story comes forward to 1941. Bob takes his son for a walk in Washington Square and Central Park. (Note the chain of association — from Greenwich Village in 1939 to Washington Square eleven years later.)

1930. Bob takes her to the party in Greenwich Village.

The story now comes back (Chapter 18) to Polly in

Washington, the Sunday after she arrived there. But it is clear that this is either the end of December, 1944, or very shortly thereafter — that is, her trip to Washington is only a few weeks later than page 1. From a newsbroadcast she learns that an Army plane is overdue in Washington and Bob Tasmin is on it. She also finds out definitely that her husband, Tom, is having a love affair with his secretary. These events launch her on another sequence of memories, involving her romance with Bob and acquaintance with Tom and eventual marriage to him. The sequence runs from Chapter 21 through Chapter 26:

1930. She becomes "unofficially" engaged to Bob.

1938. In the course of a talk with a friend Polly says that her long engagement to Bob killed her love for him.

1931 (probably). Tea at the Fultons'; Polly expresses advanced ideas.

Fall of 1932. Polly gives a party for her Greenwich Village friends. The next day she becomes "officially" engaged to Bob. A few days later she meets Tom Brett. The action now moves through their intensifying association till she breaks with Bob, tells him that she is going to marry Tom, and takes Tom to meet B. F.

Autumn, 1940. At a dinner, Polly is led to remember her honeymoon with Tom.

Here the scene returns to Washington in 1944, the Monday morning after the Sunday of Chapter 18. This is Chapter 27 and page 373. The novel ends on Saturday, page 439. We are only a few weeks later than page 1, and the final days are the foredestined end toward which the entire novel was written. But the story was already fragmented before the first word on page 1, and telling it has required all the displacement, all the parenthetical sequences, themselves fragmented and displaced, that I have listed.

I have been discussing time as the fulcrum of narrative

methods. Even more important to the effects of fiction is the simultaneity of time. Behind the focus of one's conscious thoughts is a whirl of the past in which all one's ages blend their color and movement at this moment. They are still alive; all time exists for us now. At this moment the dead are speaking, old griefs oppress us, and we are nine years old. An impulse or stimulus of this moment touches something that lived for us years ago. Each takes power and meaning from the other and from all the moments in between them that were echoes or relays of the same feeling. Time, Thoreau said, was the stream he went a-fishing in, but the image falls short of the reality: the past is a pool on which the present floats and to whose surface the causes of feeling and the meanings of our experience rise from the depths.

Marcel Proust spoke of "involuntary memory." His discovery that this faculty had a predetermined pattern was made, as Dr. Gregory Zilboorg has shown, independently of Freud, who found that pattern in the unconscious mind. One aspect of Proust's involuntary memory is part of what I am discussing here. In a letter from which I have already quoted a sentence, he writes:

Voluntary memory, which is above all the memory of the intelligence end of the eyes, gives us only the surface of the past without the truth; but when an odor, a taste, rediscovered under entirely different circumstances evoke for us, in spite of ourselves, the past, we sense how different is the past from the one we thought we remembered and which our voluntary memory was painting like a bad painter using false colors. Even in this first volume [Swann's Way] *the character who narrates, who calls himself "I" (and who is not I) will sud-*

denly rediscover forgotten years, gardens, people, in the taste of a sip of tea in which he found a piece of a madeleine; *doubtless he remembers them anyway, but without color and shapes. I have been able to make him tell how as in the little Japanese game of dipping into water compressed bits of paper which, as soon as they are immersed in the bowl, open up, twist around and become flowers and people, so all the flowers of his garden, the good folk of the village, their little houses and the church and all of Combray and its environs — everything takes on form and solidity has come, city and garden, out of his cup of tea.*

. . . [Involuntary memories] take shape of their own accord, inspired by the resemblance to an identical minute, they alone have the stamp of authenticity. They bring things back to us in an exact proportion of memory and of forgetting. And finally, as they make us savor the same sensation under wholly different circumstances, they free it from all context, they give us the extratemporal essence. . . . [3]

Yet it is more than that. Not only does the sip of tea rediscover, at the moment of its taste, a forgotten year, garden, and set of people. It calls up other times, places, people, and emotions that association has linked with them. The moment is divisible into many periods of time, and its supreme importance for fiction is that each of them enriches this one and adds meaning to it.

There are as many dimensions of significance, as many modulations and transformations, as much accretion and enrichment as the novelist is able, or may choose, to use. In passages quoted earlier from *Ulysses* one sees time as a series

[3] *Letters of Marcel Proust,* edited by Mina Curtiss, pp. 226–27.

of intermixed wave-motions playing through the consciousness of Stephen Dedalus. They greatly increase the significance of the scene; in fact, the meaning of the scene is the
present moment as it is set in an intricately composed awareness of the past. The passages I quoted occur early in the
novel. As it goes on, as more moments of the past come to
bear on present moments, with their energies still operating
and their emotions as alive now as then, they open up a good
many additional dimensions.

Proust's long novel is inconceivable apart from his use of
the simultaneity of time as an instrument of fiction: he employs it throughout. A useful analysis is not possible in the
space at hand. To understand its achievement and magnificence in full one must consider the last volume, *The Past
Recovered,* where everything that has gone before comes
into fruition, though to follow the fluctuation and inter-
mingling of time in, say, the first hundred pages of *Swann's
Way* is enough to make clear what the technique is and
how it achieves its effects.

Instead, let us see how the perception of time is used in
a skillfully written novel that is not preoccupied with it or
concerned with its extremes, Mr. Christopher La Farge's
The Sudden Guest.

The novel has only one fully developed character, Car-
rel Leckton, a sixty-year-old spinster, moderately wealthy and
of good family, who lives on a promontory that extends into
Long Island Sound. The story is fragmented but not complexly. The actual time-lapse between the first page and the
last is only that of the afternoon and evening hours of the
hurricane that struck New England in 1944. But the experiences and emotions of Miss Leckton during those hours
are significant only in relation to those of the earlier hurricane of 1938, which are in fact the principal events and

emotions of the novel. On that earlier day her niece Leah announced that she was marrying a man in spite of Miss Leckton's opposition and went off with him. This struck at Miss Leckton's dignity, pride, and possessiveness, and since Leah's husband was a Jew at her feeling of caste. Also it repeated an earlier pattern of her life and reinforced other emotions, for there had been fear, arrogance, and hatred in her guardianship of Leah, whose mother had similarly defied family opposition in order to marry a Jew.

Leah went away before the hurricane struck. After it struck, Miss Leckton refused to admit two people who sought refuge in her house; caste-consciousness, family piety, and most of all a complexly selfish instinct for privacy forced her to refuse. But thereafter her will could not prevail against disaster. While she was frantically trying to save the house and its contents — which not only had for her the value of possessions in her tradition but also objectified her will and desire — a number of people took refuge there. Among them were a humble neighbor, a worthless and sinister young man who had nevertheless saved a girl from drowning and brought her with him, a beautiful young married woman carrying her baby, and a naturalized French aristocrat to whom Miss Leckton appealed in vain for sympathy in this intolerable intrusion on her life.

There are two periods, then, 1944 and 1938. As soon as he has established the first, Mr. La Farge swings from one to the other at will, but always in 1944 it is 1938 that counts, and whenever the scene is of 1944 it is charged with significance by the echoes and relays of 1938. Miss Leckton's emotions are of both periods, but because of 1938 there are also present in her consciousness fear, anger, and significant fractions of events from much earlier times. In the end it is the sum of these on which the novel rests and which brings the reader to full knowledge. It is thus, for instance, that one comes to see what Miss Leckton herself never sees, the homosexual element in her jealousy of her sister, her anger at Leah, her diffused resentment of various men, and the sudden collapse of her will when the strangers enter her house. Without the two primary times here opposed to each other and the interaction of the subordinate times, either we would not understand her pride and its eventual submergence in loneliness and fear, or else the novelist would require many more pages to bring us by less concentrated methods to the same understanding. Her father, her sister, her sister's husband live on in both days and color what she feels and help to precipitate what she does. The fusion of time in a single moment is the means by which this story of a woman coming into an awareness of insufficiency and defeat becomes significant beyond its single character and so the means by which the larger symbol, people in the presence of disaster, is achieved. The singleness of time is a continuous part of the substance, as the fragmentation of the story into two periods of time is the basic narrative device.

*   *   *

What we have glanced at in these chapters is the illusion — all that distinguishes a novel from a treatise on manners or psychology or from a newspaper or a court record. I have discussed the means of producing it that seem to me implicit in fiction. If the analysis made here is correct, their use is to convert the substance of fiction into form, to bring all the substance inside the novel, to withdraw the novelist from it, to conceal the mechanism and structure of illusion, and to refine, concentrate, and economize. It would be idle to try to discuss the larger questions of technique, choice, proportion, the comparative values of alternatives. They are matters of the novelist's wisdom rather than his skill. He comes by them, as by any other wisdom, from the experience of effort, failure, and success, by long subduing his nature to what he works in. Furthermore, it is doubtful if even such limited generalizations as I have made here about the use of tools can be made about them. They can be discussed only in respect of single novels and what one learns from one will not help him much with others. Mostly, they are beyond anyone's analysis except the novelist's while he is working on the job at hand, and after he has grown mature he will not need to analyze them.

Yet it is worth repeating that in reasonably well-written novels form and content cannot be separated from each other, being different functions of the same thing. And it is worth adding that there is nevertheless a tension between them which on the whole has increased as the modern novel has developed.

THERE WAS A MAN
DWELT BY A CHURCHYARD

THERE WAS A MAN DWELT
BY A CHURCHYARD

THE MODERN NOVELIST must have discipline and skill. In turn he has come to make formidable demands of his reader, whose part in the relationship between them has become more muscular. If there is increased tension between form and content, as I have said, it results from a tendency to make form do more of the work, to make it carry an increasing burden of content, to pare down, strip, condense, symbolize, and suggest. This in turn requires the reader to do more of the work. Some of the best fiction of the age can be understood only by an unremitting application of the reader's intelligence. If his attention relaxes for as much as a page he may miss something on which his understanding of the whole book is intended to hinge. A single sentence in the text, one which is unemphasized or perhaps deliberately written dim, may close the circuit to discharge the potential that has been built up. The potential is not discharged if the reader misses the sentence.

The novel may be so written that most of it is left unwritten. The reader is confronted with action or emotion that would be wholly aberrant except in relation to the entire development preceding it, most of which has perhaps been suggested rather than expressed. He finds himself thrust into scenes whose relevance to what has gone before must be determined entirely by his own inference. He may have to identify not only their function in relation to the rest but even their time, place, and characters. He must bring to bear on the page before him considerable general knowledge, a vigilant attention, a memory amounting to total recall, and a rapidly working logical analysis. He must assimilate formal psychological symbols. He must complete curves of which only small arcs have been inscribed for him. He must follow several complex movements occurring simultaneously, and they may be made additionally intricate by the novelist's sleight of hand.

Thus Aldous Huxley, Virginia Woolf, and lesser novelists who have followed their leads give dynamic meaning in the novel to the modulation of thematic material. Again, the process by which Leopold Bloom's dead son comes to affect the life of Stephen Dedalus is a very important part of *Ulysses*. But a reader might entirely miss that process or the meaning of thematic modulation if he devoted less than his full intelligence to the novel. And the reader of modern fiction must be prepared to deal not only with subtleties like these which are part of the novel's organic equilibrium but also with gratuitous ambiguities which are affixed to it from outside. No one ever separated the various ages of the idiot in Faulkner's *The Sound and the Fury*, for instance, or even realized that different ages were being presented, without going back and untangling a calculated confusion that nothing within the novel makes necessary. No one ever realized, until he had been deliberately and systematically forced to misunderstand a good many pages, that Quentin was not one person but two, of different sexes and different generations. There is no value of the characters, their relationships, or the situation in which they exist that could not have been fully served without this mystification, which could properly be called illegitimate except that by means of it Faulkner achieves an effect clearly his privilege to prefer above such values.

But though criticism must grant Faulkner that privilege the reader is under no obligation to do so. They stand at the passages of Jordan and if the reader cannot require the novelist to say shibboleth, neither has the novelist any power to hold him to any password. The novelist is free to choose his effect, and every choice involves the certainty that he will forfeit some readers before he starts and lose others on the way. But the risk which extraneous mystification runs — and much extraneous technical drapery — is the reader who goes all the way but in the end decides that it was not worth his time. Did all this labor in the dark give him pleasure or satisfaction enough to justify it? Did the novelist who led him through this maze by such difficult paths in the end discover to him any refinement or profundity or illumination of experience, any beauty, any completion of himself, any wisdom or sorrow or despair — did the novelist discover to him anything that made the maze and the paths necessary? Whenever the answer is no, the novelist's position has become precarious. From resentment of extraneous additions, the reader may pass to rejection of implicit difficulties as too burdensome. *Finnegans Wake* may indeed return to the reader who has mastered it rewards that justify his effort. But there is a basic paradox in requiring any reader of fiction to "master" a novel as he would master geometry, a foreign language, or the law of torts. There will always be readers who refuse.

Beyond that there are the cults. Those who make imperatives for fiction beget cults, of which one is always dedicated to unintelligibility. Systematic criticism has a short period-icity, which swings on a divided mind. It is forever imposing ethical imperatives and at the same time esthetic imperatives that negate them, and if novelists do not accept its dogmas with any frequency, it makes the most of those who seem to. In its esthetic arc it tries to empty fiction of content, reducing it to form. Hence the enregistration of microscop-ically differentiated states of consciousness, the private sym-bols, and the curious free-floating anonymities so religiously analyzed and praised in the quarterlies. They are usually formulas as rigid as any fiction that is printed in *The New Yorker* or the *Saturday Evening Post,* the passage of decades appears not to affect the formulas in the least, and they al-most never escape into anything with which full-bodied fic-tion deals. Few read them but those who do acquire cachet. In the cults.

But one need not deal with either the extremes or the eccentricities of modern fiction in order to perceive the change that has come into it. Neither John Dos Passos nor Virginia Woolf is an extremist, but the reader of *The Big Money* and *Mrs. Dalloway* is required to do many things he is not called on to do in, say, *David Copperfield* and *Adam Bede*. We need not ask whether *The Big Money* is a better novel than *David Copperfield* or a worse one; they are in-commensurable and the question could not be answered. Yet the measure of their disparity is not what it has often been said to be. *The Big Money* has an enormous canvas and many characters, but so has *David Copperfield*. Its lines of force move intricately, but so do those of *David Copper-field,* which in fact has one of the most intricate and mutu-ally interdependent situations ever put into fiction. If Dos Passos manipulates large masses to suggest social implica-tions, so does Dickens. If *The Big Money* is a long novel,

David Copperfield is even longer. The real difference between them is other and quite simple: *David Copperfield* is easier to read.

That is an immensely important fact. There is no implication that Dickens was a shallower or more superficial novelist than Dos Passos, that he knew less about mankind or felt less passionately, that he was in any respect the inferior: the contrary of all those propositions could be argued. But also the fact that *David Copperfield* is easier to read does not imply that it is the better novel, nor that it gives more pleasure or final satisfaction to the reader. The difference is not of degree but of kind.

The modern novel has more mass and its content has been brought into much greater tension with its form, and this has produced other tensions. The reader's engagement with fiction today is a co-operation more complete than was required of him in Dickens's time. *Mrs. Dalloway* is in no sense a more profound novel than *Adam Bede,* or a wiser or more knowing or more moving one. But when reading it one must give oneself up to it far more completely. In order to stay aboard at all, one must exercise all his attention and all his balance. As a result the immediate moment, the immediate scene, has the illusion of being, if not more real, at least more important. It has a higher potential.

The mass and tension of modern fiction have enabled novelists to open areas of experience, planes of consciousness, and many themes and subjects (though very few emotions) that the novel did not deal with before the twentieth century. This development has been made possible only by great refinement and elaboration of techniques, and the reader's adjustment to the techniques has accelerated it. The more habituated to highly charged forms the modern audience becomes, the more technique can undertake to accomplish; the more completely the reader co-operates with the novelist, the greater mass and tension fiction can acquire. But the development has had other results that cannot be left out of account.

Notably it has produced a specialization of audiences. *David Copperfield* can be enjoyed by anyone who reads novels at all and the finest intelligence is not superior to it. But Proust's audience is anesthetic to, say, Joseph Cronin, and intelligence is not only uncomfortable but downright anguished in the presence of *Captain from Castile*. Dickens could reach any audience but Mr. Shellabarger cannot reach the large one that has been habituated to the interests and methods — especially the methods — of the best modern fiction.

Yet the astronomical sale of *Captain from Castile* — a phenomenon regularly repeated by books equally unimportant — does not mean merely that hundreds of thousands of people like the clichés of sentiment and melodrama, and it does not mean merely that they find in the novel solace for their manifold apprehensions or desires. It means also that the large audience which accepts the best modern fiction sometimes finds the burden put on it too heavy. It grows tired of too great strain, and it reverts explosively to the looseness, lucidity, and freedom from pressure of Charles Dickens's day. *David Copperfield* is not a book for fools; it will return to anyone quite as much as he is able to bring to it. But there is in it enough space to turn round in, and time enough to take things as they come and as you will. It has what modern fiction frequently lacks, leisureliness, and it has what the modern audience sometimes desires to the complete reversal of its ordinary taste, improvisation and spontaneity and a magnificent irrelevance.

In short, the law of diminishing return holds for the

novel. The complex and exhausting technique of *Ulysses* is employed, primarily, to make us know Leopold Bloom. At the end we do know him superbly but no better than we know, say, Becky Sharp or Huck Finn, and the accessory purposes of the novel are no better served than Thackeray and Mark Twain contrived to serve theirs. The limits of fiction have been reached by many avenues of approach.

And the novelties of experience and satisfaction that modern fiction has given the reader, the new areas it has occupied, the new possibilities it has opened, have sometimes been paid for out of principal. Sometimes in devising instruments with which to explore recesses of personality ignored by earlier novelists, the novel of our day has come out with phantoms that might have been characters if less delicate mechanisms had been put to work on them. Sometimes in striving for mass it has achieved dead weight instead. And often it has refined its substance so much that it has refined it away — in its pursuit of the mind or the truth or the society it has forgotten, and has had to be reminded by failure, that fiction is the art of telling stories about people.

*   *   *

That fact is a road-block in the way of everyone who writes about the novel: the fact that fiction is stories about people and periodically reverts with violence and acclaim to novels that are solely stories of exterior events. "Say the words a little sadly," Mr. E. M. Forster wrote in 1927, conceding the hard fact against his will, the will of a man who had striven hard to extend the boundaries of fiction and to charge it with theses and ideas beyond story, who had succeeded a little in the first effort and a great deal in the second. "Do not say them vaguely and good-temperedly like a busman: you have not the right. Do not say them briskly and aggressively like a golfer: you know better. Say them a little sadly and you will be correct. Yes, oh, dear, yes — the novel tells a story." And in 1949 Mr. Lionel Trilling, somehow able to keep his face grave while considering the thesis that the novel as a form may be dead, and able to direct toward his findings a set of notions from the new criticism (criticism is always new), said the same thing, though he said it with such diffuse abstractness that I cannot quote his words here. He said, in several pages, You can't get away from story. The novel tells a story; you can't get away from story. Everything else is added upon that.

No one who has read the first half of this book will understand "story" or "a story" to mean just fighting, flight, and fornication. Anything that happens meaningfully to people is story and any way in which people feel about it is story — after a novelist has given it form. If any certainty can be derived from the history of prose fiction, which goes back as far as written prose and, as we see in primitive societies, far back of that, it is the four-square fact that fiction is of people, things happening to them, and their feelings about the things that happen. The fact is abhorrent to some minds. We must devote a page to them. They are always censorious and unhappy and they always find that most fiction and practically all writers of it are unworthy. They try to talk about fiction as Mr. T. S. Eliot taught them to talk about poetry, and Mr. Eliot talks like a Matthew Arnold on whom a cerebral decortication had been performed. In the interest of beauty or society or true ideals they try to make fiction worthy by removing from it everything that holds it in touch with life. That is, everything which makes it art.

The revulsion against story is a desire that experience be refined so far that it cannot be recognized. It is a desire in the void: *Remembrance of Things Past* is as surcharged with story as *The Three Musketeers*. Again, semanticists and epistemologists who set out to find the absolutes of pure fiction which they believe underlie the meretricious ruck, though they may have an indulgent word for, say *Tom Jones* on the ground that it contains horseplay not unadmirable for so shallow a novelist as Fielding, usually reprobate horseplay and all other low aims. When someone is entertained they can find no virtue in the fiction that entertains him. Bernard Shaw, it is true, once proposed to open the theaters free of charge as places of moral and intellectual instruction and charge admission fees to the churches as purveyors of sensuous delight, but vestrymen and impresarios have refrained from acting on his proposal, and semantic criticism has so far shown no reason why it is vicious of fiction to give pleasure. It is a solemn province, this high place that asks fiction to be either all form, for beauty alone counts, or all instruction, for Judgment Day draws near. Its uneasiness abates a little — though not much — when it can speak of the comic but humor remains a vice. Yet in seventy-five years the novel, a form less anemic than the critical abstractions imposed on it, has so thoroughly taken over what was once a separate department of prose literature that little humor is left outside it. Or the fervor with which authoritarians dodge the word "suspense" when prospecting for absolutes. We understand that life contains something that corresponds to the word and it would seem that a novelist, properly instructed, may touch on it, but that it is improper to high thinking is shown by the search for synonyms which will mean suspense in every way except operationally. Yet even a maker of syllogisms must feel suspense until his thought comes clear and there is no life that has not felt it repeatedly as an all but unendurable strain. One wonders why fiction should avoid what all life contains and literature up to now has used to the infinite satisfaction of its audience. (Fiction shows no sign of avoiding it.) Perhaps semantics would feel less anxiety if it considered that the word "fate" will do almost as well.

Small cycles of austere thinking kill all novels except those of a particular kind; there are longer ones in the course of which the novel itself dies. Nothing has ever justified either of these deaths outside subsidized magazines where soft voices speak to one another about ideas presumably beautiful and enjoyable but, when printed, of no meaning. The novel today is the most vigorous of all literary forms. It obviously takes precedence over all others. A young writer who takes to imaginative literature in order to express his feelings or beliefs, or in order to deal justly with his experience or what he takes to be that of others, who aspires to work seriously in the art of literature, turns to the novel almost invariably and as naturally as he breathes. In the United States the drama has never yet had anything to say and at the moment poetry has nothing to say that it is willing to have heard. The novel is the form in which our culture has most often sought expression, it is the only form that seems able to express our experience, and there is nowhere any sign that its power or will is slackening. In no country whose culture seeks expression in literature is there any sign of decadence. Everywhere today the novel comes so close to being the whole of imaginative literature that distinction in any other form is so infrequent as to cause surprise. Proust no more killed the novel as a form with *Remembrance of Things Past* than Beckford did with *Vathek*. What the voices say with such concern means only that nobody is going to write *Remembrance of Things Past* again. There is no reason why anyone should. There are techniques still uncreated and all the experience of the future to put into them — and into the old ones.

So insulated is the high place and so cloistered the thinking there that one of the articles I have alluded to actually finds itself saying, "We have, for example, out of awareness of [the novel's] power demanded that it change the world. . . ." The remark is true of the high place, where even the apparitions of small poets are movers and shakers; the high place does indeed ask fallible and erring authors of what are after all imaginary stories about imaginary people to change the world. But certainly no lay reader of any novel has ever asked it to change the world, or found it changing it, and no novelist has ever expected to. Change the world? Change a light fashion, perhaps, change the accessory decorations of popular devices or assumptions, change some of the mannerisms of expression or some of the shapes esthetic dogma has taken, change some of the eccentricities of talent so far as they can be imitated — but have the sense not to try to change more. Fiction has its dignity: no one should ask it to have paranoia.

What this kind of thinking leaves out of account is the people who write novels and the people who read them: the two ventricles of the heart. They cannot be left out of account. Many different personalities write novels and some of them are given to vanities and egotisms that from a few feet away seem merely absurd, and yet most novelists have a humility about the art they practise that is lacking on the high place. In handsome costumes on dress parade they may indeed talk nonsense but never, I think, nonsense so extreme as a belief that they, singly or as the host of God gathered together, can change the world. But in their privacy the desire is to write some true things about themselves, about the world, about the life they and others are entangled with in a struggle which they desperately hope has meaning, about man's lot and what it comes to under the stars. This is a different thing, it is a far smaller thing, but every novelist's knowledge of how much he has failed shows how fearfully hard it is to do at all. He hopes to write truly, he hopes to write well, he hopes to write his way into the understanding of other men who are trying to meet the conditions of their lives and yet have time to turn to him for a little pleasure, a little enlightenment, a little understanding. He will leave changing the world to others — to dwellers on the high place perhaps, who will scorn him for philistia's low aim but whom he is forced to scorn in turn, since they are content to think out of contact with reality and to no end but vapor.

He knows that his job, far from being to change the world, is not even to write novels but to write novels to the end of being read. And the people who read novels will continue to ask of fiction what they have always asked. They want for a moment to breach the walls of loneliness and look into other lives and find confirmation and perhaps some slight fulfillment of their own, some order and significance, something life has granted to these people that it has denied them. Beyond that there is the strangeness of things happening to others that becomes a strangeness happening to them. Still farther out are the edges of the dark and the voices that whisper so terrifyingly there may be appeased or silenced . . . for a moment. There is the need that the knife be taken from one's hand and the much greater need that, even if only for a moment and even if only in imagination, one's life and destiny, and with them destiny itself, seem composed to an intelligible end. There will be great novels hereafter as there may be great novelists, a frequency saddeningly small. But neither novelists nor readers ask greatness of novels — they ask the truth about experience or, failing that, something that will seem true.

It is blasphemous to ask of art what art cannot do. But

also the art of fiction exists of human necessity. Write "Call me Ishmael" at the top of page one and from there on what happens is compacted of human need and desire, both without stint, both inappeasable. It brings the reader for only a few hours into strangeness, meaning, and fulfillment, and those hours, the sum of all fiction's hours, cannot be a large integer in the sum of his life. But he has got to have it, and a little of it goes along with him after he has closed the book. He has something that he did not have before, something he wanted, something he had to have.

It comes back to the rise of the curtain in the darkest of all theaters. Some wooden figures hang at the end of strings. But suddenly they are men, then they are me, and they may become any men or all men. In all humility, that seems enough. The operation that produces this illusion, I began by saying, must be called magical, and the need the magic serves is eternal. Where there is magic, necessity, and eternity, there is no reason to ask for more.